CW00815863

Fragments that Remain

Fragments that Remain

D Irene Thomas

NELL JARVIS BOOKS

First published posthumously in 1998 by Nell Jarvis Books
17 Moormead Close
Hitchin
Herts SG5 2BA

Distributed by Gazelle Book Services Limited Falcon House
Queen Square Lancaster England LA1 1RN

ISBN 0-9532969-0-3

Typeset by Amolibros, Watchet, Somerset
Publication of this title has been managed by Amolibros

Printed and bound by Professional Book Supplies, Oxford,
England

Contents

Part One   A Time of Hope and Expectation

1	Unwoven Strands	1
2	Novitiate	24
3	Years of Promise	46
4	Hiatus	65
5	Maryfield's War	90
6	Interlude at Penton	110
7	Arcadian	120

Part Two   A Time of Dedication and Endeavour

8	Year of Vicissitudes	135
9	Halcyon Days	158
10	Declension	169
11	Exile	180
12	Salvage	195
13	Another Life	207
14	Solitude	219
15	Through and Beyond a Tunnel	235

Part Three   Some Validations

16	Wider Horizons	253
17	Within Four Walls	264
18	Vignettes, and Sketch for a Portrait	273
19	Of Records and of Reckonings	285
20	A Look at Old Age	296
21	Some Thoughts on Transience	309
22	Last Chapter	324

PART ONE

A Time of Hope and Expectation

CHAPTER ONE

Unwoven Strands

"Well here we are last!" exclaimed my mother. "This is the Summer House. This is where I used to live when I was a little girl." Three pairs of thin black-stockinged legs stretched their furthest, and three small heads peered over a stone wall to gaze solemnly at a substantial, square and ivy-covered house with big windows, those on the bottom floor going down almost to the ground. Mother had no intention of paying a call; it was a long time since she had lived at Norton Woodseats (then well outside Sheffield), and once we had seen the house and tasted the raspberries growing wild in the plantation outside the walls she took her daughter and two little sons by train and tram back home to Rotherham - three hours of travel there and back merely to satisfy one of her sudden whims.

I never saw the Summer House again, yet, when many years after our little excursion my mother put an old photograph into my hand, I recognised the ivy-covered walls at once. She told how her father had burst in upon his family one Saturday afternoon hauling along a photographer he had met by chance in the city. His wife and daughters must leave their sewing, his sons be rounded up from the grounds, two armchairs be placed outside, so that the likeness of six children and their parents might be perpetuated in the picture now unearthed from an old album. It must have been at least sixty years old and, though

1

yellowed, was perfectly clear; through the open window behind the group mother pointed out the linen piled on the sewing table by "Ma and the girls" when "Da" has so brusquely disturbed them.

Sitting comfortably upright with arms folded he doesn't look much like the tyrant, the wilful, restless, over-versatile man of his legend - indeed his neat, short beard and direct gaze suggest stability and quiet determination. Organist and choir master, pianist and flautist, writer and composer of romping family pantomimes, he also set to music many nursery rhymes and poems ranging from Lear's *Owl and the Pussycat* to *Piping down the Valleys Wild* and others of Blake's *Songs of Innocence.* These happy simple tunes with their lilting rhythms and clear cadences - unlike his more pretentious and much inferior work - were never published but for many years were loved and sung by his children and handed on by them to their own. For a while he had toured the country as accompanist to Sims Reeves, a tenor admired by Berlioz; he organised plays and concerts and himself gave "penny-readings" of Dickens and Edgar Allan Poe from Darlington South to Penzance. An erratic, irascible, sometimes violent man, his versatility seems to have led to the squandering of his gifts in that he never had one single long-term objective. A few months after this picture was taken he was injured internally by a kick from his horse and died after a few weeks when only forty-six.

Beside him sits my grandmother wearing a flowered gown - "beech-brown silk sprigged with yellow rosebuds," says mother - with a tight bodice and skirt spreading round in ample folds. Her hands lie relaxed in her lap as she looks directly at the photographer, her face composed and gentle; she is then almost forty-four.

Behind the seated parents stand their children. John, then twenty-two, is fair with a small moustache; he's scowling somewhat, looks very resolute with feet apart and watch-chain spread across his waistcoat. Next to him Amelia, not two years his junior, looks forth sombrely from under her dark, piled hair - an aspect utterly belying one who all her life had an impish sense of fun and gay liveliness of spirit. Then comes William, the only smiling member of the group - "dear Willie", exclaims mother, "always so hopeful" - but the smile is only a flicker, perhaps better not look too lively in the presence of "Da". He too is dark like my mother, then about fifteen - my mother is short, plump of body and square of face, and it must be confessed that she has an angry look as she stares straight ahead with mouth set and eyes fixed. Peggy, next youngest, with oval face and gentle features, is slim and looks at ease, and was to grow up as the least excitable and variable of them all. Finally Madge, nearly ten, kneels at her mother's knee. Petted as a baby, admired for her transparent complexion and cloud of fine golden hair, her expression is tart, her nose too thin and pointed for generosity, and indeed she grew up feline, alternating a kittenish coquettishness, which sat on her queerly after fifty years, with a spiteful tendency to scratch when feeling unfriendly.

From their magnetic, temperamental and tempestuous father all six children inherited vitality, driving energy and easily provoked irascibility. Their impatience was proverbial; they could never endure to wait. It hurt them almost physically to stand on the brink of any enterprise and they always plunged in at once, sink or swim. Gay, hospitable, extravagant, always good company, these handsome Lees were an unpredictable lot, always fully extended and reacting in often exaggerated, over-dramatic ways to experience; their ardour and intensity of living rarely permitted them to discipline and harness their gifts to purposes transcending the excitements of their day-to-day existence.

My mother had her full share of these characteristics, in manner, in speech, in mode of living. She grew up short and dark with magnificent almost black eyes and brilliant colouring - hence called "Poppy" by her family, never Mary or Lydia, her baptismal names. She once told me that she was alone in feeling no fear of their father, relating how one day she saw him using his horse whip to punish his younger son - and I could well imagine her, dark brows down over accusing eyes, impotent but blazing with indignation - when he turned and saw her. "'What are you looking like that for, *witch*?' He lashed out at me but I stood my ground."

How my father, so quiet and scholarly, came to love and to marry the temperamental uninhibited hoyden who was my mother in her twenties is a mystery. He was then an industrious,

3

conscientious and perhaps over-serious man of almost forty, the eldest of six, and had for some years been wholly supporting his widowed mother and only sister; two younger brothers had been "very wild" (I never knew exactly how) and died before they were thirty; his sister, my godmother and always most generously kind and good to me, was a very conventional, almost prim woman; she was thin, plain and spectacled in outward appearance, having nothing in common with her three surviving brothers. Their mother, "Grandma Stuart", was only sixty-five when I was born but to me she seemed a very old lady. She always wore long black clothes down to her elastic-sided boots; spotless white lace at the neck and cuffs and cream silk shawls somewhat relieved the sombre effect; on her head she always wore a white lace cap. She therefore looked a bit like Queen Victoria, whose picture hung in her bedroom; and, like Her Majesty, she looked not exactly miserable but perhaps rather disapproving, with two grooves that ran too low down the sides of her mouth to be smile marks. She was almost as tall as my father, stately and handsome, with regular features of unblurred contour; her cream-coloured cheeks were soft and cool to kiss, their delicate lines as fine as cracks in porcelain; her cambric handkerchiefs smelled of lavender water or eau-de-cologne. She was a methodical and scrupulously tidy woman, her bedroom and its contents having "a place for everything and everything in its place" as was often impressed upon me. Gloves, handkerchiefs, stockings in tight black balls; petticoats, chemises, long "drawers" and night-gowns all edged with white lace; bonnets and caps and her spare "bustle" with its long black tapes; capes and shawls - everything in perfect symmetry exactly where it had been put. All was of great interest to me as an inquisitive little girl and I poked my nose into her possessions sometimes when she wasn't there. I was always very anxious to discover the contents of a mysterious locked black box studded with brass nails; not until I was grown up did I learn that it had contained linen sheets and a *shroud* and a bundle of letters "to be placed beside me in my coffin", which items lay there biding their time for more than twenty-two years. She professed an austere Protestantism and had never been inside a theatre or touched a playing card in her life - her puritan habits may have accounted

4

for her two "wild" sons. After my father's marriage she continued to live with him and his growing family until her death at eighty-six. In all those years I never knew her spend a single day in bed, nor did I ever see her excited or angry; she was always as imperturbable as a cat. "Grandma Stuart" was very different from "Granny Lee" who had loved the gay social life of her youth, who was still vain of her looks and wore pretty fashionable clothes and shoes, and enjoyed giving and going to parties with the two lively unmarried daughters who lived with her. I saw *her* excited and angry a great many times, but she had her own dignity and almost imperious authority, expected deference and invariably received it. My mother's family and forebears were of great and continual importance to her and she liked to remember and talk about them; of his own my father rarely spoke.

The marriage of these contrasted partners from such disparate backgrounds proved harmonious and happy, their love and devotion mutual and life-lasting. He delighted in her youthful zest and abandonment to everything she did, her high spirits, her incorrigible humour; his occasional sense of outrage was mitigated by his amused tolerance with a moustache-concealed smile that wrinkled the corners of his eyes, while her lack of artifice, her utter truthfulness, the courage and tenacity with which she coped with the mutabilities of existence excited his continued admiration. His love was expressed in the letters he wrote on her anniversaries every year for as long as he lived. To her he must have been first and foremost a pillar of constancy on which she could always rely. While her own living consisted of a series of unconnected forays and adventures - she was one of those who could extract excitement out of making a pudding - she lived beside one who, while genially tolerating her enthusiasms and exuberance, lived quietly and steadily, not battling with his world but in harmony with it. She felt for him an almost reverential affection and though her sense of fun precluded her feeling in awe of him she respected his rare judgements and, in my experience, invariably deferred to them. She maintained close contact with her mother and sisters who lived an hour's journey away, and never lost her temperamental affinity with them; yet over the twenty-seven years of their partnership her values and standards grew close to her husband's and she certainly recognised their validity.

In her old age mother loved to talk of him and their shared past, speaking always with admiration and affection and often with amusement. He had died at sixty-five, a month before her fifty-second birthday and she survived until her ninetieth year; her memory was good, her fund of stories almost inexhaustible, and often very revealing of them both.

"You will remember how terribly extravagant your aunts and Granny Lee used to be; when they had a party they would serve wines and game in season and even hot-house fruit which I would not have thought of doing, though I expect I might have afforded it. So sometimes they got into difficulties."

"One day I was paying them a visit and they actually begged me to ask your father for a loan. At first it seemed quite unthinkable but because they were so upset in the end I promised them to try and I asked him that same evening - and I felt quite ashamed for them, I can tell you."

"Your father was very good and said he'd tell me next day what he had decided. And then he sent them a cheque - and it was for more than they asked for - not as a loan but a gift, and he told them," mother looked very serious, "that they must learn to be more careful in the future, for they must understand that in no circumstances were they to ask him for money again."

"When next I went over they told me that all their worries had gone and that they could never be sufficiently grateful; they said that when the letter and cheque had come, first they had cried, then telephoned Daddy at his office and then," mother looked at me with a shocked expression, "they had all gone out and bought themselves *three new hats.*" Mother now looked aghast. "I told them not on any account to tell your father what they had done - I gave them up as hopeless." She shook her head at the memory.

"Did *you* ever tell Daddy, perhaps a long time later, maybe after Granny Lee had died?" I asked.

"*Never!*" said mother emphatically, and then most characteristically she threw back her head and laughed till the tears came. Clearly her sympathies were with her husband but how right she had been to keep the story to herself! - since his habit was to plan his life with an almost excessive care for all possible contingencies he could only have viewed such an easy-going and careless trust in the future with complete incomprehension and his gravest displeasure.

In the earliest picture of my past of which I am now aware I see myself standing in a room where my mother lies in bed her face radiant with gladness at the birth of her first son. I do not recollect seeing the child, only his wicker cradle. However his arrival fixes the date; this is late July and I must be almost in the middle of my third year. The high square room is filled with sunlight, outside the open window a chestnut waves green hands, shadows of boughs and leaves flicker and dance on walls and ceiling. I am aware of airy space and light, gay movement and great happiness.

The babe proved a child of happy temperament, healthy and easy to rear, and I shared my mother's joy at his arrival. It seems that I never regarded myself as dethroned queen of the nursery, for since in truth I had never reigned there could be no sense of displacement. Before the birth of their third child my parents had sent me away to stay with Granny, not telling me what was in store, and he was more than a month old when first I saw him. In the long white baby clothes of those days he lay placidly asleep on mother's lap as she sat complacently by a blazing fire. I knelt at her knee enraptured by this wonderful surprise but cried bitterly when my bedtime came. All were mystified but my tears ceased when I learned that the babe would still be there when I awoke next morning; he had come to stay, to be another brother. I welcomed these two coevals into my world of three grown-ups, longed to protect and foster two creatures so defenceless, all through their babyhood. I was their willing handmaid. To watch my mother nurse and nurture them, to rejoice with her in their growth and development, to help her when allowed, forged a first great bond of sympathy between myself and my mother.

For my own beginnings had been less propitious. Only two months after marriage my mother was shocked to find herself pregnant, and for some while had resented the foetus in her womb just as in the first weeks she had feared sexual consummation - for all her tempestuousness she always said she was cold sexually. Therefore I, her first child, was to be born too early to please her; worse, I was born out of turn, for I should have followed not preceded the birth of a son, and seem always to have known myself wrongly placed in the family constellation. How often I heard Mother's story! "I asked Nurse Boscill about the baby and she said that I had a beautiful daughter. I was very upset. 'A girl!' I said, 'not a *girl*, why, I never thought of such a thing - surely not a *girl*.'" I always felt deeply mortified by this story when small, and when older imagined that by its repetition she was punishing me for her own first deep chagrin.

But the story was not complete. Scores of years later, in her eighties, she and I were wandering the paths of her garden (she talking continually and always of the past, myself listening and remembering), when she again recounted this ancient tale to which she now added, half casually, "But when you were only a few weeks old I told Daddy that I wouldn't change you for all the boys in England!" I could hardly believe I had heard her aright, but she repeated her words, also saying, "But of course he and your grandmothers were delighted with you from the first." So I hadn't been rejected; disappointment had been brief and eventually I had been welcomed after all! Glad as I felt at knowing the truth, I reflected that had I known it earlier the colour of my relationship not only with her but with myself might have been modified and for the better. Not for the first time I realised that we don't always know the true facts on which to base our estimate of ourselves and our situation; this particular mental picture had been wrongly focused for more than half a century.

I was born a healthy infant but presently ceased to thrive, grew pale and puny and cried incessantly. "Try giving her a well-smacked bottom," said old Dr Taylor, but, when even this didn't improve matters, their child's almost skeletal emaciation eventually drove my distracted parents to change their doctor. They turned to the young practitioner who eventually became their family doctor over the next twenty-five years, and he quickly solved the problem; "A fine child, almost starved." Given supplements to inadequate natural feeding the prolonged crying ceased and I at once began to put on weight and make progress, but for some years I was a pallid little girl with scant straight hair and a pinched, almost an anxious facial expression. Not surprisingly, continued unsatisfied hunger and chastisement in early infancy led temporarily to poor physical development and nerves too 'highly strung".

During my early years of childhood my mother must have felt often baffled and disappointed by her pale, plain, thin little daughter with her incalculable and vulnerable nervous system who, while given to occasional defiant outbursts, was so lacking in her own fire and courage. I am sure that she never set out deliberately to thwart my childish initiatives which all too often ran counter to her own, she simply felt it her bounden duty to punish her child until she did as she was told. For I was not naturally obedient. Told "Do this", my frequent rejoinder was "Why?" and the answer "Because I say so" never seemed satisfactory. My resistance was often stubborn because I felt my very existence to be at stake - not surprisingly because the words "I'll break your will or I'll break you" seemed then, and still do seem, a terrible threat addressed to a weak though rebellious child. But though my then frequent feelings of fear and hostility led me into conflict of course, my will and stamina were at hopeless odds and I was usually reduced to shameful tears which abject behaviour merely exasperated my mother further. Whereas she had not time or patience to bother with weakness I was neither braced nor galvanised by a robust and vigorous attitude, indeed her scorn of sensitivity seemed only to increase my own. For a brief period I suppose each aggravated and augmented opposing elements in the other.

On two occasions I ran away, probably less to evade punishment than to avoid submission which always seemed much harder to endure. Of course I didn't get far - I was barely in my fifth year; I fled to the village about a mile distant down the hill where I sat on a little stone wall by a field and doubtless dramatised the situation, pictured the consternation at home, felt proud of my defiance. But I soon descended from fantasy to

9

reality; I couldn't sit on my wall forever, and what lay beyond in the distant country I didn't know, so after shedding a few tears I lagged slowly home where I cannot remember that my brief absence was either remarked on or punished. If my busy mother had noticed my absence she probably thought me hiding somewhere in the big garden - and in any case disregard was the best possible answer to my childish histrionics.

I must not suggest that I was ever singled out as victim of a maternal urge to dominate; when my two brother had to be punished they also were frequently whipped with the cane until striped with red weals and we were told, probably with truth, that had we been Grandfather Lee's children we would have fared far worse. But I am sure they were far less provocative than I had been; because they didn't feel that all control from outside was a threat to their identity they could accept authority as part of the natural order of things and generally submit to it. Moreover they avoided encounters whenever they could whereas I - probably testing my own deep insecurities - sometimes seemed almost to seek confrontation. Punishment for them was the result of wrong-doing that had unluckily come to light, and therefore, though it might cost them chagrin and tears, it wasn't resented and was quickly forgotten; for me - possibly related to unconscious memories of infancy - physical punishment seemed an assault on my right to survival and my resentment rankled bitterly and for a long time. Thus the same treatment meted out to three children predictably led to very different results: in both my brothers their self-confidence was unaffected by temporary humiliation while my rickety self-esteem was undermined and diminished by every defeat.

It is tempting to speculate on the effects of this period of conflict, and that they were not more disabling was surely due to the basic stability of my childhood life. With father, grandmother and small brothers I lived in easy accord as also of course did my mother; and I remember how for many years I would drift off to sleep to the sound of the three grown-ups talking in the room below, hardly more than a subdued murmur or vibration floating upstairs, no voice ever raised, a soothing sound, pleasantly reassuring. And through the long years of their partnership I cannot remember once hearing, or for that matter overhearing, my parents confront one another in anger. Nevertheless I imagine that certain innate tendencies emerged as a result of these early experiences. Infantile deprivation may have led to a psyche avid for everything, eager to perceive and hungry to know, with an inordinate desire to "drink life to the lees". At the same time since initiative had generally led to humiliating defeat (granting that my initiatives had been mistakenly conceived) there also developed a strong tendency to seek a spectator's role rather than a participant's. Like a wide-mouthed sea anemone my greed for experience would seek to absorb all that came my way but, like the anemone, I would choose to remain generally rooted, afraid to venture forth to master my environment or initiate fresh relationships. Therefore I submitted myself more exclusively than did my brothers to the influence of sense impressions; I was a watcher, a listener, peripheral only, a child mainly reactive to external surroundings and highly susceptible to their shaping power.

The remembered responses to the world of my distant past stream before memory's eye as a series of happenings, as though of more or less consecutive events. Standing out like pinnacles in a level landscape I also recollect moments of intense awareness wherein I knew another way of experiencing that was not in the least peripheral, when my own internal urges and desires generated responses far more significant than the circumstances engendering them - responses which were in themselves valid experiences though in a wholly different manifestation. And these, those most vivid memories of childhood which I now possess, seem not arbitrarily chosen, they have something in common. I have hinted at the first - of seeing my mother with her new-born son that bright and airy morning; that scene is still saturated for me with its associated feeling, an overriding, exultant anticipation as though I knew that from this good moment even better ones would most certainly ensue.

A very early recollection is of myself as a very small child staring with wonder at a decorated Christmas tree - frosted boughs bending beneath their coloured baubles suspended as though afloat, light blooming softly on their curves of gleaming gold and silver in dusky green recesses. All things droop or hang downwards but for the child the tree is all-upreaching, aspiring to its distant pinnacle whereon glisters a star. And the glad sensation that accompanies this memory, for again I cannot separate image from feeling, is once more of being drawn away from the instant towards something beyond reach.

When I was about five a dressing-room became my own tiny bedroom where I awoke on summer mornings to the sound of the birds - sparrows cheeping and scuffling in the ivy, thrushes, blackbirds, a skylark, singing, perhaps a distant cuckoo calling. I would lie listening half asleep till suddenly - and how often! - a thrilled expectancy would expand within me like another bird eagerly stretching his wings to meet the coming day. Impossible to lie still - I would jump up quickly, urgent to begin my coming hours, sure that they would be good. And I recall countless evenings in the swing, facing into the sunset sky where dazzling motes of light sifted away into the blue, when again my bird of morning stirred; up and up I would swing, higher and faster, faster and higher; not only the day and its morrow but an illimitable future lay before, and vastly my bird spread forth his wings and lifted himself for flight.

Seemingly by osmosis, fact and feeling have an equal share in my earliest memories, and although the first were as unique as they are vivid, the third and the fourth were repeated over and over again so frequently that I am certain that I really experienced the sense of self and situation first poised on the brink of something beyond, and then transcending themselves; I am certain that I am not ascribing to my distant past feelings now roused by remembering it. These moments stand out more vividly and were surely far more important than all my early struggles and defeats, indicating that the will had not been "broken" for all its frequent submissions to external constraints; the upsurge of an unquenchable vitality, the sensation of inner potential, the youthful belief in an illimitable future were together able to outweigh my childish impotence to control immediate circumstances.

And in any case that first mother-daughter relationship with its recurring conflicts, rebellions and submissions, was very soon to be replaced by one very different and happily destined to be permanent and positive. As I grew my health and strength improved and so did stamina and looks ("with her lovely complexion, the delicate colour seeming to glow behind her transparent skin, her large brown eyes and regular rounded features she sometimes is really beautiful," wrote my father to his sister on my sixth birthday), and such promising development after an inauspicious beginning certainly gratified and pleased my mother for whom my seeming refusal to thrive had long been a mortification. My own expectations grew less apprehensive and I began to appreciate my mother and to share in many of her enjoyments, especially her unsophisticated love of the earth and of all living, growing creatures. Eventually I was to realise - and was to continue to realise - that to her I owed not only countless happy experiences in the natural world but also my every opportunity to develop what gifts I had through her direct encouragement and her good offices with my father. There was a time when her fervour and enthusiasm jarred on my adolescent sensibilities - the folly of a schoolgirl's distaste for reactions that, however they might seem exaggerated, were in truth merely natural! - for when she expressed herself rapturously it was because she really felt rapture, as when she declared, "I could have knelt and kissed the roses," or cried, "I could eat him, I could eat *him!*" as she nuzzled the babe in her lap who crowed and laughed and waved his limbs as she buried her face in his creased neck and knees and dimpled elbows.

Our father had two dominating interests and pleasures of which the first was his love of the countryside. For this it might be thought that he had little time. Every morning at 8.30 he walked a mile to the offices adjoining the brass foundry where he was chief cashier - for a time single-handed, later with a secretary. (I suppose today he would be called an accountant, his then very comfortable salary was £300 a year.) In the afternoon he walked back up the long hill for lunch at 1.30, returned to work at 2.30 and was home for his evening meal at seven. These times and this routine never varied.

Every year he had two weeks summer holiday which were spent with his family in secluded little villages on the coast of Yorkshire. Whenever he could arrange it we holidayed in June when he considered the country to be at its pristine best, the forget-me-nots and violets and hawthorn of May mingling with June's first dog-roses and campions and honeysuckle. Often we were the only visitors and had beach and countryside to ourselves; I recollect walking a woodland path so quiet and remote that a wren felt safe to sit her nest in a low grassy bank, only blinking an eye as we tiptoed past. Paddling and shrimping, making castles and sand pies he allowed us in plenty, but walking in lanes and woods, on cliff tops and over moorland were the highlights of holiday for him.

These two weeks were simply a long extension of his habitual weekend pleasures; before my brothers were big enough he'd take me by the hand and walk with me - I so small that I just covered his handkerchief spread out on a wall for me to sit upon. (Almost the first book he gave me was Theodore Wood's illustrated *The Little Naturalist in the Country*.) When my brothers were older the whole family walked together on Saturdays and Sundays; we children used to grumble sometimes at being interrupted in our private activities - "Going for a *walk!*" as we struggled disgustedly into our lace-up boots - and always set out rather formally and sedately, three children in front (we dawdled or "misbehaved" if allowed to walk in the rear) and parents behind. But this was only at the beginning while still confined to the pavement and very soon we'd be clustered together at "The fields by the White Gate". To this point we always came and occasionally it was where we might turn back; from here we had a choice of many ways in which to walk and often stood here making up our minds. We might open the gate and pass by the footpath through the fields connected by three stiles, picking hot wilting bunches of poppies and corncockle, or stallaria, cuckoo-pint and herb robert from the hedge sides. We might visit the village with its bridge over a pebbly stream, or climb the road to the farm where in autumn we fed the squealing pigs with our week's collection of acorns carried in three paper bags. One Easter Sunday we found a lamb crying in a ditch having strayed through a gap in the hedge far too small for the ewe, still bleating in the pasture, to penetrate; Father bade me pick up the little creature and push it back through. The lamb was warm and soft and unexpectedly solid and heavy, its heart beat frantically. Reunited it attached itself to its waiting parent and drank, its tail ecstatic, while my brothers patched up the hole with interlacing twigs. Once Father gently picked up for us a rolled hedgehog and breathlessly we observed the tiny tucked-in feet and crinkled questing snout as it lay on its back on his gloved hand. In warm weather we took long trips with sandwiches and hard-boiled eggs for lunch; to the big reservoir, our nearest equivalent to a lake; to the bluebell wood smelling like hot new bread under the greening trees; and, best of all, to the anemone wood and the old water-mill by the stream. These were real experiences to be buried deep in consciousness; scores of years later, visiting the van Gogh exhibition in London's Hayward Gallery, a small canvas, hung high and unobtrusively, compelled all my attention. In the foreground was depicted a lush wet tangle of grass and frail anemones, misty trees stood behind and a haze of wild flowers beyond. Involuntarily I seemed to smell damp earth as fragrances from the past floated up into remembrance, and instead of the painted picture I saw a dripping water wheel and kingcups and forget-me-nots trembling in the spray. An "inward eye" was not the least valued legacy bequeathed me by my father.

Throughout childhood we lived in country surroundings though only two miles from an industrial town. Down in the valleys of Don and Rother lay pit shafts, factories, bessemer furnaces, steel mills and railways, a world of polluted air and water, aridity, clangour, dirt and brutal toil. Climbing steeply up and away from all this, a road of offices and municipal buildings was presently succeeded by a broad thoroughfare lined by the residences of those made wealthy by the industrial world below; beyond big double gates gravelled drives led to stables for carriage horses; lawns shaded by fine trees surrounded large detached houses with gardens imposing enough to be called grounds. About a mile above the town the road levelled out and presently the tree-lined pavements were succeeded by footpaths, hedgerows and open fields. Shortly before this, at the top of the incline, two crumbling sandstone gateposts without gates marked the top of a gentle hill that descended at right angles from the main road under a grove of arching trees; for us however it was not *a* grove but *the* Grove with houses built both sides. These were less eccentric than those built by the industrial magnates, being without the gothic crenellations or classic porticoes, the square turrets or corner towers that they had demanded of their architects. But they were well-built substantial houses, each differing in size, style, and sometimes in building materials from all the rest. The last one of all, "our house", we considered far and away the best of them all though it was probably the least pretentious. This was because beyond the redbrick walls with their stone coping lay open cultivated country, Farmer Pepper's oats and wheat and barley fields.

Here secluded at the bottom of the quiet Grove our parents reared their family although since their second daughter was not born until I was almost twelve she came too late to share my childhood. The big garden was probably my mother's least complicated, most relaxed and fulfilled joy; she was proud of her fine variety of flowering shrubs and mature trees which included silver birch, service and box, all uncommon thereabout; the copper beech and acacia each set the other off, and there was the largest hawthorn I have ever seen, of immense girth and as rugged and almost as high as the oak. Annually she gloried in the tall hollyhocks and foxgloves, the scent of her stocks and roses, the infinitely varied faces of her violas and pansies, "Do come and see this dark one, Love, - I'll declare it's nearly black!" and Father smiling assent. (Which reminds me that I never saw my father do a day's gardening in his life and like my two brothers he would not have enjoyed it if he had.)

With its rockery and fernery, its flowers, vegetables and fruit, with its wide oval lawn on one side, and an even larger rectangle of grass - the Green - on another, the big old garden was mainly valued by us children as affording fastnesses, hiding places, areas of special designation wherein to make our private worlds within the world of public family living. But although in their permanence these private worlds furnished a stable background to our childish lives, the garden also marked out for us the changing cycle of our seasonal rituals and celebrations. It gave us holly and ivy for Christmas; at Easter we rolled our eggs down the long grassy bank above the Green; we took great bouquets of summer flowers by train to Granny Lee; in autumn came apple gathering and the rows, carefully separated, lying on the attic floor down to the last lone russet of late October.

Nor was this all. The garden was bursting with life: worms, centipedes, woodlice, squirming cocoons, chrysalides turned up in the soil; ladybirds, beetles, caterpillars and butterflies, spiders, newts, toads, an occasional hedgehog came and went. Spring birdsong and mating were followed by nesting and delicate eggs inside their smooth-lined cups; soon pink naked fledgelings piped all day with gaping yellow bills - sometimes a fallen one would be brought indoors to gasp in a flannel-lined basket near the warm stove, and when these died, as they always did, they were buried under the syringa near the camomile bed. Intently we watched and marked the rhythm of the seasons; each tree had its timing, the chestnut first in leaf, the acacia always last; the very sun in the sky moved along the path of a changing arc; when he rose in summer he shone over green fields into Mother's bedroom, in winter a fiery red ball gleamed through a mist into mine. My first intimation that life was change continual, and that to exist meant living *in* a world equally with looking *at* a world, was surely hinted here in my early beginnings.

In winter we lived an enclosed and possibly over-protected existence inside the big solid house with our books and paint boxes, our building bricks and many toys and games. We watched the birds busy on the grass - the thrushes hopped, the starlings ran - the trees, the skies, the weather, always wildly excited by snowfall though we were never allowed to play in it. We had few visitors. All the way to the bottom of the Grove came Mr Applegate the breadman with his horse and hooded van; the milkman, with his jangling churns and measuring ladle to fill our jugs; like the child in the poem we thought ourselves "very lucky with a lamp before the door" and every evening came our cheerful little hunchback lamp-lighter who trudged springily up and down the Grove with long flame-tipped rod over his shoulder. Very occasionally there came a barrel organ with a tiny sad monkey in scarlet jacket gulping down the banana we'd given him while his owner ground out a rollicking tune. Mother and Father had friends in occasionally for a meal and a hand of whist; there were several days of excited rather than pleasurable anticipation when the good mahogany furniture was given an extra polish, the monogrammed silver brought out of its baize covers, and a mammoth baking day organised in the kitchen. We children met these visitors only briefly - and a tongue-tied, round-eyed trio we'd be - and then took refuge with the maid in the kitchen. There we'd sit before the black-leaded range with its spotless white-washed hearth; the 'steels' - fender, long tongs, shovel and other implements that were *never* used - had been rubbed with emery paper till they shone like silver reflecting the red firelight on to our faces as we knelt in a row on the rug.

Despite our seclusion we learned something of the world of industry. Only a few hundred feet below our fields and open spaces must surely have burrowed the dark coal seams, and we were reminded of the factory toil that had made our Grove and garden possible when we set the clocks by the workers' sirens, or when at night we saw the sky beyond the dark window suddenly flare red and lambent as molten steel was tapped from a furnace. On expeditions to the genteel high street shops of the town - the draper's little boxwood balls travelling on overhead wire to the cashier aloft in her eyrie, the "Maypole" dairy where mountains of butter were slapped with wooden spatulas into patterned pounds and half pounds by two dexterous men in white aprons - we might see women and children with enamel jugs and bowls assembling at the workhouse gates to collect free soup or dripping. Sometimes on winter evenings mother would take me with her to the outdoor Monday market where the naphtha lights waved and roared above great mounds of oranges and sweet rosy apples, and the cheap-jacks shouted the prices of their lace curtains or hardware surrounded by women with shawls over their heads. The salesmen always began with a price so ridiculously high that the women laughed aloud; then, stretching and flapping their sheets till they cracked like whiplashes or waving overhead a cluster of chamber pots, they descended the scale until a point was reached when the women sensed he could make no further reduction or he sensed that they could pay no more. Then either a woman would suddenly nod her head, and cash and item change hands, or the article be laid aside and another taken up. Under the frosty sky this was a vociferous, good humoured and brilliant scene, full of zestful energy. But there were shadows too. We often saw a mother who led by the hand her staring dwarfish child whose broad tongue hung down right over her chin, her face mottled and scarred from the fire that had destroyed her life. There was a young man, a simpleton, who would smile innocently then suddenly undo his fly buttons and attempt to "expose himself" before being whisked into a corner and "made decent".

Ignorantly I admired translucent golden beads glistening in the hair of the lice-infested, or pitied the bare red toes that sometimes protruded through broken boots. Many of the children were ragged and probably undernourished, and though aggressively lively, often puny and pale. I was never able to speak the language of these children and often could not understand it, and, when in their rags they laughed at my fur-trimmed coat and little muff, I could only shrink closer to my mother, a frightened and self-conscious child somehow separated from my fellow children. Too young for snobbery I felt that they were "different"; that I could not enter their world spelled out for me not my superiority but my inadequacy.

Though Mother and Father didn't know it, we were made more aware of this other world by their servant in the kitchen whose world it was; one would sing to us *O, Daddy don't go down the mine*; we heard of "fire-damp" and other hazards, of a brother killed by falling rock - "Look up into the sky - that's him - that bright star shining there" - and she held up a corner of the kitchen blind and we'd stare up into a triangle of darkness and feel awed and solemn and beg to be told more. When I was very small I was taken by the maid not to the park for my usual afternoon outing but down into the colliery valley not so very far below. It is characteristic hereabout that the worlds of industry and of country are often close together almost side by side, and while "Canklow" for me meant sheets of bluebells in a wood on a hillside, for her it was the name of "*t'pit*". There we visited a miner's cottage where a man lay motionless, eyes closed, on his bed upstairs; he looked sad, his face quite white except for his black moustache and eyebrows and the dark bristle beginning to grow on his chin. That bristle and the rich plum cake that I was given afterwards were indelibly printed on my memory, though I did not understand the meaning of what I had seen. We returned very late from our walk and the servant, who had been refused the extra half-day she had asked for and had therefore gone home without permission, perforce taking me with her, was immediately "given notice" by my angry and frightened mother who did not know then that I had actually been upstairs. Afterwards I imagine that she thought, as parents did and sometimes still do think, that "children quickly forget" though most adults know from their own worlds of private memory that this is only true of superficial perceptions.

The second great interest in our father's life was his love of literature, and he sought to share with his children the best experience in his power to give. Over the years we progressed happily from *There was an old woman as I've heard tell,* and other rhymes and songs along to *Gilpin's Ride* and later still to the *Ancient Mariner.* Of course Father was only available at weekends and until we could read for ourselves we turned to Grandma Stuart for poems and stories and it was she who implanted in us memories of delight, and of terror too sometimes, that were to last us all our lives. Especially I recall readings from Roger Ingpen's *One Thousand Poems for Children*; I wonder whether this marvellous collection is still in print because, omitting a few mawkish death-preoccupied and some moralising poems from the eighteenth and nineteenth centuries, it could still enthral the present generation. Nearly two hundred writers are represented apart from anonymous cradle songs, ballads, nursery rhymes and riddles and jingles, arranged in fifteen sections according roughly to theme: "The first part is intended for little children, the second part for children that are no longer little." Thus we heard our first Blake, our first de la Mare - he called himself "Walter Ramal" then - and our first Clare (Ingpen's preface is dated 1903, five years before the Symons' collection and seventeen years before Blunden's).

Our books were frequently illustrated, often by famous artists; I recall the black woodcuts in Father's eighteenth century Aesop, the Cruickshank pictures for the brothers Grimm, the illustrations in Ruskin's *King of the Golden River* (which in his sixties sometimes haunted my brother's dreams), and the sometimes alarming steel engravings in Grandma's big Bible. For she concerned herself with our religious upbringing, taught us our prayers (*Gentle Jesus, meek and mild*), stories from the Testaments where those of the Old were so much more exciting than of the New, and hymns of which the tunes mattered so much more to us than the words. I cannot recall that my behaviour, my "goodness" or "badness" was ever greatly influenced by her teachings, or that these stories were intrinsically more important than any others - indeed her singing in German of Schubert's *Erl King* was far more alarming than descriptions of the wickedness of Satan though one was imaginary and the other, as she impressed upon us, was real.

When we ourselves could read we devoured all that we could lay our hands on and Father saw to it that this was a great deal, presently giving us an open bookcase of our own. At weekends he frequently read to us never confining himself to books written especially for children but sharing with us anecdotes from his folio Boswell, or *Pickwick Papers* or Gissing's *Ryecroft*; he gave us extracts, translated as he read, from his small collection of French and Spanish books - *Lettres de mon Moulin, Pecheur d'Island, Don Quixote*; nor did he hesitate to convulse us with scenes from Sardou equally with the tales of W W Jacobs and Jerome K Jerome. Unfortunately none of us inherited his distinct flair for languages.

In my case the effects caused mother to declare that reading would be my undoing. On summer evenings I held my book close to the window to catch the last light, in winter I had secret candle-lit sessions in the attic - where the apparition of the nun in the garret of *Villette* so curdled my blood that for years I hated

21

to go up there in the dark. Mother thought that to sit and read a book in the daytime meant evasion of set tasks and duties - as indeed it all too often did - because for her real life meant work and activity. Yet supposing she had taken all the books away and made me live entirely in her world of undertakings and actions I would certainly have learned less not more of what "real life" was about. My grandmother, parents and two brothers, the garden and countryside constituted my known universe until I entered High School at eleven years old and from each and all I surely learned much; but because from infancy a secret timidity - I might almost say fear - had hampered free intercourse with the world outside I had begun very early to satisfy that need indirectly through reading.

Like small children everywhere I loved to be told a story; and like other children I often took delight in transforming myself into a Golden Bird or Sleeping Beauty or the Enchanted Frog at the Bottom of the Well. But when my reading had advanced into the world of literature, characters became much more than protagonists in an unfolding story; their total individuality was as important as their external actuality, they were beings of a quality that I could never attempt to reproduce in myself. They were my total concern. I can see now my distant self reading in my Homer translation of Andromache's last meeting with Hector, and for me Andromache *is*; behind all that Homer tells me of her looks and acts and words is the woman herself, and she is as true in her own world as I am real in mine. She is therefore elevated far above my world of everyday and by not attempting identification but instead projecting myself into, in a sense inhabiting, her character I have unconsciously enlarged myself, whereas any attempt to transfer her being into mine would almost certainly have diluted Homer's noble and heroic conception with my own puny childishness. That I understood nothing of all this at the time doesn't mean that I didn't experience it.

Mother would not have agreed; she would have said this was "only" imagination, dismissing my enlargements as escape into a world of fantasy. Certainly while absorbed in the world of a book I was removed from a sometimes unsatisfactory reality, but while the world of books and the world of reality were distinct and apart in my mind so that I never confused the two, yet I was certain that both were real and that both were true nor has any subsequent experience in life or in literature caused me ever to doubt it.

CHAPTER TWO

Novitiate

My real education began when at eleven years old I entered the local High School for Girls, but I had already been a pupil at three other establishments. For two years I had been a timid member of a small private kindergarten run by an elderly and almost certainly unqualified Miss Bolton. Here about fifteen small pupils learned their letters by making "pothooks and hangers" on squeaky slates with damp sponges attached, did simple addition and subtraction, picked up a little French from the "Mademoiselle", and in the afternoons made raffia mats or embroidered on coarse canvas - all this in a small room hung with dark steel-engravings depicting dreadful catastrophes like "The Writing on the Wall", or "The Veil of the Temple was Rent" which frightened me the more because I was taught these things had happened.

More profitably I next entered a large elementary or "council" school for girls; here the education was free and I was a member of a class of at least sixty pupils necessarily controlled by strict discipline; in the main they were miners' children and seemingly I never got over my first shyness enough to know them properly; they were a rough tough crowd but neither over-aggressive or bullying, in my experience. In the playground how I admired their skills at devising games and pastimes! - a piece of rope could be used for high jumping or a tug-of-war and especially for skipping - alone or with a partner in front, or in lines as the girls ran one after another into a long rope turned by a child at either end, or singly skipping while the rope was turned by two rivals faster and faster and faster - this was called the "Pepper" and roused much emulation. With them I joined in *Ring-a-ring o' roses, A pocketful of posies*, and *Poor Mary sits a-weeping, On a fine summer's day*, and other singing games.

With deep respect I recall teachers battling with overcrowded and uncomfortable conditions, making wonderful landscapes for us with sand and water on large tin trays, or laying out, in their brief "free" time between morning and afternoon school, ready-mixed pots of water-colours on the long desks together with a flower or a spray of leaves or berries, a separate one for each child to paint; with no aid other than a tuning-fork they taught us folk songs, when the partitions that divided class from class were always rolled back; we learned Morris dances and how to weave patterns round the Maypole (really a pillar supporting a corner of the big shed where we had playtime on wet days). Once a year there were exhibitions of painting and sewing, concerts of unaccompanied choral singing, the annual crowning of the May Queen, all organised by our busy teachers; parents paid a penny or more to attend these functions which went to swell the long-standing "Piano Fund" and a second-hand instrument had been bought and installed in a splendid celebration just before I left.

For a period I was sent to school at Harrow-on-the-Hill of which my chief remembrance is a day at London's 'White City' exhibition where we watched a beaver build a dam in a stream of running water; I came home so grown that I thought that all the knobs on the doors had been lowered in my absence.

I entered the Municipal High School with a "Minor Scholarship" and remained there for seven years until I was eighteen. I set out on my first morning proud of my pleated tunic of green serge, the green and gold band on my hat, my leather satchel with plimsolls and shoe-bag inside. The school seemed to me more like a palace than a prison-house with its bright airy rooms surrounding the tall balconied assembly hall, its broad stairways and corridors, the delicious clean smell of beeswax on parquet. I was placed in "Form 3" with some thirty other "scholarship" (i.e. non fee-paying) pupils each with a chair and her own private desk; that first morning these were stocked up with new exercise and notebooks of various colours and sizes, History and Geography and other text books, French and Latin primers, Scott's *Marmion* in green cloth covers, *Pride and Prejudice* in red; a pen, pencils ("HB" and "B"), an india-rubber and a box of strange instruments (compasses, dividers, protractor and set-squares) were also distributed. I was dumbfounded at all this largesse and kept opening my desk to gloat over and especially to smell the books and stationery, a first surrender to the allure of private possessions and a private place to keep them in.

It was some time before I could take these things for granted, or my teachers and fellow pupils, and I spent hours in observing and ruminating on appearances and behaviour. I might be gazing at the teacher seeming to hang on her every word while wondering why, even in summer, Miss Wright's nose remained red at the tip. I could spend hours merely staring from my seat on the back row at the heads of the girls in front - long braided plaits with ribbon bows, carroty red wire tied back in a stiff bunch, dull dark wings either side of a square head, silky tendrils held back in a slide, a haze of gold like an aureole in a shaft of sunlight - more often than not to be pounced upon by an irate teacher and given "lines" or detentions for not knowing the answer to a question that I hadn't even heard.

These girls and I climbed the school together from our greenhorn Form 3 to 4b, a year ahead of the next "new" girls, to 4a where we were insubordinate and earned ourselves a bad name, to 5b where some of us began to take lessons seriously, to 5a where we sat for the "Senior Cambridge' examination, and then for a few the eminence of two years in "the Sixth". Over the years we grew into an identifiable group; as one victim we groaned under the tyranny of martinet teachers, slavishly aped our current favourites, behaved like a mob, ruthless and cruel, when we teased and defied an inexperienced junior teacher - and were all of us horrified one day by her tears for really we liked her very much - and often did good honest work for those we could both like and respect for their enthusiasm and drive, their endeavour to understand and be interested in us, and who never affronted us with perfunctory teaching. Most of the staff were graduates and specialists and I suppose even the youngest - those in their early thirties - must have been born around 1880 so that none were far removed in time from the beginnings of academic education for women and many possessed the pioneers' sense of vocation and dedication. Our first headmistress we knew only as a short plump benevolent figure with a shrewd and kindly twinkle in eyes behind large spectacles who rustled through the hall and corridors in a black silk academic gown and who once a year entertained the whole school with a lantern lecture illustrating her holidays abroad in the Near East or her water colour copies of Egyptian papyri scrolls. She retired early in my school life and was succeeded by a first class Cambridge mathematician who came to us after holding an appointment in the US.

On the whole my schooldays were exceedingly happy and I flourished in a world where delight in books and learning was encouraged and extolled, and where my greed for knowledge could be fed to the top of my bent. I was *excited* by learning; it wasn't for me a serious business - at least not in the beginning; I wasn't a hard worker or at first particularly successful, I simply rejoiced in the expanding worlds revealed through the various "subjects", exhilarated by the experience, the sensation of discovery. It was no fault of the teacher in maths that I was for so long a failure in her subject. Had I ever been shown what figures represented then they and the abstract symbols of algebra would never have seemed so strangely arbitrary. In early childhood by dint of repetition I had learned my multiplication tables and knew for example that seven multiplied by eight equalled fifty-six in the "seven-times' table and that in another entirely separate table, the 'eight-times", eight multiplied by seven came to the same thing. For a very long time this to me was simply coincidence. Had I been given fifty-six counters to group in sevens and in eights and other possible combinations I might have understood something of the basis of numeracy - I doubt if I realised that multiplication was simply to add any given number a certain number of times. Such an abysmal numerical illiteracy at my age would not have been conceivable to my teacher who probably put down my incompetence to lack of reasoning power although I could understand and do quite well in geometry. Thus for an hour a day for six years I attempted to absorb instruction in what was virtually a foreign language, eventually achieving sufficient understanding to reach matriculation standard, and during my final year at school I had thankfully laid mathematics aside forever. While this lasted it had been a wasteful handicap of bewilderment and impotence.

With adolescence I noted with interest the breasts that bulged beneath the gym tunics of my contemporaries, myself still undeveloped; I noted how from their coltish carelessness they had grown into attractive creatures who took an intense interest in themselves and their appearance; they also had sessions in which they discussed their relationships with boys. Their experience seemed to consist of giggling encounters, hand pressings and furtive kissings, all seeming of great importance to them and very mysterious to me. Of course I knew my friends' brothers and I had two of my own, I exchanged quick cousinly pecks with my male relatives, had kissed at Christmas party games, and had on one occasion been rather disagreeably handled when, of all people, my own mother's uncle had felt amorous and I had very firmly resisted his advance. On the whole I thought boys boring - they were noisy, untidy, often dirty and given to horse-play among themselves; their violent games and rough and ready approach to life didn't attract me. Maybe my submission to my private enthusiasms was basically sexual but this was "unlocalised" sex, and at that stage more valuable to my development than any titillating playing at the real thing would have been. In any case I had been a "late developer"; I was almost twelve years old before I learned "the facts of life" from an older schoolgirl. I found the facts unacceptable; that the dignified and serious adults I knew really behaved at night in bed as I was told they did, and especially that organs that I associated with excretion were brought into play were two circumstances that I could not come to terms with. I laid aside this knowledge while I pursued the far more exciting topics that then engaged my mind.

My father was gratified that eventually English literature became my overriding interest and my continued and deepening absorption in character made me especially attracted and impressed by the playwrights. My reactions grew to be very different from his, being such as he could never know or for that matter would wish to know for they were quite alien to his nature. His approach was always measured and deliberate, and his attitude objective. He could appreciate the broad humanity of Chaucer, Cervantes, Shakespeare, Dickens; he could argue learnedly with a host of references as to whether Hamlet's madness was real or feigned, and he greatly enjoyed textual criticism. I sometimes thought that he saw characters solely as literary creations, rarely as prototypes of real humanity and without his claim to understanding I was perhaps more able to realise the actual nature of Hamlet's dilemmas and indecision, or Lear's turbulent passions and poignant final acceptances. I remember one winter night sitting close to a bright fire downstairs after everyone had gone to bed, immersed in the last scenes of Marlowe's *Dr Faustus*. His struggle seemed as real, as elemental as the wind howling in the chimney and the soft hiss of the snow on the window pane; his final invocation, "O lente lente currite noctis equi!" shook me to the heart (as surely Marlowe intended that it should). At breakfast next morning when I had to explain why I had gone so late to bed my father regarded my reaction as rather excessive; "After all it's only a book."

Maybe his attitude was good for me. For my approach was invariably subjective and only rarely could I see a play or poem apart from my own involvement, my literary experience being a vivid collection of unrelated sensations. During the warm evenings of summer terms I studied in a corner of one of the attics that I had fitted up with a chair and table and a shelf for my books. From the square casement window under a pointed eave I could see beyond the horse-chestnut tree over the hedged fields down to the coppice of whispering poplars at the bottom; alone up there in my "realms of gold". To this day the smell of whitewash on hot summer days can evoke that life, so intense, so narrow, so unaware of all that might lie beyond.

Nevertheless towards the end of my schooldays I had begun a little to mature. From being sensuously delighted by a poet's use of assonance, rhyme, rhythm and other devices, I became aware of how these wrought their incantatory effects and how their use differed from one poet to another; became more conscious of what had been unconscious associations - recognised for example that the word "little" could mean something very different from the word "small"; even the powerful reactions evoked by the personages of whom I read so avidly I could sometimes examine from outside myself, thus realising that Tennyson's Arthur was a pathetic hero while Homer's Priam had tragic dimensions.

All this was elementary, but dedication and enthusiasm resulted in success at school and my mother, growing ambitious for me, persuaded my father (who grumbled: "She'll only get married at the end of it all," - a not uncommon reaction in those days) that I should seek university entrance. Neither my parents nor myself explored any possibilities, however, so that in my final summer term just before all universities closed down for their long vacation my headmistress discovered with consternation that I had applied nowhere for admission, an almost incredible state of affairs that I can only ascribe to ignorance or passivity or the fact that my whole mind's attention was directed into one single channel - at this juncture W B Yeats and the *Celtic Twilight.* She urgently sent for me and I duly filled in and despatched the necessary forms - Redbrick or Oxbridge - all the same to me so long as my almost obsessive interests might continue and advance as now. When at the eleventh hour I was accepted at Leeds I had no idea of my singular good fortune. The School of English Language and Literature claimed to be the second best in the country, the best being Sir Walter Raleigh's at Oxford whither very soon the distinguished faculty at Leeds were to depart - happily not before I had benefited from their tuition. Mary Morgan Kane, the teacher to whom no tribute of mine could ever express my debt, wrote to me from Larne; "I am very glad you will be under Professor Gordon - real human person.

Mind," (she added perceptively) "that you don't get too rarefied."

When I went to university I was, though bookish, an ignorant romantic child, whose most important life to date had been lived inside a head peopled by imaginary personages, perhaps substituting for people in real life, and whose knowledge of life outside home and school was virtually non-existent. The only firm ground under my feet was my love of literature and I had not the faintest inkling of what university life was about - no student could have gone up less prepared than I. When I left home that bland October afternoon I was bemused, as I had been all summer, in the Celtic twilight of Yeat's *Secret Rose*, and had some vague picture of presently arriving in my "study-bedroom" where I would work surrounded by books. Next morning found me in the Great Hall of the university, one of a surging crowd of hundreds of grown men and women, attempting like them to register myself as a student with the appropriate faculties. Their numbers, liveliness, their articulate purposeful know-how almost alarmed me; many of them - it was 1920 - were ex-servicemen of the First World War whose age and experiences made them different in kind from mere sixth form scholars like myself. But this wasn't the whole explanation for I found myself equally floundering and feeling bewildered at Weetwood Hall among the women students of my hostel not only on the first day but for the whole of my first term. True there were four other "Freshers", but they had paired off at school before coming up and if they felt isolated it did not appear. For myself the second year students in their grown-up clothes - I had just put up my hair, only just emerged from a gym-tunic - seemed almost larger than life in their self-confident thrusting activity, and it wasn't conceivable that I should ever feel their equal in anything.

The hostel, a fine Elizabethan hall with Tudor ceilings and some William Morris glass on the ground floor, housed some thirty young women between the ages of eighteen and twenty-two, and was set in well-kept grounds some three miles from the city, the main university buildings, and the other somewhat drab halls of residence that accommodated the main body of women students. During my first month I walked the whole distance there and back - six miles a day - from the hall to the college buildings for lectures. The walking I didn't mind except that it set me apart from my fellows all of whom - apart from two lucky ones with bicycles - went part if not all the way by tram. I kept to myself as though I felt ashamed of this economy, as possibly I did. My parents, who probably thought of university as simply an extension of school, had decided to allow me ten shillings a month pocket money, but at the end of my first week after buying essential note and text books (many of the latter second-hand) and paying certain obligatory subscriptions, I simply had no money left for tram fares. Ultimately I wrote home of my difficulty and thereafter I was given an extra £1 at the beginning of every term though my weekly allowance remained at half a crown, i.e. thirty pence, until my fourth year. My parents could comfortably have given me more but I never asked for it, and although many students certainly came from much poorer families I do not believe that many had to manage with less. I learned to plan and to choose among priorities - if I bought a cup of coffee in the refectory after lunch then I couldn't have the tram in the evening, a first elementary lesson in the art of balancing desires against assets.

Of the students in my hall of residence a few came from wealthy homes, a few from poor ones, the majority from comfortable backgrounds like mine; all were working for degrees - in mathematics, physics, chemistry, medicine (the Leeds Medical School under Sir Berkeley Moynihan was famous), modern languages, history - and a few, not specialising, were taking general or "Pass" courses. The Warden, also on the staff of one the science laboratories, was considered unusually young to be in charge of a hostel; she had been widowed during the war and was courageously tackling her present job in a highly original way. Mrs Redman King's approach was very different from that of the older women who ran the somewhat spartan establishments in College Road; for example at dinner each night we were dispersed at separate tables taking about six students each according to the place cards which she had herself set out; in this way we were obliged to meet and talk with others not of our own particular age or study group and perhaps not invariably those we would ourselves have chosen; thus all unknowing we came to learn one of the social graces. It was an unwritten law that we always changed before coming down to dinner and she herself, elegant and striking in bright silks - rusty red, emerald green - would preside from top table where there was never an élite and everyone sat there several times each term. We stood behind our chairs until she entered, pronounced her "Benedictus Benedicatur" and sat down; a lively babel at once ensued but there had been a brief moment of formality and even those who would never have admitted it must have been inscrutably influenced by her standards and attracted by her glamorous looks, slender figure and beautiful spun-gold hair.

It was rumoured that Sir Michael Sadler, the university's Vice Chancellor since 1911, had promoted her appointment against some opposition from the more conventional; at all events it was clear that she shared his enthusiasm for contemporary art of a kind not acceptable to the majority. From my first week I had been both startled and fascinated by what to me then seemed very strange pictures; paintings by the Impressionists, the Cubists and by "Abstract" artists hung in the passages and corridors of the university buildings; we had one in our common room and the Warden had several in her large private sitting room. These were on loan from Sir Michael who had been championing their cause for a considerable time and possessed works by Cézanne, Gauguin and other notable artists of that period in his considerable private collection. Yet perhaps his most valued contribution to the growth of modern art in this country was not as a collector but, like Sir Edward Marsh, as patron and promoter of work by young and unknown artists in whom his practised eye saw promise. Among many others, the brothers Nash, Mark Gertler, Jacob Kramer, Stanley Spencer and later Barbara Hepworth and Henry Moore were encouraged by him in their days of early obscurity. Often I heard the Vice Chancellor's pictures derided, and when he gave to Eric Gill the commission for the university's war memorial many of the citizens were outraged and, as I seem to remember, it was actually defaced. But he continued undeterred, not arrogant or obstinate but enlightened and discerning. In appearance he was astonishingly youthful - his face, fresh of colour and smooth of contour, had an open eager expression; his eyes revealed candour; his manner was energetic, enthusiastic; seemingly he lived adventurously in the search for excellence in many fields of endeavour. I met and spoke with him only once and that not until my third year (when it was his private secretary who undertook to type my thesis); I heard several of his talks on individual artists (on Blake he was memorable); probably there were many like me whose eyes were opened to new ways of seeing through the artists' work so freely laid before us in our impressionable years.

On the first night of my second term Mrs Redman King invited me to accompany her after dinner to a symphony concert in Leeds Town Hall. The Leeds subscription concerts had an international reputation but although almost nineteen I had never yet heard a symphony orchestra play. Dazzled by the glittering sense of occasion and the excited anticipation of the packed audience I took my seat to listen to works by Haydn, Schumann, Brahms. Certain themes and cadences, the ebb and flow of the rhythmic pattern, its surge and momentum, the virtuosity of performance that was obvious even to my untrained eye and ear, wrought upon me greatly. When at an unprecedentedly late hour for me we emerged into the cool night air and the bright lights of City Square I was almost speechless. Through reading I already knew the rare delight of being wholly gripped by a work of art but had never known the reinforcement of sharing it simultaneously with a great audience. This night's concert marked my entry into music's world of "unworded" experience; to this day I am unable to analyse or describe in any adequate way what music intrinsically *is*, yet at its noblest it can move me on to another plane of existence.

The word "academic" is sometimes used perjoratively to describe a cloistered life of narrow interest but paradoxically university life was immeasurably to broaden my outlook as these experiences of a mere four months had indicated already. Which was all very fine, but after all it was for the sake of academic study that I was in Leeds, and of course I did give much more time to my books than to looking at pictures or listening to music. But in the beginning, of these three interests, my studies had least impact. During their first year, Honours students in the English department met only the junior lecturers whose tutelage was to me a grievous disappointment. Lessons at school had been illuminating and lively, based on close study and appreciation of the texts, so that I found the reading to me of lectures often prosily delivered, which dealt with "schools", "trends", "influences" and other abstractions from literary history, very dull and even boring. If we did study any texts I find that I cannot now remember what they were. Others shared my reaction. In the other three subjects obligatory that first year we did better: Professor A J Grant was lucid and authoritative on medieval Italy on which he had written a standard book; Dr Soltau's not yet disciplined grappling with Gauthier's *Trois Grotesques* gave us something real to bite on; and a Mr Bibby with whom we studied Virgil's *Aeneid IV* demonstrated conclusively that a Latin sentence might be read without transposing the order of the words - for me a revelation. We had been taught at school first to discover and translate the main verbs and the nominative cases that went with them, then to seek subordinate clauses and relate them to the main statement, ultimately arriving at an English version of the Latin original. Once I had grasped how to let the Latin words drop into consciousness one by one, building up a cumulative edifice of meaning I found myself *reading* not laboriously translating; and through what had once seemed arid hexameters Virgil unleashed the passionate love and hate of Dido, an injured and bitterly frustrated woman. For the first time moreover I was not reading mainly for subjective reasons but during these sessions knew the exhilaration of mastering intellectual difficulties - no question of being "carried away" but rather of getting a grip on, bringing the mind to bear upon, a text. This was for me, at that juncture, an invaluable discipline.

35

At school the schedule of lessons from 9.15 to 4.15 had allowed little time for more than casual relationships with my classmates and of course we were quickly dispersed at the end of each day; here between lectures in the college or in the evenings up at the hall there were plenty of opportunities for getting together. I had absolutely no idea how to avail myself of them. At first I had been overwhelmed by the sheer numbers and the seeming self-assurance of the great body of students. As I grew more familiar I perceived how the mass consisted of many smaller groupings and in my own groupings I began to be acquainted with the individuals, either among the hostel inmates or in the nucleus of prospective English specialists down at the college. But of course I had no experience of people except those long familiar to me at home or at school who accepted and took me for granted; on such an already established footing I could be relaxed and natural and generally au fait - which was why I now found it easy enough to talk about our work with my own study group; the topic was neutral and impersonal and I could join in without inhibition.

But I wanted more than this for I was fast becoming as interested in the living people by whom I was now surrounded as I had so recently been absorbed by imaginary ones. Perhaps because for so long I had devoted myself to characters in books (maybe a relic of infancy's insecurity) I tended to feel, if not afraid, then certainly nervous of strangers until quite sure they meant well. Yet I so ardently wanted it to be otherwise! Too vulnerable in my frailty to come out of my shell, my only attempt to initiate a relationship had resulted in failure - inevitably since all the interest had been on my side, and from the first there had been no reciprocity. During my first year a senior woman student up at the hall, like me and unlike the majority not closely attached to anyone in particular, had drawn my attention by how different her personality was from anyone I had previously known. I suppose her outside attributes were for me unusual - black hair combined with intensely blue eyes, feet and hands small and cared-for, a gold signet ring on a little finger, clothes and footgear neither flamboyant like some nor poorish like others, just quietly excellent; her suits were tailor-made, her blouses of tussore silk - she came from a southern county and to my superficial judgement her speech and manners seemed smoother, more polished than those of the north. All in all she was for me entirely original and unusual in style and behaviour wherefore my interest grew. She sat with her contemporaries in hall, travelled with them down to the college, attended lectures in another faculty, so that it was some time before we were acquainted. During my third, the summer term, when I had put away my books for the night, I would regularly go down the corridor to her room for an exchange of news and gossip; there seemed no physical or emotional involvement on either side, it never occurred to us to touch or to kiss but she suffered my evening visits and listened tolerantly to my talk while I avidly absorbed all that she told me of her past and the strange and unknown south.

We agreed to correspond during the three month summer vacation and I wrote after a week or so, and getting no answer, I presently wrote again. I wrote three times in all and during the last six weeks of silence on her part and, I confess, of considerable pain on mine - for obviously my feelings were entangled with my interest - I found myself not merely surrendering to my sentiments but also beginning to think about them. In real life thus far I had known strong emotional experience only as a small child in conflict with my mother with whom (except for two intensely felt and never forgotten battles and defeats in adolescence) my relationship had long ago grown into one of simple taken-for-granted affection. My present pain however was the result not of defeat but of rejection. Of course this hadn't been deliberate, was merely the result of indifference, or laziness, or of having something better to do than to write letters to a junior - that I was honest enough to realise this didn't make it any the less hard to endure.

To my childish frustrations I had reacted with tears and anger and outrage, all of which had usually in the course of a few hours, with no effort on my part, simply subsided and dispersed. In this present situation, at first still child-like, I was aware only of my distress with no idea of how I might deal with it; yet presently discovered that I was mustering my forces not dissolving, that, instead of an emotional response to a situation, it was possible by examining it to develop an attitude towards it.

It was then a cardinal discovery that the feeling self which fluctuated with circumstance could be dominated by a still, central, unchanging self that could assess a situation, think out a way to cope and, most important of all, then act accordingly. I was determined not to write a fourth time; turned my attention in another direction; set about weaning myself from what I clearly saw could never have been a fruitful association. The matter was small enough perhaps but this deprivation taught me one of the most important lessons in my young life and marked a very important stage in my beginning at last to grow up. That I could deliberately give up what I so ardently desired, could determine not to seek it again and abide by that decision taught me that an integrated human being could endure frustration without feeling defeated, that although one might often be at the mercy of outward events quite out of one's control yet submission was not the whole answer; acceptance yes; but one's reaction need not be abject or ashamed but sturdy and self-respecting too.

Later on in my life at Leeds I was to know many intermittent moments of intimacy with my contemporaries though these tended to be one-sided for I remained still a receptive vessel, less now because of self-distrust but that I had very little of myself to communicate, whereas my fellows were inexhaustibly exercised over their own affairs. Since listening was my function, advice being neither expected or given, it could only have been my undoubted interest and concern that made me the confidante of so many; I don't think I ever tried to draw people out. I heard of hopes and fears, of private family relationships, desire for marriage and children, of secret ambitions and misgivings; all was indeed, though important to individuals, yet predictable of their group, but to me it was a marvel to learn of what went on behind familiar facades. The one sensational confidence came in my final year from a contemporary with whom I had no relationship whatever; she told of how, a year before, she had foolishly allowed a stranger met at a dance in her home town to take her for a drive; how, after she had accepted a little petting, she had been cruelly raped and left to crawl painfully home. During the next term at Leeds with increasing horror she had realised her pregnancy, and in the next vacation, at the fourth month, she had contrived a self-abortion using a long knitting needle and had been dangerously ill as a result. She spoke first in the third person, telling the story as of another then during my speechless reaction confessed that she spoke of herself; "Nobody knows but my mother and the doctor." Neither of us alluded ever again to this confession and I very often wondered whether she regretted it though it may well have done her good; she need not have feared for its safety for I never betrayed even a trivial confidence.

This story was three years away in the future and I now return to the beginning of my second year and a very different being from the "Fresher" of twelve months before; I knew the world to which I had begun to belong and had a better idea of what a university was about; having learned some control of myself and my reactions I was less tethered and constrained and my failed correspondent became one among many who were of interest to me without emotional tie-up; having passed the "Intermediate" examinations of my first year I could now concentrate entirely on my chosen subject; soberly and with keen anticipation I settled down to my studies.

"Now in your second year," said Professor Gordon, "you can really begin to know academic freedom. There will no hurdle until you sit for your Finals two years from now; you have time to browse in the fields of literature." George Stuart Gordon, head of the English School, was presently to become first Merton Professor then Master of Magdalen, and eventually Vice Chancellor at Oxford; his colleague in charge of the department of English Language (Anglo-Saxon, "Middle" English and Philology) was Professor J R R Tolkien, also with an Oxford professorship - and his *Hobbit* saga - ahead of him in the future. His lectures were characterised by great fervour and when reading aloud - almost declaiming - the Anglo-Saxon texts he could be exceedingly impressive enunciating the proper names - Hrothgar, Heorot, Hygelac, Beowulf - with tremendous relish; but when it came to commentary and exposition he was sometimes barely audible. He spoke often hurriedly and had a tendency to swallow his words; very frequently myself and others would meet together afterwards almost despairingly to compare our sometimes incoherent notes. It was a pity that the valuable tutorial classes or seminars in his department, in which we read and discussed our essays with members of the faculty, didn't extend to those not specialising in English Language. Professor Gordon, with his small ex-infantry officer's moustache and rather aloof bearing, gave an excellent series on Shakespearean Comedy, stylish and almost over-polished yet full of human sympathy and humour. When as secretary of the university English Association I came to know him as correspondent and adviser I found him always genial, time-generous and helpful. It seemed a disaster when we learned that he was to leave us for Merton College, Oxford, and would not be in charge during our third and final year though he would be external examiner. No one could have been less like the suave and scrupulous professor than his successor, Lascelles Abercrombie.

He was then known to us as one of the "Georgian" poets, to whom Rupert Brooke had bequeathed, as to de la Mare, part of his estate. He came as head of the whole department of English Language and Literature, not specialising in poetry alone but covering a wide range from Shakespeare to Thomas Hardy including a history of criticism and a course on aesthetics. With him works of literature should be not life-escaping but life-enlarging and enhancing, and his approach was as powerful intellectually as it was strong emotionally. In his lectures, delivered in a rasping vibrant voice and entirely without notes as he paced his rostrum, he often related literary experience to its basis in real life and humanity. In my work for the Association I was often grateful for his help, more than once when I kept an appointment with him in English House at nine in the morning he would be at his desk where he had been at work all night, the light still on, himself pale and unshaven, the green eye-shade still pulled down on his forehead. He it was who while recognising my sensitive ear for the use of language, my unusual verbal memory (by no means always an asset as later I came to realise) and my real delight in literary excellence yet pointed out two crucial elements still lacking in my equipment - experience of life and intellectual judgement.

My three year course was finished. I had passed out head of my year with the English Literature Prize for my thesis - "alpha plus" from both himself and Gordon - and I visited his home to discuss the book list I had made to buy with the award. "I see that you ask for Huxley's *Crome Yellow*. In that case you should really include *South Wind* by Norman Douglas but for which the Huxley could hardly have been written." He was amused at the frivolity of this choice among the classics of my selection and afterwards gave me good advice; "Yes, I see that you feel, actually experience much of what the writer intends you to feel; for myself I generally know very well what he is aiming for which may make it hard to feel - sometimes a real deprivation. Nevertheless remember always that feeling isn't enough. Never allow yourself to become merely a sensitive instrument at the receiving end of literature."

In some such words Lascelles Abercrombie confirmed what had already been made clear by another and much greater poet, W B Yeats. During schooldays the word literature had meant bound books on shelves whose printed pages could evoke almost an infinity of response, and little else mattered but that response, the impact of the writings upon my private sensibilities; I was well on the way to becoming a young aesthete or at all events over-"rarefied" as Miss Kane had realised before I came up - but I doubt that I understood her meaning. Therefore writers were not for me people in the sense that other people were persons, but beings set on a remote pedestal almost apart from their creations, and thus it had been with naive reverence and awe that from my first year I had beheld the practising men of letters who frequently delivered lectures or read their works at the university. Masefield, de la Mare, Chesterton, Drinkwater, Galsworthy, Binyon and many others famous then but less illustrious now - I saw and heard them with feelings akin to Browning's disbelief; "Ah, did you once see Shelley plain?" and

I do not suggest that it is misplaced to revere those gifted and singled out from ordinary humanity. So that I was already "agape with veneration" on the night when W B Yeats mounted the platform. I was at first almost wholly absorbed in attempts to realise his actuality and to relate him to his books. And certainly his striking appearance and bearing, the glasses on their long ribbon, the flowing tie of violet silk, the beautiful soft yet resonant voice slowly intoning his poems like incantations were as romantic as any romantic child's idea of a poet could be. But he presented another image when he began to speak of the genesis of his work and what lay between the first conception and the bringing to birth of his creation. He discussed *Innisfree* probably because he could count on its being familiar to a large audience, and sought to penetrate behind the finished poem into the unconscious gestation of certain thoughts and images and feelings that had long lain fermenting in his mind; he described the utterly irrelevant sequence of events that had suddenly brought the necessity of the poem into consciousness, and - more easily comprehended - the craft and labour - we use the same word for the physical process of bringing to birth - whereby he had transmuted his vision into the poem itself, in which last phase the writer became the "word-smith" that the Old English poet said that he was.

Yeats did not attempt to discuss "genius" or "inspiration" for supreme creativity is surely a mystery, a gift heaven-sent by which he himself seemed almost bewildered - Pushkin has denied having any idea of how his poetry came to him - yet the analysis disclosed much. Henceforth I should study the artist's intention and method of work, not only his creations; thus mercifully not growing into the aesthete that I might so easily have become. I must already have recognised the artist's exceptional powers of observation, insight and recall, but the necessary brooding of experience before attempting to convey it I had not even guessed at, nor appreciated the sheer toil and skills of the fashioning - Eliot's "turning of blood into ink". It was crucial to my development that I should begin to realise that all works of art were in essence attempts at communication, and that however shapely or intricate or absorbing or sensuously beautiful the symbol devised for this purpose it existed not for its own sake or for art's sake (still less for my sake) but in order to convey some inner sense of meaning. That the meaning should come to seem as important as the symbol was a wholesome shift of viewpoint, one much nearer to truth and reality, the heart of the matter.

Lascelles Abercrombie had concerned himself as closely as Professor Gordon with the affairs of the English Association and had read the Mss for a booklet of original verse written by members. With help and advice I had arranged and seen through the press the first and second issues of *A Northern Venture* which included several poems by Professor Tolkien (which are now listed in his bibliography as among his earliest published works). The founder and first chairman of this lively association had been a third year student when I became secretary in my second; he had come up in the last year of the ex-servicemen when he was only seventeen and must have been the youngest student of his year. He had neither the soldiers' life experience nor the training of the scholars for he had been at work in a bank from the age of fifteen and had gained university entrance by hard private study, yet after three years he had emerged as a man teeming with ideas, one who could fire others with his enthusiasms, knew how they might best be brought to fruition, could speak his mind on a platform without nerves or self-consciousness. I could not judge of his skill either as a debater or organiser, in which activities I had little interest, but his fellows recognised his quality when, while he was working for his Master's degree, they elected him President of the Union in the university's jubilee year.

So far I had taken no special interest in members of the other sex except in so far as they foregathered equally with my women acquaintances in circles of shared interests. With my two fellow sixth-formers at school I had tacitly accepted the single-mindedness of our celibate teachers - it had seemed incongruous when two had married young serving officers during the War; moreover my friend's mother who believed strongly in women's emancipation and had worked among others with Eleanor

Rathbone in Liverpool, had frequently impressed upon me and her daughter that men generally tended to impede the self-fulfilment of women. At university I was so engrossed in so many interests that when two very different men, the one briefly and tentatively the other with sincere and long devotion, had sought more than my interest, I thought their attentions merely a nuisance, as spoiling and complicating what had been simple and enjoyable. Maybe something may be excused to ignorance and inexperience but the fact remains that though in the beginning their attentions may have flattered my vanity in the end I treated both inconsiderately and selfishly and felt nothing but relief and freedom when they ceased. Neither had roused in me a spark of sexual response.

My relationship with "FG", my colleague in the association, began very differently. Since in the beginning I was learning all the time his capacities rather than his character first impressed themselves on me. I saw that when the others present were concentrating on detail he was appreciating an entire situation, seeing wherein lay its essential components which he could then pluck out and place in new and fertile relations one with another. He had a seeming inborn ability to judge situations and people; I never saw him uncertain and tentative like myself. He had something of Abercrombie's rugged stature, his carelessness of appearances, his unswerving honesty of mind; both were knit into life by a simple but immensely strong integrity very different from the fragmented world of the senses, and both were so unpretentiously and naturally themselves that it was impossible to feel self-conscious or constrained in their company.

It seemed that first FG's gifts, then his virtues, eventually his actual selfdom were gradually revealed to me; out of merely working together, not out of a sudden sense of need or reciprocity, over two years grew slowly our recognition of what might lie between us. And then to meet him unexpectedly would generate in me an almost electrical response that thrilled me through. He was my first love and rightly then I knew that he would be the only one. We didn't believe in announcements, engagements and rings, but our compact was made before we left university though it was more than a year before our parents knew. With him I felt no temerity, no need of self-protection for there seemed no danger of domination, no servitude in giving oneself freely to another when each had trust in the other's goodwill and understanding; but it was mutual knowledge certainly not similarity or affinity of outlook that was our basis, and each was forever discovering new aspects of being in the other's so different identity. One of us was still fluid, still capable of growth and development, the other already firmly established and my love recognised the unconscious and absolute authenticity at his core. Much might be written about our relationship then so young and green, its experiments and disappointments, its occasional disillusionments and glorious fulfilments, but now I shall say simply that our partnership was to stand unshaken by the stresses and strains of lives more severely tested than those of perhaps more fortunate humanity.

Chapter Three

Years of Promise

My mother's support since school days seemed to her vindicated when I had achieved a degree, Father's quiet pleasure in my citation as prize-winner was perhaps a more discriminating reaction. As for me I felt as much relief as satisfaction, encouragement from any source was evidently still important, and it was a pity that I did not spend my postgraduate year (working for a diploma in the Department of Education) to better advantage. Much of this time I frittered away in a ceaseless spate of extra-curricular activities - dances, dinners, meetings of too many societies, parties; at first beguiled by the novelty of this untried style of living at the end of two terms I was utterly sated by the social whirl and vowed never to be so wastefully enticed again.

The following year, in my first teaching post, I fell into another trap. In the year 1905, twenty years before my predicament, in a letter that I did not read until sixty years after it had been written, Professor Gordon described his sensations when freed from academic constraints.

"A long education...puts you in a strong prison of dogma, and it gives you one or two [tools] to break out with. It doesn't give you the tools at first, it gives you plenty of time to become acquainted with your prison...You are amazed you didn't notice [the tools] before; and even when you have got them, you may require to use quite prodigious patience and ingenuity to break prison with them. When you do you almost faint with the strength of the sun and the air."

My own adjustment took time; like a mettlesome foal brought up in confinement and suddenly finding myself free I scarcely knew which of the alluring ways before me I should follow. For the very first time it seemed that my mental life was under my sole control, no "set books", lecture time-tables, periodical examinations of progress. But to speak of "control" is nonsense as applied to my activities during a year when although my days were employed in teaching duties some evening hours and all my weekends were mine to do as I liked with. The freedom, the possibilities proved intoxicating. Eagerly I devoured works by contemporary English, French and Russian writers ignored by my degree syllabus; after Greek plays in translation I went on to Jane Harrison's studies of the myths; visited city art galleries where the Italian Renaissance almost burst upon my senses; attended concerts, and after a brief infatuation with Wagner discovered Bach to whom my allegiance was to prove lifelong. It was all intense, but undirected, undisciplined, even as I now think, absurd. Like the child I had been, swinging at sunset under the hawthorn tree, I again saw the future as infinite with possibilities and no one single lifetime's endeavour could possibly encompass all I desired of life then; that circumstances or my own limitations might prove obstacles to attaining all that I sought never even crossed my mind.

There was something of a greedy acquisitiveness perhaps in all this; and also there may have been in my temperament, hitherto concealed by timidity's fear of defeat something of the unbridled urgency, the desire for all-out activity of my maternal forebears; perhaps there lurked in my unconscious tendencies so vigorously deployed by my mother, maybe that was why I had been so long in learning to submit to her will. During these two somewhat febrile years after graduation I largely worked this out of my system and eventually knew of a truth that I was my father's daughter, for whom aridity and exhaustion would result whenever I surrendered to the desire to grasp more than my hand could hold.

Of course I owed many new experiences to my financial independence. From the very beginning, out of my monthly salary cheque I regularly sent a fixed sum to my parents whereby eventually was repaid their investment in me; when I paid for my lodgings and for my keep when at home or away on holiday there was usually a monthly balance of five pounds - maybe a very little, but ten times my allowance at Leeds. During the first year I spent it all. I bought books - FG and I informing each other of our every purchase so not to have duplication in our eventual joint collection, and I also joined the "Times Book Club"; later I acquired a gramophone, and recordings when I could; there were rail fares and tickets for an occasional theatre or concert; at the end of the year I had a bicycle and a small camera to record my explorations. Come to think of it although a car has now superseded the bicycle, not until quite late in life have I had resources more than would provide for self-maintenance and such modest satisfactions as these, and am glad to have kept my life simple and free of the preoccupations that great affluence - equally with great poverty - may bring.

Meanwhile FG was using these same years to better advantage for himself and other people, working as sub-Warden at the Bensham Grove (Quaker) Settlement at Newcastle upon Tyne under the splendid Miss Lettice Jowitt, giving WEA lectures in the evenings and gaining an intimate knowledge of life in what was then industrially a depressed area. We corresponded regularly and at great length, each visited the other's home so that we managed to meet several times a year though never often enough. One bright spring morning after one of his visits I walked alone beside a greening field; I remember how the sun was hot enough to be felt and that I carried hat and coat the better to feel its power. I glory in it and at knowing myself loving and beloved. As I step forth buoyantly I am suddenly brought to a standstill by the fusing of two delights, the outer and the inner, in a brief moment of unfathomable youthful bliss. When I walked on I felt that together we could do anything, anything…

To have worked certain tendencies out of my system had been a great but nevertheless a negative gain. But I came eventually to a more balanced and coherent way of life for a positive reason - by the time that I began work in my second appointment I had discovered my vocation. Since my seventeenth year I had hoped to teach my chosen subject, my long education always had that end in view, but only now did I discover that this could be my prime objective to which I could give my best with no kind of reservation. The pleasure in satisfying my own need for experience through the arts was channelled into putting others in the way of obtaining it. For the next three years I taught English in a secondary school for girls and also worked with adult students for the WEA.

As teacher I sought that pupils and students should experience to their utmost capacity the actual work that lay before them, to bring them into the closest contact with it and then, on that foundation, to discover its implications and meaning. My first aim was most certainly enjoyment without which at the beginning I should have nothing on which to build, and this applied equally to the simplicity of an eight-year-old's approach to de la Mare's *Nicholas Nye* as to an adult's long study of Hardy's *Dynasts*. I did not aim at increase of knowledge but at extension of experience and I avoided arousing the over-subjective reactions that had so dominated my own first approaches. But I believed that over and beyond the study of single works, in good literature there was inherent a liberalising quality, that under its influence the reader might, as Matthew Arnold had said, be enlarged, enlightened, illumined. But this was incidental, not a conscious objective. By laughing at the light comedy of *The Rivals* my sixteen-year-olds experienced one aspect of life in the eighteenth century; and when two years later they read Swift's *Tale of a Tub* they learned of another. Mainly I hoped to reveal that good books could be good company and, like good company, "turn a stream of fresh and free thought" (Arnold again) upon aspects of life we have ceased to notice, or never noticed, or seen and taken for granted. For in the final analysis creative reading is the ability to bring to life the actualities which the printed words on the page are there to convey.

I had no problems of discipline; the healthy hearty girls of rural Lincolnshire were far easier to handle then the sharp-witted but comparatively puny girls of my own not so distant schooldays, and by interest and engrossment I usually managed to hold their attention. In the beginning diffidence and nervousness did hamper my first approach to adult classes but not for long; once all my attention had focused on to the work in hand there was no room left over for self-consciousness and fear. An almost lifelong delight in entering through words into worlds beyond instant reality, enhanced by the more recent discovery of an always latent empathy (which I do not elevate into understanding) with my fellows, were now both brought into play. Many of the masterpieces of English literature are dramatic and since the interplay of character on character is intrinsic to all drama it is possible that my best lectures and lessons were in this field. Be that as it may few joys could have been greater than the one I discovered in opening up for others the avenues that not very long ago had been so gladly discovered by myself.

Apart from work satisfaction I much enjoyed the general conditions of my life at this time. The school buildings stood on a hill above the clean market town with its slender church spire - designed by the architect of Salisbury and very nearly as high - clearly visible from the grounds. Close by the school a pleasant creeper-clad house in its own gardens housed some boarders and a few members of the staff but most of us lived in "digs". We numbered eighteen or nineteen and between us covered a dozen subjects; we shared a bright and comfortable common room where the atmosphere was stimulating, relaxed and happy - very different from the acrimony and feuding that had so startled my inexperienced self from the very first day in my previous appointment. Our headmistress, wholesome, crisp and lively, was an alert good-looking woman in her early forties, three of four of her staff were obviously older, most around her age, a few of us still in our twenties.

At weekends we were often glad to share our individual enjoyments with others of similar tastes - some made music together, some took riding lessons or played games, some of us on our bicycles explored the clean and placid countryside with its beautiful small churches and manors, and I no longer went alone to theatres and concerts. The friend that I made here was not on the school staff but a musician whom I first saw when she gave a public recital of old French *Bergerettes* (traditional "shepherdess" songs), wearing a costume and exquisite white silk wig both nearly two hundred years old; her voice was light but sweet and true, I found the performance enchanting. When we were acquainted I learned of her aptitudes - that she held Academy degrees in pianoforte and singing and had pupils in both; that she had studied "Eurhythmics" in Geneva and when we met was enthusiastically guiding groups of small children to respond with spontaneous movement to the rhythms of music; it was interesting that Dalcroze had been first brought to England to demonstrate his methods at the instigation of Sir Michael Sadler of Leeds. In her hands this wasn't a "subject" to be taught, nor a drill and discipline like ballet, but a liberalising experience. She herself certainly had a liberalising influence on me for she carried her considerable abilities with a buoyant and almost careless delight in their exercise very different from the solemn earnestness of the specialists at Leeds. I may add that in the school staff room I also discovered that real proficiency did not imply over-seriousness about oneself and one's work.

FG and I married four years after going down from university when we were both twenty-six. A year previously he had been appointed "Tutor-Organiser" to open up adult education in the countryside of Devon, the work being funded by the Carnegie United Kingdom Trust. For five years we lived in a village lying between Newton Abbot and Torquay in what was then the quiet, that is "undeveloped", valley of the little river Aller and only a short drive from the sea. The south west of England was entirely new to me and I was delighted and astonished by the colour of the heavy red soil, by the lush and brilliant green vegetation, by the thatched and white-washed villages, and by the mild soft air that seemed almost another element. But as I began to explore with FG this large and beautiful county - and I continued to give evening lectures for a while - I soon learned not to take everything at its picturesque face value; the communities were often exceedingly poor, a farm labourer then earning about thirty shillings a week; neighbours and families sometimes feuded bitterly one with another; housing was inadequate and often primitive - a pretty village smelling sweetly of the apple wood smoke rising from its chimneys might house three generations in a single tiny dwelling; we knew a family with twelve children living in two adjoining cottages where the smallest ones shared a bed with their grandparents. In those days remote hamlets seemed almost cut off from the outside world or even one from another.

After marriage, like my mother before me I was happy to know and honour a lifestyle very different from my own. During the years just past I had spent the school terms in lodgings, and holidays at home with my family, meeting fresh people mainly as colleagues, school pupils and adult students, settling myself alternately in Yorkshire or Lincolnshire and there being engrossed, usefully (I hoped) employed, and also happy and contented, but not until now that I shared FG's enterprising free-wheeling mode of life did I realise how narrow and restricted my own so far had been. With him - in corduroys and tweeds, jacket usually unbuttoned, pipe in mouth, pockets bulging with more pipes and tobacco pouches - how warmed and enriched and loosened-up my life now grew to be! We were welcomed and entertained by denizens of rectories and manors and farmsteads in the country and by professional men and women in towns; I hold in specially happy memory our visits to what had once been a priest's house, a beautiful long low dwelling, an "L" enclosing a prolific garden deep in a hollow combe, home of a traveller settled again in her native county with her two Spanish servants, her pony and trap, her collection of glass and silver and old lace; we also went often to Dartington where the ancient banqueting hall was now in process of restoration and re-roofing by the Elmhirsts as part of their reconstruction of the parish after decades of neglect.

Thus I began to meet my fellows by no means only on the plane of literature or the arts, to enjoy the simple give-and-take of uncomplicated relationships and, best of all, to discover with some mutual affection ripening over the years into friendships that proved to be lifelong. It was a happy discovering time for us both, and we were at the same time so caught up in the reciprocities of our young love that I sometimes almost felt incredulity at the joys that now filled the days and the nights.

Almost two years after our marriage our elder son, Philip Stuart, was born in a pleasant house in Torquay equipped and staffed as a maternity home. Although FG and I were prepared to acknowledge that the entry of a child into the world was a commonplace occurrence already many millions of times repeated, yet the arrival of our own seemed to us both a near miracle. With wonder we beheld the tender body and limbs, the slate-grey eyes, the hair finely etched on an oval pate, the tiny perfection of all his parts down to the pink transparency of his smallest toe-nail. He and I had a room with wide windows opening over a June garden and it was during the unaccustomed leisure of our stay here that I began to write in the first of the notebooks that I have kept ever since. I indulged in any young mother's hopes and dreams for her family - pictured babies crawling on sunny lawns, toddlers lurching through green grass with fistfuls of buttercups and daisies, youngsters working, playing, holidaying at home and abroad, imagined another generation carrying our seed into the distant future.

But when eventually we went home practicalities proved far more rewarding than dreams and fantasies although at first I had so much both to learn and to do that each day I was thankful if I managed to get through all my domestic and maternal duties - never in my life before had I laboured so hard physically nor ever felt so rewarded. At the end of each day I would thankfully undress and go to bed where I fed the babe for the fifth and last time. When he was changed and laid down in his crib I would simply lie back and sleep as instantly as he. The feeding times were my intervals of leisure and delight when I nursed my baby as satisfied as a purring cat with her kitten. But for him these were periods of intense effort in which he brought all his strength to bear; he would press upon me with outspread hands, work his head, push with knees and feet, his face flushed with his exertion; then suddenly tired and satisfied he would let go and fall asleep, the milk drops wet on his chin. He showed a similar concentration in the attentive gravity with which he moved his limbs and splashed in the bath. Those three busy months my notebook contained only brief jottings of growth and progress and then, after the engagement of the healthy practical motherly Dorothy who relieved me of most of the physical labours of housekeeping, I had once again some time every day that I could call my own.

Our infant's rearing fortunately differed from my own for he assimilated his food and put on weight steadily; in the mild clean climate he could live outside twelve hours out of twenty-four, growing into a brown and bonny infant so chubby, jolly and friendly that for a time we called him "Toby" - the name seemed to suit his small compact personality, his throaty chuckling laughter. Presently he was taken for walks in the lanes, sitting alertly in his pram as one about to see marvels, intently listening to sounds, eyes brightly observant as a bird's; like a bird's also were the soft and croodling sounds he often uttered before he went to sleep. And while he certainly enjoyed his regular routines he also accepted without protest changes in food, and new things in life - playpen, high chair and safety harness for his pram. Remembering stories of my own antagonism to guidance and my early lack of enterprise it was good to watch a development without fuss or conflict; I hoped he had inherited his father's spontaneity, quite unselfconsciously taking himself and his world for granted and so feeling at home in it.

Whereas I had learned to walk and run at a very early age, accompanying my father on his country walks when very small indeed, Philip had been so late a starter that I consulted our doctor who laughed at my concern, told me that no child should be compared with textbook "averages", and that since he was active and lively and looked so fit and sturdy he would catch up in his own good time. By his second birthday he had become an independent toddler who joyously paddled in the sea in his canary yellow swimsuit or played barefoot in the short fine grass of the downs above the village while I watched him from a bank of the pale and scentless violets that grew up there on thread-like stalks. By then his eyes were brown though his hair remained fair, softly windblown on top with curled tendrils lying in the nape of his white neck; the mottled flesh tints of his arms and legs had turned to gold from his second summer's sun. I held him up to see in a hawthorn bush a thrush sitting arched and unmoving over her eggs; then we sat beneath and I gathered those rose-tipped yellow flowerlets we called "socks and shoes" and stuck them between his plump toes. His presence seemed sweet and wholesome as he manfully trotted around, all fresh and sunny, completely all-of-a-piece, his steadfast gaze reflecting some inner and lovely integrity. To him I had already begun to convey my two worlds of delight - my mother's love of living growing things, my father's rhymes and stories. But being FG's son he was more intelligent than imaginative, a doer not a dreamer, and together they would eventually share pleasure in constructive skills away out of my reach.

We hadn't embarked on parenthood with a set of theories or with any predetermined "system" of upbringing. The only definite pronouncement on FG's part that I can remember was that it might be valuable for his son to do a job of work for at least a year, preferably outside the United Kingdom, before entering an institution for professional or academic training. More negatively I hoped that there should be no repetition of the conflict of wills recollected from my own childhood, and let feeling, certainly not theory, guide my approaches. Of course it helped that we had a well-nourished and therefore healthy and contented child to foster whose equable temperament and cheerful temper caused him usually to take pleasure in co-operating with his parents. I had found as a teacher long before I married that the young are essentially creatures of potential, containing within themselves embryo possibilities that can only be guessed at, and that these in fact may be greatly superior to those of the adults put in charge of them - or, as I would prefer to put it, to whom they have been entrusted. Only time will show. For me the duty and delight of motherhood would be to promote the growth and unfolding of a dependent yet unique and entirely original being. My mother and both her parents had believed it their duty to assert adult omniscience and authority, to secure unquestioning obedience, almost to treat children as material to be moulded into an acceptable shape. If FG and I had no predetermined system we certainly had a definite conception of our function; we recognised the integrity of the young, desired to promote their self-respect and do nothing to diminish it. Hence physical punishment was never administered, indeed the very idea of punishment for "wrong"-doing seldom arose, the discipline of simple cause and effect being usually sufficient. Even a very small child can appreciate that if he doesn't at least help to put his toys away then there may not be time after his bath for his bedtime songs and stories. When Philip asked us why a thing was to be done he was given a reasonable answer that he could understand and just as with adults we found that consideration was usually repaid with consideration.

We had never intended to have an "only" child but after a period of poor health and an eventual operation my plans had to be postponed. Recovery was disappointingly slow so to ease my convalescence and to give him companionship Philip was driven by FG to spend every morning at the nursery school at Dartington Hall. He was three years old in the middle of June when FG was offered a travelling fellowship by the Rockefeller Foundation to study rural extension departments in the universities of the United States. At the same time a private trust offered me a grant together with some wonderful introductions so that I might go out to study America's "little theatre" movement. It was suggested that while we were away Philip should become a boarder in one of the "children's cottages" attached to the school (each housing perhaps half a dozen children of around his age together with their temporary "mother"). At first I opposed this scheme though in the end I accepted it. FG's fellowship was important but he refused after my recent illnesses to leave me alone at home in full charge of Philip while he was several thousands of miles away for a whole year. At the same time to uproot Philip and take him with us would be out of the question since we would be travelling long distances with no settled home even if I forewent my opportunities in order to care for and companion him. It was urged upon me that while for FG such an opportunity might not come again there could be no real disadvantage for Philip if he lived for three terms in a climate and surroundings to which he was accustomed, in one of the cottages that already he knew as well as the staff, his fellows, and the school's general way of life. Before making a final decision I again consulted our doctor about Philip's gait - he trotted rather than ran and walked like his paternal grandfather with what FG called an "old sea-dog's" sway and swing. Again I was reassured and the doctor declared in addition that maybe the outgoing liveliness of the school with a premium set on activity and freedom was exactly what our little boy then needed. But although I accepted all this I deeply regretted the parting. We duly vacated our house, loaned our furniture and goods to an impoverished composer musician we knew, and at the end of August FG sailed to America where I joined him after I had settled Philip in school in late September.

For both of us the American experience was enlightening and encouraging and exhilarating almost beyond belief. My letters of introduction were my only recommendation yet heads of university drama departments and directors of civic theatres, to say nothing of established playwrights, poets and journalists generously took endless time and trouble to enlighten a complete stranger from Europe with nothing to stimulate their kindness but her intense interest in what they were doing. After three months work in New York City we set out to study our contrasted objectives; in a Ford V8 we drove south through Virginia down to New Orleans with stops for study at Washington, the University of North Carolina, the Tennessee Valley Authority and so on; thence from the Gulf of Mexico up through Texas and across the south west to the Pacific, returning by a northerly route via the Salt Lake desert and the Great Lakes back to the Atlantic. It was the time of Roosevelt's "New Deal" after the depression, and FG recorded on cine-camera evidence of the industrial or agricultural problems he was studying while American economic and social history was in the making. At the same time the natural background to the spectacle of intense human activity was impressing itself upon us - the vast and varied panorama of what we realised belatedly was not simply politically a country but geographically a continent with tremendous variations of climate, terrain and animal and vegetable life. In those days there were no airways and the train took five days to cross from one ocean to the other; in remote parts of the south west even the splendid roads we traversed sometimes turned into dusty unmetalled highways where already Roosevelt's labour force was hard at work engineering the roads of today. We are glad to have travelled when in southern Texas we perforce crossed the Mississippi by paddleboat, went from San Francisco to Berkeley by sea across the Golden Gate, traversed deserts where the gas stations were so few and far between that we carried spare fuel and a supply of drinking water. But this is not the place to retail our story but rather to record a debt of gratitude we can never repay for the immense generosity and kindness of this land and its people.

I returned to England some weeks before FG in good time for Philip's long summer holiday. The *Leviathan* was to dock at Cherbourg and merely stood by off Plymouth for the passengers for England to be taken ashore by tender. It was a glittering June morning when I came on deck to see the wooded cliffs of Devon green above the sea and smelt the sweet land breeze - a good moment, the sense of achievement enhanced by most happy anticipations. In a very few hours I had arrived at Dartington where the children from the cottages were playing outside and Philip and I had recognised each other. I didn't say much at first - afraid of being "sudden" - but he led me by the hand to show me his garden and picked two flowers with stems almost a yard long; I gave him a coloured postcard of the *Leviathan* to show him how I had come; this he took away to show his small friends one at a time, standing a little away and pointing me out to them. That night I went upstairs where he lay in bed and he seemed to be feeling shy for he talked in a whisper and wasn't merry as he had been all day. I kissed him then for the first time and he responded naturally enough and next day and onward we were as companionable as usual - more so now that he could talk and share himself with me. I sent FG a long letter telling him all that we had said and done during the week I stayed in Totnes visiting the nursery school at least once every day; Philip had not lost his swaying gait, and although he clambered up the ladders and slides and bars he was noticeably slower and less agile than the other children.

In September FG returned and took up his new duties as head of the Rural Extension Scheme run by the university college and Philip returned to school. I had been asked to give a course of lectures on modern American literature and included in my survey the "little theatres", their playwrights and repertoires, and this caused some of the students to want not merely to study but to perform plays by contemporary writers. Because I had returned from the US full of enthusiasm and desire to put to use what I had learned (for though I had a little experience I had not before that journey studied techniques and method) we decided to experiment among ourselves privately to see what might come of it.

All this time FG and I had been house-hunting and living in furnished rooms in Exeter, our musician having departed to take up an appointment abroad without divulging to anyone what he had done with our belongings. When after weeks of time and trouble they were found in storage and thence moved into the house we had taken, FG and I drove down to Dartington to bring Philip home. We knew that he was delighted at the prospect of a house and garden of his own but all the same wondered how he might react when it came to the point of departure. He was very self-possessed. He awaited us in the cottage doorway wearing a scarlet sweater over his corduroys, his hair glinting gold in the sunshine; he watched his cases being carried out and stowed in the car, then he marched down the path. He turned at the gate to call goodbye and wave his hand then he got into the car and set his face forward.

He never thereafter seemed to hanker after this world and his friends and I concluded that he had made no close ties with anyone or anything there; very readily and naturally he would allude to happenings and people as they occurred to him, and some of these recollections were highly entertaining, but apparently this was a piece of life he had lived and concluded without regret; now he simply turned the page and engrossed himself in the next chapter.

An artist's impression of D Thomas, based
on a photograph taken in the 1930s
(Artist - Vicki Poulter)

Topsham is a small estuary town on the Exe river famous for salmon fishing and ship-building since the twelfth century (Chaucer speaks of Topsham sailors). Hence in a quiet side road - Rope Walk - we had discovered "The Woodlands", an unpretentious cream-washed house standing behind double iron gates; there was grass in front, a dark Irish yew by the pillared porch and an ancient contorted and beautiful arbutus shading the path. Behind lay a small cobbled courtyard with an old pump and beyond this an oblong of grass under apple trees with borders on three sides - genistas, myrtles, a tree erica, cascades of forsythia and cydonia on the walls. A gate at the bottom led on to a wide empty paddock - splendid for kites. In scale this was small indeed compared with my childhood's garden but we hoped that its seclusion, its simple comeliness together with its seasonal constancies might give to Philip a similar sense of security and continuity.

After the long break in our family life we allowed a year to pass before he restarted schooling but he never felt dull or lonely as there was always so much to do. Throughout the year we had a great many walks - to the big water-mill with hope of seeing one of a pair of kingfishers, down to the old quay where timber boats from far-off Russia sometimes lay anchored, in the "Forest" where in autumn the tiny cyclamen thronged under the cypresses, along the causeway by the estuary - very exciting at full tide with a good wind blowing - to the churchyard high above a broad promenade where the fishermen's nets hung to dry on poles, into the fields by Clyst St George where - in those days - the rabbits scampered and played, a trip by ferry to the other bank of the river - though never when the swans were nesting. In summer there were picnics and parties beside his little pool and sand pit, followed by tea on the grass afterwards with his growing circle of small friends Binkie and Walter, Hilary and Robin, Brian and David. At weekends we sometimes drove to the sea. One summer we stayed in a quiet guest house in Highgate Fields thence visiting the Zoo, Kensington Gardens, taking river trips to Greenwich, Richmond and Hampton Court, visiting the Abbey, the Tower, watching the Changing of the Guard. Every night after his bath, he dictated to me his memory of the day, and so completed his *Holiday Book of London* which I have still, stapled and bound as a gift to his father. (I see now that we should have sought a publisher.)

Although Philip and FG were often engrossed in their Hornby trains with the big lay-out on a cork-floored room upstairs, in the making of Meccano working models, in kite flying or sailing little boats that they had made themselves, there was always time for a reading session daily with me; we shared all my old favourites and also read books quite new to me, the *Pooh* stories for example - not as "whimsical" as I had been led to expect except perhaps for Christopher Robin himself; in the year of publication we read the first of the *Hobbit* books wherein the bravery of "little people" sometimes could bear comparison with Homer's "mighty men"; and the *Dr Dolittle* books by Hugh Lofting where fantasy and adventure combined with sturdy common sense and a wholesome humanity. By the time he could enjoy *Bevis* by Richard Jefferies he could read it for himself.

When he was six he had lost the square stocky contours of his "Toby" days, his face had lengthened and so had his nose, his hair, now almost as brown as his eyes, was cut short and smoothly parted. Every morning he attended a small kindergarten in Exeter of about thirty pupils in age ranging from four to eight years where he was quickly happy and at home. The school was a simple cedarwood building of two rooms at the end of a sunny garden; in summer a Kate Greenaway picture when the small chairs and tables were brought outside to stand on matting spread under plump little apple trees, the sunlight gleaming on grass and beds of flowers and the children's hair. Here the children were allowed to develop naturally without being over-stimulated. There was a timetable; and work as well as play; but the children's liveliness had plenty of scope so long as they didn't spoil things for other people; whenever we visited the atmosphere was one of busy and happy engrossment.

There was no kind of competition. Philip here was to acquire two splendid assets - an excellent grounding in writing, spelling and the basic elements of arithmetic; and an unemulative and co-operative spirit. (And when in his tenth year he entered a boys' school where competition was intense - class lists in every subject every week, terminal and examination precedences and all geared to the Common Entrance examination - he could adjust without stress and do well without emulation.) Just now however he was simply a cheerful and intelligent little boy whose disposition - especially towards ourselves - seemed unusually frank and spontaneous, so that he shared with us many of his joys and perceptions and school experiences - thus behaving very differently from my brothers and myself who would not have dreamed of sharing such confidences with the "grown-ups". I had no specific ambitions or hopes for him other than a desire that his life should continue to open, his innate qualities expand. But always I saw his future suffused as it were with a kind of radiance.

This was a happy time for us all. As well as organising adult education for the college FG was now broadcasting regularly at first from Bristol and then from London, and from the scripts, many of them first published in *The Listener*, came some of the material for his book *The Changing Village*. I was now directing the work of The Exeter Drama Group into which the first small nucleus had now expanded. I found that I had very definite ideas about the aims and function of an amateur group of players, especially feeling the necessity of long hard work in the service of a play before attempting a public performance; I insisted from the beginning that because amateurs lack both the experience and the technique of professionals they must allow ample time for gestation and so far they had presented only two plays a year. At the same time amateur players should not imagine that their audiences come primarily to see their acting; they have come to see a play of unusual interest adequately staged, lit and presented, something imaginative and suggestive. Over the years we were to give our audiences works by Chinese, Russian, German, American, Czech and British playwrights, all of which our audiences would have had to travel a long way to see, even had they been in production in this country at all. By the June of Philip's seventh birthday I had begun in my mind to plan further ahead though I told no one of my ambition to give to Exeter what Nugent Monck at the Maddermarket Theatre had given to Norwich with his amateur players; however we now had a nucleus of players capable of working constructively together,

63

had known success, had created an audience for ourselves, so that such an objective was by no means entirely out of reach.

During the mornings of Philip's second summer term, while he and FG were in Exeter and the soft-spoken and efficient Freda was at work indoors, I would work outdoors at my prompt copy, preparing for the autumn's work. After the snowdrops the plum blossom, now the summer flowers. Like the garden our lives seemed to possess a built-in certainty, and very propitious for us seemed all the omens then. The news from Central Europe seemed as far away as our own "Abdication Crisis" now sunk without trace. All seemed set fair; our buds had blossomed and now we might look forward to the fruits. Our hopes were high.

CHAPTER FOUR

Hiatus

By the following year all sense of security and stable continuity had disappeared from national life; incredulously we watched men dig sand-bagged trenches and erect barricades on the outskirts of the city of Exeter. For this was 1938, the year of Munich, and after that graceless reprieve all knew themselves vulnerable and read the posters (IT IS PEACE) with only momentary relief. We had felt the ground slipping from under our feet and thereafter obsessively watched and waited on events in Central Europe while Britain prepared for the actuality of war, postponed but now seeming inevitable.

That same summer our kind old landlord died suddenly and we had to find another house; with great regret we left Topsham and Philip said a reluctant goodbye to the water mill, the birdbrake, the "Forest", the country walks and estuary vistas and our many picnic places. Our new home was high above Exeter looking over city and river across to Haldon Hill with its marching firs on the skyline, the site and layout being sunny, spacious and airy, set in a large and prolific garden. The building, tall and solidly constructed of grey granite, would have looked severe but for the giant magnolia that covered half the walls, and clematis and passion flower festooning the windows. A lofty conservatory with tessellated paving, fringed pool and layers of white staging was attached to one side and this alone was as large or larger than the whole ground floor of Topsham; inside grew an almost bewildering variety of plantings, grevillea, red and white camellias, stag's head and tree ferns, the tall Norfolk pine, the datura heavy with exotic sweet perfume. Though the house was much more convenient, having no attics or coal cellars, and the high square rooms with their big windows must have been healthier, yet Maryfield for me always lacked the gentle human warmth of Woodlands and I never grew familiar although we lived there longer.

These events certainly affected the current of all our lives but far less profoundly than did another enforced change, this time of outlook and objective - an alteration equally unpredictable and unplanned. In March, three months before Philip's eight birthday, I had made a note that our hopes for a change in his gait and general mobility were not being fulfilled and that I - but emphatically not FG who believed he would eventually outgrow these "habits" - had begun to feel very concerned. Only a week or two later we put him to bed with a temperature and suspected measles; this proved to be a feverish chill and with treatment his symptoms cleared up rapidly. Naturally he had to recuperate after the high fever which our doctor told us was a not abnormal reaction to infection in a child, and he made a docile little patient content to rest and listen to stories and presently to sit up and read to himself. At the end of a week he was still pleased to remain where he was with no desire whatsoever to be up and dressed, and after waiting a few days when my persuasions had failed it was at FG's insistence that he somewhat tearfully suffered himself to be dressed and brought downstairs. We were distressed by his reduced agility, at which he himself evinced not the slightest concern; we realised presently that we could not ascribe his present difficulties (for example with climbing the stairs) to weakness after a brief lie-up in bed and since he did not improve with time and practice we decided to seek expert advice.

Our doctor arranged an appointment for us with Mr Norman Capener in Exeter and we counted ourselves fortunate that a specialist with an international reputation was living and practising so near; we had every hope and belief that he would be able to explain and ultimately to solve our problems; we had met him briefly once at some college function and though his clean shaven square face looked genial enough my impression had been of a man almost formidable in his expertise, assurance and authority. I hoped that he would not alarm Philip and told him in advance that Mr Capener's children had been pupils at his own little school; fortunately at the interview Philip wasn't at all nervous but chattered away quite naturally until sent off to the receptionist to look at picture books in the waiting room. As soon as we were alone we were questioned closely - had there been in ourselves or our families any history of muscular disability? The answer of course was none whatsoever and I privately longed to leave speculation and come to the solution of present problems. But I had not to wait long. Not looking at us directly and speaking gravely and quietly Mr Capener gave his verdict; beyond any doubt Philip was in the early stages of a metabolic disorder of the muscles, a very rare condition, of which nothing was known either of cause or of cure, its worst feature being that the sufferer could only get worse, the muscular weakness being invariably both progressive and irreversible.

Minutes seemed to pass while I tried to comprehend the meaning of these words - I sat stupefied as though in the silence following an explosion. At last I managed to stammer out; "Get worse? You mean he won't improve?"

Still speaking quietly yet weightily and with absolute certainty the specialist repeated; "He will worsen. He will continue to walk for a while as now, then only with help, then not even with help. He will be confined to a his chair, he will -" and at this point FG got to his feet. I saw his ashen face without the least concern, heard him say, "Excuse me," saw the nurse come, take his arm and lead him out. I remained behind asking question after question - was research being conducted into this problem? - he knew of nothing significant either in this country or America; what about the medical literature? - unfortunately negligible; could not deterioration be slowed up? - this depended on basic constitutional factors and the maintenance of good health without debilitating illness; would other children born to us be at risk? (a hypothetical question yet I asked it) - if, as we had said, there was no history of muscular dystrophy on either side of the heredity, then Philip might be regarded as "a biological sport" (I winced at this) and other children should be normal.

Eventually I stood up. "Forgive this painful, this exceedingly painful interview," he said, and I saw his damp forehead as he rose, "but it would be cruel in the extreme to encourage false hopes. In the present state of medical knowledge the disease can only progress to a tragic conclusion and it is only right that you should be prepared. I know of no practitioner, I know of no treatment, that can alter the outcome in any way whatsoever. I am desperately sorry but there it is."

While resting in bed recovering from shock, that very afternoon with white lips FG expressed his determination to fight the predicted degeneration with every means that science and medical expertise could offer. Watching the little boy happily playing under the apple trees beneath the bedroom window I could not match such strength of mind and purpose, and that for a very good reason - faintness had obliged FG to leave the room before the consultant had divulged the final outcome, and I could not increase his distress by telling him of it now. At first simply incredulous I had seemingly against my will been overwhelmed by the certainty of the forecast; that, and the commiseration with which so famous an authority had spoken seemed to leave me with no choice but to accept his verdict. After a period of wandering blindly up and down the street attempting to collect my fragmented mind, stunned into a kind of stupor, I had gone to father and son in the waiting room and we had driven home. The effect of this acceptance was to cloud my faculties and render me mentally inert, not only for that day or that week but for a very long time to come.

On the other hand next day FG's exertions began; he sought advice, wrote letters, studied the literature and daily reported to me his findings. In the space of a month he had made appointments with a Mr Roper in London who had specialised in physical education - at Eton and Bedales and in Scandinavia - before devoting himself to remedial work; he had succeeded in helping some famous patients whose problems had seemed far more intractable than Philip's were now. Before we met I had exchanged several letters with him - he wrote in a large clear script on big sheets of smooth paper and was given to headings and subheadings and sub-subheadings. His style was very precise and formal; "I have set aside Saturday 23rd, from 11 a.m. till 12.30 for you. My room (Drayton House, Gordon Street) is in the western part of Friends' House which is in Euston Road, opposite Euston Station. There are two lifts, and you will find me on the top (3rd) floor." He wrote "and", "street" "road" always in full. A page of his upright clear handwriting, with perfectly even spacing and a consistent broad margin on the left, suggested a lucid and very deliberate habit of mind.

He was an unusually fine looking man, I thought, when eventually we met outside Drayton House; in his formal London suit with monocle hanging from a black cord he looked like a distinguished diplomat. Philip was very intrigued by the eyeglass, and very matter-of-factly Mr Roper told him that since only one eye was faulty he had no need of two lenses and Philip accepted this at once as plain common sense. RER, as I came to think of him - though I would have never dreamed of so addressing him during the years I was to work and correspond with him - was probably then in his sixties; he appeared taller than he really was because he stood always very upright holding a Roman emperor head erect on straight shoulders - flexibly however, with nothing of the fixed stiff stance of the professional soldier. His hair was silver, his colouring clear and healthy; his long upper lip and chin clean-shaven; his rather thin mouth gave him an almost ascetic look; he had a fine forehead and a bold nose, and he looked with a cool and very observant eye. To this I was sensitive - he watched how Philip walked, how he got in and out of the lift, and I found such immediate concentration a little premature and too noticeable. (I imagine that at this time my judgement was warped by private pain and the bewilderment of having no idea of the why and wherefore of our problem - it seemed a strange necessity that we were there at all.) But Philip, who like his father possessed the happy gift of unselfconsciousness, was quite oblivious and at ease with RER from the beginning, and delighted that his room proved to be a small gymnasium.

That first morning RER made it his business to make it very clear to FG and myself that he had nothing to contribute by way of medical expertise; he was not concerned with diagnosis, prognosis, or with pathological research; he would be concerned entirely with problems of movement. During the ten sessions Philip and I spent with him after FG had returned to Devon I saw how he approached each individual as an entirely fresh and unique problem. He began by careful examination of physique as related to difficulties, and proceeded thence to observe how attempts had been made, often by mistaken and even by harmful methods, to compensate for them. He thought the rolling gait was definitely due to shortness of the ankle tendons and that these could gradually be made more elastic by daily exercise and gentle stretching. Moreover he found this problem had led to many other erroneous patterns of movement or to extra unneeded movements, perhaps because nerve messages were being sent to the wrong muscles and some powers therefore were "forgotten rather than lost". At the end of our fifth visit his plans "for re-education" had clarified; during five more he devised exercises and activities to preserve existing powers by ensuring that all joints should be moved once a day, and to combine these activities so to create new ones. At the same time it was essential to avoid stress and fatigue; "for Philip this is poison." In this connection he read his school reports with approval not because they were "good" but because he liked the teachers' approach to education; "Philip continues in a spontaneous way to find joy in all school activities"; "He has a happy way of acquiring knowledge" and so on. (Certainly the "good grounding" he had acquired by the time he left kindergarten at nine years old stood him in good stead for always.) Philip thought the visits to the gymnasium great fun and was delighted at the prospect of having slides and bars and ropes of his own in house and garden when we got home. (One day, in the middle of some explanation, RER inverted himself and proceeded with his exposition gravely standing on his head; Philip dared not laugh and the pair of us learned that the change of posture had an excellent therapeutic effect.)

It was necessary that I should learn something of muscular anatomy and also three types of simple massage; when Philip was amusing himself on some safe piece of apparatus I would sit with RER at the desk while he explained the mechanics of movement illustrating with neat little pencil sketches. RER had,

I am sure, quickly sized me up as incapable of independent judgement or initiative which at this time was certainly the case; but he always proceeded as though I was as objective and intelligent as himself. These were matters hitherto entirely unknown and I found much very difficult to grasp; every topic he placed before me impersonally almost as though it were a problem in engineering and the close attention this entailed on my part made our sessions as valuable for me mentally as they were for Philip physically. At night when Philip had gone to bed, I studied the page proofs of RER's forthcoming book, *Movement and Thought*, an examination of fundamentals and a study of individual problems; like himself the book was deliberate and meticulous; I discovered the value of objectivity; that I hadn't defined an object when I had described it nor necessarily knew a fact when I had given it a name; I must not think that I had dealt with my problems by merely arranging them. With humility I submitted to new disciplines, deferred to expertise, learned all that I could and did what I was told.

We returned with a very full programme and an appointment to visit Drayton House again after six months to check progress; this was to be our last London consultation though we continued to work under RER's direction and kept in constant touch by correspondence; his practical suggestions and his whole mental approach had been enormously helpful to us all.

In the beginning I had difficulty in combining the normal running of my household with two sessions daily of massage and special exercises, the need always to be present when Philip used his slides and ropes and bars, and writing for RER each week a detailed report. It was with disproportionate effort that I embarked on my new aims in life; not merely seeing the world obscured by a haze of pain and distress but being hampered by the strange sensation of moving in some palpable resistant medium as though the very air were heavy and opposing. I could not emulate FG who seemed as though stronger for the challenge he had accepted - almost exhilarated by it; he had never accepted that there was nothing we could do. Continually he urged me not to allow the situation to dominate, said we must do our utmost to avoid becoming circumscribed and himself lived out his resolve in his outside work. But for me this was an impossible demand. At first I managed every day to perform to the best of my ability the work RER had assigned; his approach was completely realistic, not my own secret and futile "however can this thing have happened?" but, "let us set about coping with the problems of movement that now confront us."

During this difficult time my current journal became of great private importance, especially because reading Mr Roper's book had reinforced my conviction that I had no capacity to think in the abstract logically and coherently in my head - a weakness for which no sensitivity of perception or understanding of isolated ideas can compensate. I used my notebooks from now on for puzzling my way through my current problems - it seemed easier to think things out if I set them down on paper - I could test conclusions, see discrepancies, begin to see where we stood. Again I realised, as at university, how much more important was an attitude towards experience than a merely emotional reaction, more, that at this juncture feelings were not merely irrelevant they were a positive hindrance, that I must develop strength of mind and will ignoring sensitivity. For one with my temperament and natural affinities these were hard lessons.

Over the months I gradually rose from my first shocked torpor but, because RER spoke only of amelioration never of cure, I had no hope that we might alter the outcome. Nevertheless I realised without denying the ultimate prognosis that our efforts might at least use and conserve all proficiencies, and within some such framework I kept despair at bay, began to rebuild my shattered will, geared and dedicated my whole self to this one over-riding purpose. Devout and honest labour kept fear at a distance and the creeping worm of doubt; sometimes I felt, obscurely and irrationally, that if only I tried hard enough there must come the reward of ultimate success; more primitive, vaguely moving below the surface of consciousness, was a strange sense of attempted propitiation.

It must have been now that perforce I laid aside a typescript in first draft of a MS awaiting drastic revision and rewriting - a recording of our year's travel by car over a wide spectrum of the United States, this crossing being then what it would not be today quite a considerable achievement particularly over the mountains and deserts. I had called my document *Span of a Continent* and cherished hopes of making it good. In present circumstances it seemed shameful that I minded thinking - rightly as it turned out - that without much more time spent than was now at my disposal it would never see the light of day. But I did mind. I laid aside my 70,000 odd words where I would be unlikely to come upon them, astonished at my intense regret.

Philip's general development continued to delight as he steadily expanded and unfolded, far too much engrossed in his endless activities to see my secret preoccupation, while for my part his daily self-fulfilment as before remained an important objective. But the parental hope of building upon the child's endowment as basis for a future member of adult society had been removed, and to this the only adjustment was to pull down a shutter to screen off foreknowledge; as the child himself did, I sought to find in each moment its own validation. Eventually this worked, but an important dimension had been removed from the perspective from which I saw our lives.

Despite the upheaval of removal and settling in and all our new activities we retained Philip's usual summer pattern; mornings at the Garden School, afternoon picnics in the country or at the seaside, tea-parties for his friends to play at the pool by the sand pit, which delights were this year augmented by games on the new equipment. And now came "Molto" into our household, given to FG as token of appreciation by his students at South Molton, and when he brought home this tiny Sealyham puppy Philip received a friend for life. He was an eager, enterprising delightful little fellow, full of zest and energy, bright eyes glinting through his tangle of white hair, so plump and frantic that if he ran too fast he fell over his fat furry feet; he hurled himself into every activity that Philip devised, they rolled and tumbled together on the grass, played games, and under FG's guidance Philip taught Molto obedience and good manners. He also was responsible for measuring the puppy food, keeping fresh water in his bowl, daily exercise and some grooming. Squatting down before Philip, looking up for ideas - ardent, expectant, mouth wide and tongue out, panting with excitement and energy - even motionless he suggested ebullient movement, endless expectancy of joy.

All in all memories of that summer are of hard work and many moments of real satisfaction; when we kept our appointment with RER in the September we were all of us happy at Philip's marked increase in agility and general freedom of movement. There followed a good autumn term and our first Christmas party in our new house.

Philip much enjoyed school, his friends, his teachers and his lessons, and gladly embarked on the next - (Easter) - term. But there were hazards and in the next spring term in company with many of his small friends Philip was laid low by three separate bouts of infectious illness, from each of which he recovered without complications. During illness all that mattered was to fight the infection and to win; it was relief, thankfulness, almost a triumph each time I had put away the thermometer and brought him downstairs. And he soon looked fit and well, his health and good spirits quickly restored; but after the last bout, really measles this time, his muscle power had again diminished; again he showed no sign of frustration, no anxiety for himself - it seemed to be mainly not to disappoint us that he co-operated so manfully in all that we attempted; nevertheless he could now walk only short distances unaided, it seemed that we must accept a new situation and work within fresh limitations.

But, before I had become daunted or Philip discouraged by the set-back, FG removed the pedals from his little old tricycle and seated upon it with no weight upon his feet and using his legs as oars our son was able to propel himself easily, speedily and safely all over the house and garden; soon he was able to use the apparatus and enjoy most of the exercises and games of the year just past. This was enormously heartening to us all. For Philip it must have been satisfying to know that he could virtually go at his own volition wherever he liked, and especially to do so under his own power; perhaps it was a relief to find himself accepted on his own terms neither asked nor attempting to perform the impossible. And FG bought an almost adult size tricycle on which Philip was delighted to pedal himself out of doors; we began again.

At this time of restoration of activity and effort came our first hope of tackling the root cause of the muscular problem - while of course continuing under Mr Roper's supervision to combat the results. Through a scientific friend we heard from an Austrian doctor now in London doing research into biochemistry for Hoffman la Roche of the famous Swiss pharmaceutical firm. They would supply us freely with certain chemical products, both tablets to take by mouth and ampoules for injection which had seemed helpful in certain cases. "*Most encouraging! - so let us try,*" she wrote. Results could be negative but had never been harmful so after discussion and medical consultations we accepted this proffered help and advice, agreeing in our turn to forward reports. FG especially was sanguine of this new development; "at last a really positive approach"; it was just a year since the prognosis.

Having by this accepted that Philip's condition could only be explained as due to an exceedingly rare genetic mutation, and in this new atmosphere of hope, FG and I at first welcomed my second pregnancy but in the third month, as soon as she heard of it our new adviser wrote again. While the mutation theory was probably true, in her experience once dystrophy had occurred there was a "strong familial tendency" for it to appear in subsequent male children. She advised that I should be given the same therapy as Philip to help the unborn foetus. It would be true to say that had we known this fact four months earlier it is unlikely that our second child would have been conceived. Abortion wasn't considered; perhaps all would be well; I might give birth to a daughter; but our first instinctive joy was sometimes commingled with dread and sometimes even superseded by it, and while FG was kind and considerate and helpful at the same time he was often silent and grave during the longest six months I can ever remember. We were both - inevitably - afraid, I think. (Yet looking back today I can see how

75

much our lives would have been the poorer had this child never lived; and the world he lived in, too. However insignificant was the corner of the world he shared with us it is out of such falsely considered "insignificances" that the whole is built after all.)

That year's winter continued long into the calendar's spring; the wind blew cold and the trees remained bare, interminably bare, under the sad grey skies. Bird song, sunshine, green leaves and warmth - had such things been, could such things ever be? How unnatural and deeply wounding it seemed that to no one, not even between ourselves, did we speak of or rejoice in the life that was to be. Yet of course they passed, those long, black days and weeks, and eventually, the spring sunshine poured hot through open windows and in the garden below hundreds of varied narcissi covered the steep banks under the flowering trees.

Philip returned to kindergarten in the summer, taken and brought home in the car - as also were many other pupils whose homes were not within walking distance; it was astonishing how he was enlivened by renewal of companionships, the lessons ("This morning we had *newts*"), and the welcome he received - "He has quite woven himself in," said his teachers. And he discovered, and I thought this of value, that many of his friends had been home suffering from the same illnesses as himself, nor did they show excessive surprise at his reduced activity, perhaps thinking only that he was taking longer than they had to convalesce.

The international situation continued to deteriorate and I think about now everyone in the country received a leaflet "If War should come". After the Drama Group's touching and beautiful performance of *Children in Uniform* we had all sensed that our work was unlikely to continue. A month later I travelled with FG on one of his regular journeys up to Broadcasting House while Philip stayed for a few days with a friend at her seaside bungalow; in London's parks the tulips stood wide-petalled in the sunshine while newspaper placards proclaimed Hitler's latest sinister dealings with the Sudetan Germans, and the feeling in the streets was tense with expectation and anxiety.

On our return Trude Ehrenberg, a Jewish refugee from Hitler's Austria, came to live with us and to help me as one of the family. Short, stout, spectacled and nearly always cheerful, how welcome was this homely Austrian girl! We tried to help her build her new life by giving her a pleasant room where she could entertain her fellow exiles and her English was so fluent that it was easy to feel her as one of us; though at first Philip had been a little doubtful he soon grew to tolerate and in the end to like her well. We had outings in the woods and on the hills, and musical picnics on the moors, Trude stepping out sturdily in front with her accordion "squeeze-box", Molto and the rest of us behind.

We wanted to celebrate her birthday in a way she would like and discussed plans with one of her friends. It seemed that the cake should be decorated with fresh flowers and Philip and I puzzled how to contrive this, eventually making a tiny circular hole in the icing and lowering a glass container into it with moist cotton wool at the bottom. Into this we inserted a nosegay of miniature roses; maidenhair fern from the greenhouse completely hid hole and container and the pink roses and pink satin ribbon encircling the cake made a confection at which Philip clapped his hands; "Oh, won't Trude be pleased!" She refused a private tea party for herself and friends and we shared her fête with them. One of the guests asked as she nibbled a macaroon; "Why is it, in Vienna, that we call these little cakes 'widow's kisses'?" "Of course it is because they are so *sweet!*" cried Trude, and she laughed and blushed and looked almost pretty. That evening I found on my pillow a letter written in her stiff stilted writing on thick blue crinkled blue paper thanking us for making glad "a day that could, dear Madame, have been so sad for me".

Next morning she made one of her rare allusions to her recent experiences in Vienna, adding to my astonishment, "And yet, you know, I could not help but applaud Hitler as he rode down the Ringstrasse!" She spoke almost complacently and though I could perhaps understand her being momentarily carried away *then*, I simply could not understand her tolerance now; no use asking her to explain, I simply gave her up with the unspoken cliché that human nature is often very mysterious.

When he was nine it was time for Philip to leave kindergarten and we therefore arranged that in September he should enter a preparatory school, so called because it aimed at preparing boys for public school entry. Norwood was a mere ten minutes walk from Maryfield and we all went along to meet the headmaster and his wife; in a pleasantly matter-of-fact way it was accepted that FG should bring him every morning on the tricycle and call for him again at midday. Once he was in the classroom seated at his desk Philip would look and be treated no differently from any other pupil. We returned in good heart bearing with us the various items of his uniform - shirt and tie, cap and blazer. When he put them on we realised how much he had developed. Under the smooth dark hair the same brown eyes looked steadily but the round stubby features of childhood had subtly lengthened into an oval face with a good nose and a more resolutely moulded mouth and chin. The child "Philip" in socks and sandals was about to become "Thomas" the satchelled schoolboy in a world of "maths" and "languages" and "order marks".

Not until the seventh month did I look over such of Philip's baby clothes as had not been given away, and bought materials for making little vests and jackets and night-gowns at which I worked in my room upstairs; with Trude's help I made a few rearrangements in the house. I would not consider the purchase of other nursery equipment until after the birth, and had deferred even these minimum preparations to the very last moment as I was unable to visualise or with certainty count on a successful outcome. By the time that our expectations had become known to intimates among our friends, although I could not feel their unrestrained delight at least I had somehow ceased to feel apprehensive misgiving for the child's sake. Philip's joy touched us both deeply. Simply now that all reasonable preparations were concluded and a case packed ready for any sudden eventuality I awaited the outcome with calm. During the next two months slowly a sense of being quietly carried along towards a new situation began to permeate all I did, and as I grew more burdened so I grew more self-contained; I withdrew and let the days drift by with an increasing sense of peace and composure. We often had tea in the garden, dog and cat stretched beside us in the sunshine and I saw the group as listener and spectator of the talk and laughter, in a kind of animal placidity, enclosed in a private world of my own.

Meanwhile like thousands of citizens all over Europe we had put our affairs on a war footing. I had assembled an "Air Raid Precautions" case of essential foodstuffs as advised by the government, our safeguard against enemy interference with supplies. FG had buckets of sand and a stirrup pump on landings and stairways in case of fire from incendiaries. A heavy door at the back of the house in the courtyard opened directly on to the wide stone stairway down to the empty wine cellars under the kitchen and storeroom. The cellars were hewn out of the solid rock on which the house was built, clean and dry with electric lighting, and they made an ideal shelter with canvas chairs stacked in readiness in a corner. A joiner cut a large wooden trapdoor in the storeroom flooring and to it fixed a flight of wooden steps so that we could get below quickly in case of emergency without having to go outside to the courtyard. Moreover this gave us an alternative exit from the cellars in case the other was blocked. Beside the packed suitcase of baby clothes stood a dreadful "respirator" with its mica face-piece like a small window in the top, and stout strap fastenings, designed for the protection of infants from poison gas; from now on every man, woman and child in the country was obliged by law to carry a case containing his grotesque gas mask whenever he went out, and to keep it always at hand in a known place when at home. FG had enrolled as member of the "Observer Corps" whose function was to chart the course of enemy aircraft flying over our area. Our friends had become "Fire-Watchers" and "Air Raid Wardens" who patrolled the streets to check the complete screening of lights and kept vigil at their posts. In September Great Britain and the Axis powers were officially at war.

Early in October our doctor called for me with his car - for of course ours was laid up "for the duration" - and at midnight we drove to the maternity home through a city dark and deserted, all houses close-curtained ("blacked-out") all street lights turned low. I had refused for so long to look beyond each present day's instancy that the coming birth had seemed a possible event rather than the advent of another human creature and I had scarcely pictured a real baby actually wearing the little garments I had made until I had handed the suitcase over to the nurse and entered my bedroom; I had almost felt disbelief when I found there a cot with tiny pillow, and the blanket already turned down, then as I stared incredulously involuntary joy had flooded me through. Next morning I felt the same incredulity when I held our second son in my arms.

When FG came in after taking Philip to school he saw a fine child (weighing nearly two pounds more than Philip had done) and we both felt a surge of hope and relief now that the long waiting was over and we could make plans for the future even though the war and our circumstances limited the possibilities. In spite of everything I could not help feeling happy and enjoyed the felicitations of visiting friends and the delight of Trude and Philip. She was voluble with home news and important with her responsibilities and her success in her role as mistress of Maryfield. Philip was curious as well as pleased, very interested in the babe's feet and hands and asked a lot of questions; curiosity satisfied, his talk was all of school fellows and the masters and the entertaining habits of his new pet, a hamster in a two-chambered little house that because he "liked the sound" he had christened "Machiavelli". However he was content that his brother should, more modestly, be called plain Richard Stuart.

During two weeks of inactivity and comparative solitude I tried to look at our family situation dispassionately and honestly. Thankfully I contemplated Philip's present and positive assets and while it might be difficult to forget the prognosis, whenever I thought of it I determined also to imagine the chance of a scientific breakthrough to nullify it, and meantime to keep all anxiety to myself. My feeling of solicitude would provide energy to ensure that nothing that could be done to make these children well and strong should ever be left undone, and for the rest I would turn my back completely on all matters that I could do nothing about in any practical way. Many months must pass before the babe's future could even be guessed at, we were all four in good health and the country as yet mercifully unassailed by the enemy; we might therefore hope to enjoy an interlude of family happiness, and so far as it lay within my power I determined that we should.

Richard was asleep tightly wrapped in his shawl when we came home and I laid him down into his waiting bassinet; Trude was upstairs, Philip at morning school, FG at the telephone, and I had a moment alone. After the almost continuous sound of opening and shutting doors and busy nurses' feet here was complete quiet; there was a rustle in the ilexes as a current of air stirred the curtain, and I felt an intense thankfulness at my return before I went upstairs to unpack and begin anew. At long last I was able to discard my maternity dress and changed into my tweed suit and maize-yellow jersey. As I stood at the airing cupboard stacking a pile of clean nappies Trude stood at the head of the first stair landing. "Ah!" she exclaimed, "Ah, madame, what pleasure to have you back and now to see you look like this! Before I could have no idea—" and she coloured and laughed. "This is my usual shape," I said, and we laughed together. After two weeks down in the town the house on the hillside seemed wonderfully light, bright, spacious and airy. To my relief Richard slept until after Philip's return and we all lunched together "like old times", as he said with a big sigh of satisfaction.

The expected hostilities being long delayed, over the next six months the nation had a breathing space, and at Maryfield we watched our baby thrive and grow while with accustomed equanimity Philip adjusted to his school, made new friends, and combined interest with proprietary pride in his small brother. He kept fit and well all winter and was as happy and successful at Norwood as at the little "Garden School" doing especially well in Latin, French and mathematics. At the end of the first week he had brought home several "lists" - the weekly head of class in each subject being given the list to take home as trophy. His lists grew to be routine and we were glad that he took all this in his stride, FG declaring that he valued his sense of proportion as much as his success. At Christmas and Easter he had both "Star" and "Form" prizes; not indifferent to success he wasn't in the least elated by it; he read his books and put them on the shelf and became absorbed in holiday pursuits with his friend Martin. Since his aptitudes were neither bookish or laborious we believed his success due to a wonderfully clear intelligence - not that he knew a great deal, but that he had grasped and understood and so could use effectively all the knowledge that he had. To listen to his chatter, school meant fun and camaraderie and a varied assortment of fellow beings - he could be most entertaining when recounting stories of boys and masters. It did not seem that his handicap made him feel different and we supposed that he didn't feel so because in essence he wasn't "different"; a microscopic chemical deviation in his make-up had not turned him into a different person. His good looks may have helped; a stranger seeing that class of boys would only have singled him out for that reason, if at all.

Another letter - the third - arrived from la Roche when Richard was about six months old advising that he be given reduced doses of Philip's daily medication and therefore a crushed white tablet as prescribed was regularly incorporated into Richard's vegetable puree. Until now I had succeeded in my resolve not to contemplate a problematic future but this letter brought a serious possibility forcibly back to mind. What I could do in a practical way I did; I gave the baby his bath upstairs to give freer scope for his vigorous splashing, slapping and plunging around in the water; I let him play naked in his playpen in front of the fire and outdoors when the weather was warmer; I was even tempted to exercise his limbs, but would not, lest I do more harm than good. But I soon discovered that labour on the practical level could not drive out of mind the implications of this last letter - disquiet might be concealed, it could not be prevented. With Philip we had no previous experience, no other child with whom we might compare him; now I knew what might have been unrecognised warnings in his infancy, and during the next few months, in a small notebook kept apart from the journal I noted dates of Richard's crawling, dentition, standing, walking, shape of feet, size and shape of calf muscles. These compulsive observations were entirely for myself, indeed I felt sometimes ashamed of them, yet this little book must have served as helpful outlet in a time of almost sickening anxiety, during which I managed at least to keep feelings tangential to my main endeavour.

Until June 1940 people spoke of a "phoney war" though uneasily aware of the shapeless future under which menace the whole of Europe lay. But although hostilities had not begun our world was changing fast. Many of FG's colleagues had left for war work elsewhere and we knew that he himself might be called up at any time; Trude's linguistic gifts had been requisitioned and her place taken by "Di", an untiring healthy girl from a farm between Exeter and Crediton; every eligible male in the Drama Group had been mobilised; we were virtually separated from all but Exeter friends because petrol was only issued to civilians with special duties. Yet although so many had departed, the city was almost over-populated, being full of "evacuees" from London, the narrow pavements thronging with young mothers with toddlers and fleets of perambulators. Later there arrived Miss Elsie Fogerty with her now almost exclusively female School of Speech Training; then the London School of Medicine for Women.

To this influx from outside Philip owed his school friend Martin, whose parents had left Bristol to avoid possible air-raids and all three were living with his grandparents a little higher up the hill, in a large house with a beautiful garden and superb views over the city and the course of the river Exe. Martin must have been, if not lonely then a bit isolated at weekends and soon it was the regular thing for him to spend part of Saturday with us; we were a lively household with dog, cat and baby, and upstairs a big playroom with model trains and rolling stock, Matador and Meccano, and all the children's story books and toys and games. During the holidays he came down almost daily, and eventually I asked him to invite his mother to come one afternoon for tea. I was delighted when she came to meet the woman I had several times seen in Hoopern Fields, striding forth buoyantly in brogues and tweeds, with a fresh eager look on her face. Edith must then have been in her late forties; I discovered that her husband had instructed and trained FG's group of the Observer Corps - Paul looked like a handsome subaltern of the 1914 War, which indeed he once had been, though now his elder son was called up and in the army. When we returned the visit we met Grandpa Read, a big fine active man of eighty with large sandy moustache and booming voice; and Granny Read, small and delicately made with a gentle face under silvery hair, wearing a narrow black velvet ribbon round her throat and generally a fichu or touch of lace at the neck. We came to love this cheerful warm-hearted household endued with a simple all-embracing kindliness; Edith herself, with the laughter-lines at her eyes and the corners of the mouth, had grown up spontaneously and without complications just as she herself was uncomplicated and spontaneous. It was good at the time of my secret anxieties on Richard's behalf, then at their worst, to know such a person, and a home whose life progressed so smoothly and straightforwardly.

That same summer Susan B and small daughter Carola came to live near us. We had met briefly a few years previously shortly before her marriage to a young naval officer after which she had lived in Singapore where he was stationed. I remembered well her gaiety and sense of fun, her sudden spurts and gushes of laughter, her youthful and unselfconsciousness enjoyment of her happiness. She wore her shining dark hair parted in the middle and drawn back into a knot in the nape of her neck; her face with its small red mouth, wide forehead and fine eyes under this demure hair-do made a piquant and delightful contrast. Nor had her appearance much changed when she paid her first visit to Maryfield bringing her little girl. But we knew that her husband had been aboard the *Glorious* sunk in the ill-fated Norwegian expedition and now she had no certainty of knowledge other than that the ship had been lost and her husband posted "missing presumed drowned"; that before the ship went down he had been seen attempting to launch a cutter; and that there were islands where he might even now be receiving shelter from the inhabitants supposing he had managed to reach land.

After she had settled in her new home with her elderly mother and little girl, Susan came very often to visit us and my own private anxieties were dwarfed when I imagined the terrible fluctuations between hope and despair that her uncertainties must have caused. For her part she sympathised warmly, even at this time of her own trial, with all that we were attempting for Philip (it was only of *his* problems that I spoke the other being too painful even to hint at). She frequently helped at weekends when I had no help from Sunday afternoon until Monday morning when Di arrived on her bicycle from her weekly visit to her distant village, and we had long talks while the three children played together or when we took them all out for a walk - talks often grave with unuttered feeling though never with emotional surrenders. With the brave and gallant Susan I was to enjoy a brief friendship intensely valuable to us both.

The "phoney war" ended suddenly when France and the Low Countries fell before the Blitzkrieg of June 1940, and it was strange and dreadful to see contingents of the British Army, rescued by the flotillas from Dunkirk, marching, or rather shambling through our streets, gaunt exhausted men just landed from the Channel into the estuary of the Exe, without their arms or equipment, or even without uniform or adequate clothing. Despite the desperate situation England was not "finished", as Ambassador Kennedy then reported to Roosevelt, but prepared to wage war and resist attack to the bitter end. And so the air "Battle of Britain" marked the next phase, and it was on the night of the first attack on the city of London that FG departed thither, having been seconded for work at the Ministry of Labour. With brief periods of leave at widely spaced intervals he was to live away from his family for nearly six years.

Richard was then almost a year old and during the following months my anxieties on his behalf were sometimes allayed though not dispelled. In truth I had grown obsessed with my concern and not a week passed in which I didn't use the little notebook (always kept apart from my journal) to record moments of relief or what almost was anguish. I had vainly hoped that he might develop earlier than the "average" for that might have set my mind completely at rest; when this didn't happen I hoped that he might be "average" which he just managed to be

85

- this at least meant that he was some months in advance of his brother at the same age in all the successive stages of his development. I sensed, as I posted my long letters to FG telling him the lively doings of the family and especially of Richard's growth and prowess how my life had begun to be lived on two levels - were it possible today to compare one of these letters with a notebook entry of the same date the contrast might seem startling, although both were perfectly true. Although such reserve with FG perhaps seems extraordinary since my feelings prolonged over so many months were surely natural, yet I think in some strange way that keeping them from him and from everyone else must have been, in the long run, strengthening.

Early in December I was disquieted to hear from my "daily" that she had been in recent contact with a case of measles in her lodgings; our doctor agreed that we must do our utmost to prevent Richard becoming infected at the age of fourteen months and I especially feared that the side effects might be as severe as two years before in Philip's case. There was a serum which conferred some protection if used in good time, and he made an appointment for me to consult the pathologist at the hospital that same evening. I had to wait about half an hour in the laboratory, and because I was perhaps tired, or unused to doing nothing, or daunted at this sudden unexpected emergency, my spirits were at a low ebb when at last he hurried in. He quickly galvanised me for he was a lively voluble man, short, ruddy, very quick of speech and movement, very intensely concentrated upon the matter he had in hand. He explained what his injections would consist of, its immediate value, length of time of the possible immunity conferred. Why, he wanted to know, did I so urgently want to use it all, and he pricked up his ears at the words muscular dystrophy, "an inscrutable thing" on which he was sure he had read some recent paper. He told his assistant to bring in the year's files of *The British Medical Journal* and *The Lancet* and while I waited he went through them - all of course unbound and without index. Rapidly and impatiently he furled through the pages, flung them down, rubbed his chin, passed his hand over his head once or twice, then went over them all over again, still rapidly and jerkily though perhaps more methodically until he found what he wanted. He handed the document over and waved away my thanks. "Take it with you. I'll collect it when I come up to perform the injections - as soon as I have got hold of the serum."

It was very dark outside in the black-out, it was late and cold. But I could not wait until I got home to read the paper. Every dimmed street lamp cast down a faint blur of light on to a patch of pavement immediately below and I made for the nearest one and under its pale gleam I half-incredulously read what had so chancily come into my hands. The paper, written from a London dispensary, was in two parts. First the writer described researches abroad on animal muscle whereby withholding essential vitamin E from the diet had produced the various changes associated with the human dystrophies, normality being restored by re-administration of the vitamin. Secondly he described individually his own clinical experience with more than a score of patients treated with vitamin therapy; many had improved "dramatically"; just as importantly none had lost ground where deterioration might have been thought inevitable. He concluded that this form of progressive muscular weakness resulted not from a disease but from a deficiency, and that therefore it was curable.

Almost three years had passed since the prognosis during which time this work must have been undertaken and concluded; it might well be the "breakthrough" of FG's constant hoping. Some such thought crossed my mind as I put the periodical back into its envelope, but instead of feeling relief and joy I seemed almost to be trembling with fear; inwardly I was numb as I pushed my bicycle up the steep hill between the shuttered houses. I decided to make further enquiries and the following morning wrote and posted a letter to the author in London. Thereafter time almost stood still; the injections were given; I returned the periodical with heartfelt thanks and received some further encouragement; Richard did not develop measles. Eventually I received an answer to my letter, beginning with the words; "I am quite certain that very very slowly we can cure your son."

The next three months were filled with increasingly buoyant activity. I wrote telling Mr Roper of this new approach and early in the New Year he came down from London to spend a few days with us. I was a little nervous of this visit, hoped for no heart-searchings but rather to behave as though the successful rearing of both children were a foregone conclusion, but in truth my hopes were as yet tentative and uncertain and I could not quickly discard recent preoccupation. When he arrived, outwardly unchanged, tall, spare, well-groomed and distinguished, I met his searching look as we shook hands, but he spared me verbal questioning, and when I had taken him to his room I came quickly downstairs. Philip, easy and natural as usual, was very pleased to meet him again and to introduce his small brother already beginning to walk. RER welcomed the new possibilities and subsequently wrote at length outlining his suggestions, having first taken the trouble to meet and discuss with FG matters not broached in Exeter.

After this visit I explained to Philip the meaning of a vitamin deficiency and how we aimed to correct his own imbalance; in his turn he revealed his hitherto unspoken belief that his several illnesses had left him with weakened limbs but that he had always expected them to return to normal. He would soon be eleven years old and until now his attitude of easy acceptance had been a mystery; now we had his confidence.

Presently the London doctor sent to us a colleague who had worked for a period with him but who now, as part of some war-reorganisation, had been directed into general practice at Tiverton in Devon. She was probably about fifty, white hair cut short like a man's, direct blue eyes in an alert intelligent face, country tweedy tailored clothes, quiet manner, speech clear and to the point. When she had obtained all the data she required I took the opportunity to ask her a great many questions and she indicated the need for further research; at the same time she felt that we should concentrate on the possibilities opened up by what we already did know, and I was only too thankful to do this.

Eventually this acceptance lessened the need for effort and struggle because if we encouraged and continued every possible form of healthful activity and at the same time made good the known deficiency then we might, without battling, leave the result to nature. And as the disastrous prophecies of three years before receded into the past no longer was willed effort required to disregard them. The clouds rolled back, the horizon expanded, and life seemed even brighter than before because of the supervening dark - which now began to seem like a temporary interruption of our old way of life.

These things happened not suddenly but slowly, a joy that seeped through to irradiate all living. So that when one afternoon Richard and I walked out in the rain, his Wellington boots twinkling through the puddles, his waterproof and sou'wester making bright blue reflections, I knew an upsurge of the delight first experienced in my own infancy; once more the dimension of futurity had become the dimension of hope, Jane Austen's "sanguine anticipation of happiness which is happiness itself."

CHAPTER FIVE

Maryfield's War

To Blake's affirmation that "energy is eternal delight" I now discovered perhaps a corollary, that out of great joy may spring the flow of energy in full spate. Certain it was that in the months of happy enterprise that now ensued no burden seemed too heavy; in his absence I buoyantly shouldered all FG's responsibilities in addition to my own, almost glorying in my labours now that an attainable objective lay ahead in the future. The journal was virtually laid aside and I picked up my pen instead to write my twice-weekly letters to FG in London; Richard's little notebook was forgotten (it turned up twenty years later and I glanced over its contents, realised that it had fulfilled its purpose, and consigned it to the dustbin). A handful of the old Drama Group had come up to Maryfield to read plays once a week but the effects of war work and the black-out had soon ended this. Edith and Martin, Susan and Carola, we saw regularly as a matter of course, and my own better expectations seemed to augur for Susan that, although she had no news of her husband after almost a year of uncertainty, she must not relinquish her own now wavering hopes. ("It's so absolute, darling, so final. That's what makes giving up so terrible.")

Though not in close touch with many old friends we were soon welcoming new ones. About now one of FG's friends at the BBC wrote telling me of the plight of his son, just called up and stationed with his unit in Exeter where he knew nobody - could I do anything? So having met and liked Michael I arranged for my neighbour's seventeen year old Bunty and her fiancé together with her cousin Mary and two or three others to meet at Maryfield one evening a week to drink coffee and get acquainted. After the first evening I would take in the coffee tray and leave them to their fun - a merry crowd, often sitting in a big circle on the floor in front of the fire playing "vingt-et-un" or talking. Mary was lovely of feature and colouring but suffered from the disadvantage of being more than six feet tall. However Michael topped six feet three inches and their engagement and marriage was a happy sequel to their Maryfield friendship (they wrote me long afterwards a grateful letter - I have speculated sometimes on the height of their offspring).

Shortly before Easter I met outside the dairy a friendly somewhat untidy woman with a baby in a pram; I took her for the child's grandmother, perhaps yet another Cockney "evacuee", so I was surprised at her cultivated speech and still more at hearing that the infant was her baby daughter Ursula; she had another little girl at convent school and two sons, the elder at Dartmouth Naval College, the other at school in Reading. I liked her squareish build and rosy honest face and asked her to try to visit us and in a very few days she did; she turned out to be a motherly practical kindly-disposed woman who was living for the day when she would be re-united with her husband, an official with the Ministry of Agriculture in Kenya. Before leaving she rather diffidently asked me whether I could possibly put up Adrian, her second boy, for his approaching Easter holiday; she and the little girls would be able to stay at the convent but she had no suitable plans for him; he was fond of small children and family life, it would be "a marvel" for him to stay in a companionable home and a great relief to her of a rather pressing problem. I gladly agreed; he was thirteen, Philip nearly eleven, Martin younger, and I thought they might fit in rather well.

In due course he arrived, not at all like his deliberate and stockily built mother, being slim and fair with a very lively open look and sudden impulsive movements. Kaye came with me up to his room on arrival and helped unpack his case. "Put these here," she said pointing at the chest of drawers. "And these there; then they'll all be ready and in order when you pack your case to go." "Oh I say, mother!" he expostulated, "don't talk about me going before I've even arrived!" He cocked his head at us with a most engaging and comical look at his mother followed by a loud schoolboy guffaw. He swarmed downstairs on the banisters and made friends with Richard, picking him up and talking to him as though he'd known him for years, Richard for his part delighted to respond. In spite of being older he proved an excellent companion for Philip and Martin; they were rather a quiet pair and the exuberant Adrian enlivened them considerably, convulsing them at mealtimes by asking for "the sneezing powder" when he wanted the pepper, and tilting dangerously on the two back legs of his chair as he burst into one of his frequent explosions of mirth.

While he was with us we had several air-raid "Alerts" and we frequently could hear the raiders and even an occasional bomb, not aimed at us but jettisoned to lighten their load as the planes passed over the estuary back to their continental base. One raider was brought down in the sea and Paul - Martin's father, head of the local Observer Corps - joined us in our walk one afternoon to show the three boys where another had crashed in open country. Adrian, Martin and Philip excitedly followed Paul's pointing finger and thought they could see a distant smoke rising though I could see nothing but the woods and the fields. Two men had baled out to safety, one had perished in the plane, and as we stood just below Paul's look-out post - the peaceful countryside now veiled in spring's soft green - it seemed an unbelievable business. But it could be real enough at night when doors and windows rattled, and especially on the two occasions when I had actually seen the flash of an explosion. I had then roused my household and taken them to sit close to our shelter in the wine cellars until the "All Clear" signal. The boys usually slept well and rarely heard the sirens and to me my times of listening and watching seemed next morning like a bad dream of the night. Nevertheless during this holiday I had upstairs playroom and downstairs study interchanged to make a day/night nursery of the big room downstairs where Philip and Richard slept in the greater safety of the ground floor.

By now Richard had grown out of babyhood into an agile, lively and enterprising infant very different in looks and temperament as well as in build and colouring from his dark and equable older brother, being blue-eyed with fair skin and hair, and apt to fly into passions of rage when grub screws refused to come out of door handles or closed cupboards would not open. He was going through the exploratory phase with tremendous concentration - when all was quiet we used to tremble, and his forays and escapades kept us in a state of almost continued vigilance. Needless to say such almost ceaseless activity to me was relief unspeakable. At the same time with the dog and cat and all his toy "animals" he was always tenderly solicitous; he was affectionate and loved to play with other children while Philip, Carola and Martin were all devoted to him. There were endless charades using the big chest of "dressing-up clothes"; the mothers, Susan and Edith, Kaye and I, were available to help and to applaud, while Richard was always most co-operative, suffering himself to be dressed up by the others, and always portentiously solemn - perhaps overawed by all the older children. I wrote to London with news of all the doings:

Even without Adrian and Martin, by calling in Di and me the younger ones managed a playlet yesterday. Philip was Emperor of Arabia in scarlet robe ensconced in a draped chair as throne; Carola his Favourite Concubine (!) in Dresden Shepherdess costume; Di in blue was Princess Violetta of the Kingdom Adjacent; with her the Heir Apparent, Prince Bulla, (Richard) with a scarlet fillet on his head and a piece of gold lace for a cloak hanging from his shoulders; I was Slave as well as Grand Vizier. The Emperor was peremptory, the Shepherdess Concubine a picture of childish innocence, the Vizier pompous, the Princess inclined to giggle, the Slave abject and grovelling, and the Prince very solemn especially when plighting his troth to Carola's best doll. The Grand Vizier at this point got into trouble for remarking that 'in those days people did get engaged young', the Emperor ruling that asides were *not* allowed, 'they spoilt everything'.

"How I wish you had been here to see Richard, the little Fairy Princeling..."

Toward the end of the holiday Adrian's brother visited us with his mother; he was on last leave having been posted to his ship after successfully passing out from Dartmouth. Michael was just twenty-one, like his mother square of face and of build, and looked well in his blue uniform with its gold buttons; Kaye looked proud yet troubled, but Philip and Adrian were mightily impressed, especially when he said, "And I've got a *battleship* - can't say which for security reasons but it's incredible good luck at first posting," and tipped them a lordly ten shillings each on his departure.

Before Adrian went back to school Kaye and I agreed that he should spend at least part of his summer holiday with us and that his small sisters Alison and Ursula with their mother should come as well - Martin and Philip were jubilant.

During the summer term, stimulated by the holiday endeavours Philip and I now embarked upon the writing of two short plays using the characters created by Hulme-Beaman in his well-liked *Toytown* radio series. We collaborated very happily, building up our situations ingeniously and improvising the dialogue as we went. The value of these weeks of often hilarious labour lay in the success we had in devising the structures, that within these we created comical incident, and best of all that both plays were completed as whole creations - we really had succeeded in making something, something not merely begun but finished in all its aspects. I had them typed and sent them up to *Children's Hour*, where they were read "with considerable amusement" but of course returned because the characters were the author's copyright. We ourselves however put them to use on several happy occasions.

During FG's summer leave one cloudless morning he and I left the children in charge of Di and Susan, and took the train to Dulverton; after lunching at the inn we spent the whole afternoon wandering in the woods above the river Barle. We were then both thirty-nine but we might have been nineteen, walking hand in hand, resting among ferns in the shade or beside small glittering streams as if we had no care, as though the day would last forever. And during Philip's summer holiday Di took full charge of Richard for a week at her home while Philip and I holidayed in the same area. We seemed tireless; he and I and the tricycle covered fifty miles that week. I see at this moment a curve of white road following the bend of some little river; woods climb from the water's verge up to the hilltop; here we have paused to take it all in. This instant is indelibly printed upon memory - a picture not important, with no underlying significance, yet still unforgettable - why this out of all the other moments that I might now remember?

But although despite FG's absence this was the happiest summer we had known since Topsham in 1937, the year 1941 was a tragic one for Kaye and her family. During an enemy engagement in May, by a thousand to one chance the battleship *Hood* had been hit by a shell which had exploded in the magazine; the ship had literally blown up and virtually the whole ship's company had perished - there had been only three survivors. The disastrous news had been immediately broadcast to the nation by the BBC seeking thereby to forestall enemy announcements jubilating at the destruction of the Royal Navy's proudest vessel, and this meant that it was with brutal suddenness that all next of kin heard of their loss. Kaye's young Michael, one of the junior officers, had not been among the survivors and she had been sitting quietly listening-in with her hosts, Judge and Mrs Thesiger, when this bolt had fallen on her out of the blue; she had scarcely known a carefree moment since he had put to sea, and now anxiety was succeeded by a more terrible certainty.

In less than a week she came to Maryfield. She could not speak of her boy by name, only of the loss of the *Hood*. She looked aged and exhausted. "He's gone. But what to do?" She opened her hands and spread her arms in a gesture of helplessness and emptiness, then rose, her face working, and walked to the window. I shared her helplessness. What was there to do? What was there to say? Nor were feelings at all assuaged when, after long pursuit, the great enemy ship *Bismark* was cornered and sunk, also with great loss of life. The insane wastage, the huge grief and misery of warfare, the horror, clutched many hearts, British and German alike.

The August visit of Adrian and his family could not repeat the gaiety of his Easter holiday. He was sobered by Michael's death and probably also by the sense of now being sole elder brother of his two small sisters, and his parents' only son. The other children, Philip and Martin, Carola and Richard, and Kaye's two little girls, were full as ever of liveliness and zest, and maybe the mothers, each with her private load to carry, Edith (her son now on active service) and I as well as Kaye and Susan, were glad to immerse ourselves in the doings of little children whose concern was solely with their present moment. Kaye was extraordinarily brave but inevitably had her bad days when speechlessly she seemed to enter wholly into her grief; no one could reach her; she was alone, remembering and suffering dumbly.

On one such day I suggested that we went down with her two daughters to visit their convent school. The Reverend Mother met us in the kitchen garden and we walked the narrow paths between the vegetable plots in the sunshine looking at the apples and pears and plums while the children ran about. Kaye's face remained bleak and stony and she found speech difficult. Little Alison found a rosy windfall in the grass and came to ask the Reverend Mother if she might eat it. The old woman said she thought it ripe enough, and taking the fruit in one hand and child by the other turned into the greenhouse, the rest of us following. Just inside the door stood a pipe with a tap which she turned on, rolled up her black serge sleeve and held the apple in her little red hand turning and washing it in the flowing water. Kaye watched as intently as the children, her face softening, and I recognised this to be a good moment though I could not have said why.

Later as we walked back up the hill she told me all she could remember of Michael's early childhood.

Before Autumn term began Kaye suggested that she and the two little girls might live at Maryfield on a permanent footing joined by Adrian in his holidays. It was an excellent idea - if I would cater and cook she would shop and take over the gardening; if Di (now married to a young soldier) were called up we could manage without her; if either was unwell the other would take over; and the children would continue as playfellows. If only, I thought - then, and very often afterwards - she had spoken earlier! But most unfortunately I was firmly committed until Easter to accommodating three medical students from the college - had felt unable to refuse since with the accommodation available I was lucky not to be put in charge of "evacuee" children, a difficult assignment for a parent with my special cares and responsibilities.

All the same I had been reluctant to accept these students although they all - Pamela, short and dark, business-like and brisk, Catherine, fair and gentle and soft-spoken, and Seeta, shy and silent, a beautiful young Indian - made me eager promises if only I'd be persuaded. No wonder they were so anxious to come, said Kaye; FG's study to work in and two large airy rooms upstairs, a beautiful house and sunny garden - compared with the "digs" they had probably inspected elsewhere Maryfield must have seemed sheer luxury. I told the girls frankly of my difficulties and for their part they offered to make their own beds and keep their rooms tidy, said they would be out from breakfast until dinner at least five days out of seven, and would in all ways give the minimum of trouble...

They turned out to be very agreeable guests and all their promises they scrupulously kept; moreover they were so regular in their ways that we could almost live by a timetable. But by their Christmas holiday, after the girls had been with us three months, I realised that perhaps I had undertaken too much, though had we been a normal household there might have been no problem.

During the previous year I had successfully managed the trips to and from school with Philip and the tricycle, every morning and every afternoon; though Saturday afternoon was free, this meant four times down and four times up the steep Pennsylvania Hill on all the other days; I had taken over FG's gardening and the business running of our establishment; and had not neglected my own duties or Philip's daily massage, exercises and use of the Roper apparatus. It had been a full programme but I had not found it difficult. I had thought that the students' stay might be similar to Kaye's with her children but of course it was very different. In the first place Kaye's family had always visited during holidays when there were no time-and-energy consuming journeys to and from school; their visits lasted for about three weeks, not twelve as now with never even a free weekend; Kaye had in fact lightened my load while for these young women I felt responsible in a special way for their health and comfort and for getting the best value out of their rations; it had been that much easier when we had all eaten our main meal midday and had the last one all together in the big nursery playroom after which there had been plenty of time for three of us to tidy up generally and put the children to bed; now, although the girls dined at six to give them a long evening for study and they always departed upstairs with their coffee tray immediately afterwards, a main meal had to be served and cleared up before Di and I did anything else, and even she, so good tempered and patient, once spoke crossly of "that old dinner".

Almost inevitably I grew more and more engrossed; the only outside engagement that I can remember was an evening judging the one-act play competition at the college; my letters to FG grew shorter, less lively; instead of reading by the fire after the boys had gone to bed I often dropped asleep over my book. After going down from university I had discovered that with me absorption in doings and dealing with *things* more often than not led to a dishevelled state of mind - I might have inherited some of my mother's zest for being consumed entirely by each day's activity, but whereas she sought this constantly and enjoyed it, I really, like my father, temperamentally required times of quietude in which to ruminate my experience. Now such opportunities came rarely and the purpose of my toil was simply to get it done which isn't real work, only labour; only for and with the children was my life in those days valuable in the true sense of the word.

Both boys enjoyed excellent health during the whole six months of the girls' sojourn, and although I looked vainly for positive improvement in Philip's condition I remembered the words, "very, very slowly", and told myself that I should be thankful that he was growing normally and showed no sign of the predicted degeneration. Both, I am sure, knew I was burdened and did all they could to help me. I recall leaving them in the playroom on one of Di's half-days while I tidied up the evening meal, "blacked-out" all the windows, turned down their beds, prepared for baths. I felt very tired and sat down for a moment in the hall before I listlessly opened the door and went in to collect Richard. The room was perfectly tidy! - every single toy and game away in drawers and cupboards, and two lively faces awaiting my surprise. "Your room for the evening," said Philip, adding with characteristic honesty, "It's a good thing you've come - we were wondering whatever to do next!"

On the whole hope for him held firm though sometimes overwork and lack of FG's supporting presence made me uncertain; on the other hand Richard continued to reassure with his general development and the delights he discovered in his own small world - boys and girls, rain and sunshine, birds, flowers, insects, his own dog and cat - he enjoyed them all, and was absorbed in observation and activity until, in white nightie and little blue jacket, rosy and placid after his bath, I tucked him into bed for the night. Once as I was about to lower him into his crib I knew a rare feeling of despair when I really felt that I could not go on (probably only tiredness at the end of a long day but none the less real for that). The instant of self-doubt held me motionless, my face perhaps revealing more than I knew. At that moment Richard placed his arms about my neck embracing me tenderly before placing two kisses gently on my face. I laid him down and he snuggled in happily for the night, but then and afterwards I felt astonishment - not because he had never before either kissed or embraced me (he was then only two) but that he had done so at just this moment. With or without the success I longed for, I felt my labours not entirely vain with such tokens of trust and affection to uphold me.

Whether coincidence or whether a baby heart had somehow sensed my need (and why not?) of course I could never know. By April change was in the air. Our three student friends departed; Kaye telephoned me to say that she had discovered a house and would at long last have a home for her family at Newton Poppleford; Sue came down one afternoon to say that Carola was accepted as pupil at a school for the daughters of naval officers and that she herself would then go to work in Cambridge. She had now been widowed two years; in her face a new sweetness replaced the impishness I remembered - and found it painful to remember. She knew her going would be a loss to me and came down oftener than before, always beautifully groomed and dressed and smelling delicious - then my only friend who used perfume, but with such discretion that one was only aware of an elusive waft of a suspicion of fragrance. She spoke slowly now, almost dreamily; moved smoothly, was always calm but; "We never took our heavenly times for granted. We always knew we were specially specially *fortunate* to have married one another." How I wished I could have done more for her! She reassured me; "I shall always think of you as a godsend, darling."

Meanwhile the days grew warmer and longer and when FG came down to spend the first weekend in May it certainly was pleasant to have the house entirely to ourselves. He spent some time checking over the air-raid equipment because the previous week incendiary bombs had been dropped on Exeter - one through our conservatory roof which had burned out harmlessly on the tiled paving. Edith had sent Martin away to friends in nearby Crediton, remaining herself with Paul and the old people in the big house up the hill. FG greatly enjoyed his brief respite and decided at the last moment to spend an extra night with us, returning to London early on Monday instead of Sunday night as usual.

We had all been asleep for some hours when I was awakened by the "Alert" signal ululating its minor wail and I sat up in bed to listen for enemy bombers and when I recognised the pulsing reverberation of their distant engines I got out of bed without putting on the light and raised a corner of the black-out curtain. I was appalled to see hundreds of glimmering lights falling out of the sky over the sleeping town; all was strangely quiet, the planes seemingly at a great height, but the stealthy descending radiance of their flares lit up the whole city, a clearly exposed target, and there was no mistaking what was about to happen. I roused FG and we instantly betook ourselves with the children down the steps below the store room into the rock-hewn wine cellars; Philip had a blanket, Richard and I had picked up a coat as we sped through the hall, but with all our haste we had barely erected the canvas chairs before the raid began. FG would not allow me to go back for the dog and cat but closed the trapdoor and we prepared to sit it out.

During the next two hours we remained like animals huddled together for safety in a hole in the ground while - unlike animals - our own kind sought to destroy us. The noise was tremendous and almost continual; sometimes we attempted to crouch deeper, heads bent, into our chairs as a dive-bomber seemed about to penetrate our fastness, afterwards exchanging looks of relief at near-misses; we could not attempt to talk and none of us showed fear - we behaved as though helplessly accepting a cataclysm of nature; by the light of the bare electric bulb I mechanically read the metal labels on the old wine racks - Hock, Burgundies, Claret.

At last there came quite a pause and we hoped all was over, that we would presently hear the "All Clear". Richard miraculously slept in my arms, Philip was awake and calm - I suppose it was about two o'clock in the morning and as nothing seemed to be happening FG, veteran of many London air-raids, proposed to ascend the steps to the kitchen and make tea. We sat shouting hopefully up to him as we waited for the kettle to boil, and he shouted down to us that Molto was safe in his basket, and the kettle beginning to sing.

With dreadful suddenness a dive bomber approached with an almost unbearable increase of sound. There was a sudden burst of gunfire just as a bomb came shrieking down and hit the earth so that it shook. There ensued a long and terrible confusion. The huge rending explosion was followed by instant darkness, the house shuddered, drew in upon itself, seemed to cringe, then with a tearing of wood, shattering of glass, riving apart of masonry and metal the fabric was sucked apart by the blast and flung aloft and around to fall back again to earth in a pouring down of debris that seemed to go on forever. Eventually silence; and pitch darkness. Before anyone had spoken I had handled both children, then as though from a long way off FG's voice called from above, "Are you there?" and I said, "We're all right - and you?" "Yes, but the trapdoor's covered with rubble - I'll have to get to you from the back drive." I switched on my torch but could see nothing whatsoever, and had clicked the switch vainly several times when Philip said quietly, "If you are testing your torch, Mummy, you'd better wait until the dust settles," thus explaining what I was then too dazed and stupid to understand for myself. While we sat breathing the smell of powdered plaster and granite rubble in the silence of another lull I became aware of water trickling steadily down the wall behind me, probably I imagined from a fractured water main, a very disquieting thought. I said nothing, and presently tried the torch again and could now see that the cellar was intact together with the steps leading up to the kitchen. I felt it imperative to get us all above ground as quickly as possible so I laid Richard down in my chair and climbed the steps. Although I pushed at the trapdoor with all my strength it was immovable. Without hesitating Philip agreed to sit with Richard alone in pitch darkness while I went with the torch into the adjoining cellar whence the wide stone stairway led to our alternative exit to the back courtyard. This cellar was also undamaged though the treads of the stairs were smothered with blocks of torn granite and masonry; yet at the top of this rough incline there flickered a rectangle of red and lurid light signifying that the heavy outer door had been blasted outward not inward as I had feared. By crawling and clambering over the debris we could get outside - a tremendous relief this. To this open door now came FG from the drive, almost unrecognisable as also was I, both us covered in a grey film, features, hair and eyelashes thick with bomb dust, coats like ashy cerements. With him came a uniformed and helmeted warden who agreed that since the worst appeared to be over we should all get above ground - he did not think the water immediately dangerous but there was a risk at any moment of further subsidence of the house. Since the falling of the bomb there had ensued a long lull so we quickly brought the boys outside - but where then were we to go? Both our courtyards were piled with rubble from the outhouses from which the dust was still rising. Across the road, behind beech hedges actually blazing and crackling, the houses stood upright with roof tiles crinkled and gaping black windows, but Maryfield had no walls standing on this side; from what had been roof there now crazily tilted and protruded laths, beams and timbers at all angles, while the water tank had been blown up into a tree. In the valley a great conflagration in the city cast an intense reflected glow up into the sky by which light the grain of brickwork and even the minute veining of the young leaves on the trees appeared with floodlit distinctness.

Obviously it was better to go up rather than down; mercifully the lull continued, we passed Susan's house still standing, and went on the big house of Martin's grandparents. The glass of the outer porch lay smashed in the entry but the house stood solidly substantial; the warden knocked and shouted and they brought us in. The contrast with the scene of fire and devastation was almost shocking - carpeted floors and curtained windows, cabinets of glass and porcelain intact, Granny, Grandpa and Edith together with their cook and her small daughter all clean and composed, while we all looked ghastly behind our coating of powdered white plaster, the children in blanket and eiderdown, ourselves in coats over our night attire. We sat all together under the stairway in the central hall and very soon heard the thin steady note of the "All Clear". We waited a brief while, then the boys were given a couch with blankets and pillows to sleep in the drawing room, FG and I were given big chairs in the hall and the rest went upstairs to bed. Not until next morning did Edith know of Paul's safety when he returned haggard and exhausted after his night on duty at the Post exposed on the hill, all the time suffering acute suspense for his family down in the target area. Even after the "All Clear" it wasn't a quiet night for the fires burned noisily, and delayed action bombs continued to explode long after the last plane had departed.

Next morning, after some sleep, cleaned up and dressed in borrowed clothes we sat to take stock in the "Barnburgh" garden where the first roses were opening, the long lawns glittering in the sun, the birds singing as though nothing had happened; we were bleary from lack of sleep, I felt tainted from my experience of evil, felt that we tarnished the lovely garden as I sat on the grass beside Paul and for no reason he savagely dug holes in the turf with his penknife. I could see an intact gable of Maryfield above the trees and for a while hoped in a few weeks to be back at least in a corner of the house and starting again. Paul and FG went down to investigate, returning to say that the house was uninhabitable, that we were literally homeless. With thousands of families all over Europe during those years of wastage, we had endured the experience of going to bed in a well-ordered, seemingly permanent establishment, to find ourselves next morning possessed of little beyond our night attire, not knowing where we should live in the future, not knowing indeed where we should find a bed for the night. The men had discovered that a thousand pound bomb had exploded outside the high brick wall at the rear and that only two yards difference would have meant a direct hit on the house and the end of us all. The blast had caused havoc - the house was almost a shell with our broken possessions scattered all over the floors. They had found the Sealyham asleep and well on a pile of smashed granite and plaster but no calling or searching had revealed trace of the cat. Very luckily both men were there when faithful Di arrived on her bicycle from her usual Sunday at the farm and their presence mitigated her shock at finding the ruin on the hill; but other friends were less fortunate and didn't know of our survival until the final casualty lists had been posted.

They brought Di up to "Barnburgh", then FG and I went down to the city where owing to the destruction of the Post Office it was not possible to wire friends and relatives the news of our safety; the whole of the centre was gutted, reduced to huge piles of rubble, and elsewhere whole areas were cordoned off while delayed action bombs were exploded; over the ashed and skeleton houses hung a terrible smell of powdered rubble and smouldering timbers, dust hung in the air and made the eyes water. Vans were patrolling the shattered streets distributing food and drinking water; money and coupons for petrol and clothing were handed out at Relief Centres, casualty lists were posted with anxious queues lined up for news. The whole of High Street from the Guildhall to St Sidwells being a wilderness of rubble, it was in unfamiliar shops in little side streets that we used our new "clothes coupons"; luckily FG's main wardrobe was intact in London but he was now, like myself and the children dressed in clothes borrowed from our friends at "Barnburgh" even to shoes and underwear; we hoped eventually to salvage some things.

By teatime having packed our new combs, toothbrushes and handkerchiefs and fresh (borrowed) night attire, with a special allocation of petrol we prepared to drive to Crediton in Grandpa Read's car. There temporary hospitality for homeless refugees - our present designation - had been offered by many householders; Edith and Paul decided to come with us to join Martin already staying with friends but the old people preferred not to move. On either side of the road we saw many little groups preparing to sleep in the woods and fields, either homeless or unwilling to sleep in the burned city, while here the quiet country lay steeped in the golden sunlight. At the top of the lane to Di's cottage we dropped Di and Richard to stay there while we were taken in by the retired headmistress of the girls' grammar school, a warm-hearted and hospitable woman who gave us baths and a meal and a long night of peaceful sleep. For a few nights Richard slept on pillows in an open drawer in my room; he seemed undismayed by sudden changes while Philip remained calm and collected as always - apparently such reactions were usual when children were not separated from their parents.

Next morning we used Crediton Post Office to send off telegrams, and FG spoke to his office and was immediately given "sympathetic leave". Since Di could easily cycle the short distance into Crediton every day and Martin and his parents were staying quite near, for three days FG and I were able to drive into Exeter in our borrowed car knowing the children companioned and in good hands. We found it possible to get into the house and at once found Philip's two tricycles intact together with Richard's push chair in their places under the stairs; we also collected Molto and arranged to board him out at the kennels where he was always taken for "stripping" - which association made him a very sad dog when we took leave of him. We managed briefly to see some of our friends, including Susan and Carola, all of whom were safe and well; Grandma and Grandpa Read sent messages, he being delighted to see his car, laid up "for the duration", out and moving on the road again. But, apart from putting our names on the books of such estate agents as had premises still standing, we spent most of the next three days at Maryfield proceeding from one urgent task to the next, working all day in the debris and driving back at night to friends and family.

We wrote off linen, carpets, pictures, silver, glass and china, but were able to advise the salvage organisation that some bedding and larger pieces of furniture were worth rescuing. We found some clothes and shoes in drawers and cupboards all of course filthy but otherwise undamaged and on the first day I had been glad to find my store of spare linen intact inside an undamaged chest on the back landing; next morning the chest was empty, as also were the rose beds, every budding bush having been dug up and removed. We had moved about gingerly when we first got inside, but soon with expert familiarity we crawled and clambered over the granite slabs blocking the stairway up to the windowless study where on the second day the books were damp after rain had penetrated through the holes in the roof. From the empty window frame FG lowered them to me in buckets and I stacked them in bundles on the path below whence we carried and stored them in the comparative safety of the locked garage together with all the files and papers we could rescue from the litter on the floors; already much was stained by the brown of bomb-dust and damp - *Comedies* of Terence, 1773, Stirling Brown's *Southern Road* with the poet's warm inscription on the flyleaf, and, in the playroom, books that my father had read to me and that I in turn had read to Philip and Richard.

With FG beside me I worked steadily and methodically but one afternoon alone I grew demoralised and wandered aimlessly around picking up valueless relics - a glove puppet, a soft blue velvet elephant, building bricks, and was astonished to discover in a corner pile of glass and plaster the scattered contents of Philip's "Treasure Box" - a scrap of the original alabaster from the top of Cephren's pyramid, a broken wing from the painted Indian rain bird, the blue potsherd from the Arizona cave dwelling. Wrapped in cotton wool were the framed miniatures of his great-great-grandparents. I found a few scraps of the Royal Worcester mug that had been our first household possession, which led me to a foolish futile search for the small gold-rimmed

Crown Derby bowl which we had bought together instead of investing in a conventional engagement ring. And suddenly the misery of all this wanton waste and destruction was too much to bear and I simply squatted down in the rubble and wept over my violated Lares and Penates in primitive grief for what had once been symbols of a love and a troth and a faith. But - I asked myself eventually - what did these things matter since I still had the living reality through which, after all, these symbols were invested with value? And before FG was back I had mopped myself dry and composed myself.

Small wonder that, weary after a day of digging and delving I the woman, the home-maker, outraged in a basic instinct, while the three males slept soundly, passed long, wakeful, ceiling-staring nights. Much had happened since the days of hoping and planning under the apple trees of Topsham, and this near-disaster and uprooting pressed the truth well home that far from having chosen and directed the way our lives should flow we had increasingly become mere flotsam and jetsam tossed about by random events. This present situation resulted from a stream of happenings set in motion in places far off and by forces unforeseen and unimaginable five years before. Our survival was by a freak of chance just as the deaths in the *Hood* had been due to a gunner's aim going wide and hitting the powder magazine. I must have known before this that chance equally with character has a say in human destiny, but to discover a truth by experience is different from knowing it in theory. I had been ignorant, and therefore the idea of individual impotence was now a strange notion, unwelcome, hard to accept and get used to. Now I faced up to the fact that every day and to everyone things happen that have not been willed to happen - natural disasters, climatic catastrophes may be triggered off by sunspots millions of miles away or by subterranean forces within the earth's dark interior; the inscrutable behaviour of viruses may affect whole populations; we do not choose our genetic endowment - what could be more random-seeming than the meeting of the chromosomes? To me then there seemed little that we did to guide or govern, rather individuals lived amid a swirl of chancy circumstances - which surely included the jostle of incompatible human aims as all Europe was discovering now.

As I too had now tardily discovered for I had not really faced up to the full implications of the revelations of five years before; with some disdain I contemplated old assumptions and anticipations so much at variance with subsequent experience of reality - the wonder was that I had lived half a lifetime confidently planning and guiding my own lifeline and that until five years ago so much of what I had hoped for - and *more* - had come about.

We now heard that the children and I would be taken as temporary paying guests at the large rectory of a nearby village by the kindness of the incumbent and his wife and early next evening we therefore left Crediton, loath to leave but not wishing to impose ourselves too long. The rectory proved to be a Georgian country house with a well-kept garden and large conservatory; the wife had beautiful old furniture and while she was showing me our room upstairs I congratulated her on her good fortune in living in such surroundings. She did not respond at all, seemed distant or absent-minded, and I imagined that she found our arrival unwelcome. But perhaps it might only be for a short while. At dinner, although friendly, our hosts were grave and quiet and more than ever I felt that our arrival was a mistake. The rector's wife excused herself immediately after the meal and he offered to show me over his conservatory. We examined and discussed some wonderful exotics, and then suddenly changing from a quiet conversational voice into a dry grating tone he said, "Mrs Thomas, we heard this afternoon that our only son has been killed in action." He added abruptly, "It is terrible. Terrible."

Too shocked at first for speech I stood up stupidly beside him still holding upturned in my hand the flower I had been admiring, and then in a rush saw how desperately he and his wife would wish to be alone and by themselves, how very inopportune our presence must be. Sympathetic words would be meaningless and anyway he could see my feelings well enough and so, with no idea how it could be managed I said that we would try to leave if we could in the morning, tried to express grateful wonder that they had allowed us to come at all. He broke in almost eagerly, jerkily; "Yes, yes, if you could possibly find elsewhere - I really don't think my wife has realised properly yet—we didn't feel there was time to put you off this evening— she was really looking forward to having you—but when she has taken this in it will be terribly hard for her—her only son—if you were to go I could perhaps take her away for a while—" I would not let him continue but asked to use his telephone and left him motionless, standing staring at his plants. We rang up Edith and Paul immediately and in the morning they telephoned with valuable news. With Martin they were staying with friends in the converted coach-house of a large residence on the hill above Crediton town. Their hosts' mother, a Mrs Montagu, owner of "Penton", the big house, now offered us the whole servants' wing - four rooms, bath and back stairway - empty and available for us to rent until we should have found ourselves a suitable furnished house.

CHAPTER SIX

Interlude at Penton

We first saw Penton on a warm rainy morning when the beeches in the drive dripped over wet bluebells sprawled in the long grass - a big white house with classic portico; under the pillars an erect, lean and militant woman in WVS uniform awaited our arrival. Miss P's vigilant eye and ear had probably long been on the look-out for us and now she brought us indoors marshalling us before her through a long corridor into a large drawing-room. The big front windows were completely boarded up and a green sub-aqueous twilight filtered into the room through tall tree-shrouded windows at the far end. Here we sat down and Miss P introduced herself as sister of Mrs Montagu's son-in-law to whom we owed our present hopes and opportunity. I supposed she was then in her middle fifties, her head was small and restless like a bird's, her face red with a small prim mouth and keen eyes that darted appraisingly over each of us in turn. Very soon she was plunged into plans - her plans - for our future; she spoke volubly, her high colour increasing, and in spite of myself a protective shell began to stiffen my responses even although I did not doubt her good intentions.

Maybe she did tend to seem bossy but when I had lived under the same roof with her for some four months I had learned to appreciate her real value though in the beginning with some difficulty. Philip, always perceptive because of his objectivity, later identified her with Rabbit in the *Pooh* story books. It was an apt comparison. Like Rabbit extremely efficient and practical, and possessed of inexhaustible nervous and physical energy, she enjoyed organising and pushed people round in order to do it; often she seemed officious; yet she was as innocent as Rabbit of malice or unkindness and, as I was to discover, used herself tirelessly and selflessly in activity - and in talk - on behalf of other people.

When Mrs Montagu came in Miss P departed, for here was the real mistress of the house. She had no need to assert herself simply because she possessed natural authority and as a matter of course expected deference to her wishes. Her voice and manner were then, as always, quiet, unhurried and composed, and the projected arrival of ourselves to double her household so soon after accepting the catering - though not the housing - of Edith, Paul and Martin she calmly accepted in her stride. Underneath a cloud of white hair was a squareish face with gently rounded features of a pleasant clear cool colour; at seventy-eight she was an Air Raid Warden doing her night's vigil once a week at the Post.

In many ways she was remarkable. To be a good naturalist as well as gardener and bee-keeper was nothing unusual but to be able not only to understand and maintain but to construct a radio set most certainly was; she had been and I believe still was closely associated with the weekly journal *Time and Tide*, had shared the interests of Colonel Montagu her late husband whose African and valuable Etruscan collections filled glass cases on the main stairway, in halls and passages and in his study; she was apparently an authority on the tracks and lifestyles of certain gypsy tribes on the mainland of Europe. Concerning these and other proficiencies we learned from other people, never from herself.

But now she was concerned with the problems posed by the infant Richard because when I had dealt with Maryfield and its remaining contents I must concentrate all effort on the search for a furnished house, and this was the more urgent because now that we were no longer responsible for three medical students Di might at any time be called up for war service. The meals at Penton were formal, the menus unsuitable and served at times quite unrelated to a toddler's routine. Mrs Montagu suggested that while Di was still available she should sleep at her own home, a cottage not far off in the country, and cycle over to Penton every morning to take charge of Richard in my absence and especially to prepare nursery meals for them both at his normal times and generally to preserve his accustomed routines. Edith would keep a watching brief, and with Martin and Philip we hoped he would soon settle down.

While Mrs Montagu talked her daughter Zoe had entered, arms bent at elbow, hands clasped before her waist, head demurely cast down, her usual demeanour and, as I discovered, very concealing of her real self. She was a plain little woman with dull straight hair cut short, wearing a drab dress rather severely cut. She didn't join in the conversation but sat still, as quiet and unobtrusive as a mouse; yet the downcast silence hid much. Although she often sat as at this first meeting, silent and a little apart, she was all the same much regarded and deferred to, for her observation was acute, darting and quick, her insights and judgements revealing and shrewd. Presently she took us upstairs to see the bedrooms, mine containing a child's crib equipped with pillows and bedding sent down by her married sister; she looked pleased at my great appreciation of all this and led us to the playroom bare and empty but for a big table and a chest of drawers, but light and well ventilated with lots of space to play in. There we agreed our terms and decided to bring ourselves and what possessions we had that very afternoon.

So FG departed and less than a week after the air-raid we embarked on our new life. Every morning I would dress Richard and bring him downstairs to caper around in the kitchen and courtyard impatiently watching for Di until she arrived to prepare their breakfast and take it and him upstairs. Meanwhile Zoe had descended to rake out and refuel the "Esse"; she would be in her dressing gown waiting to take her bath after Mrs Montagu, and when a gush of water told her it was available she went upstairs, leaving to cool in the sink the horrid pans of "lights" she had been cooking for her cats. At about nine o'clock her mother descended and donning a clean blue and white checked apron she proceeded, leisurely and in high dignity, to prepare breakfast for eight. She was a competent and resourceful cook producing interesting and original meals out of our pooled rations and her own ingenuity - but she refused to be hurried. Often Miss P, Edith, Paul and I stood hungry-eyed in the kitchen awaiting the trays at ten in the morning, while Philip and Martin relayed urgent messages to us from the dining room ("Tell her we're starving!") which I need hardly say were never delivered. Eventually we sat in formal array round three sides of the long dining table, Mrs Montagu, apron removed, the unflurried hostess, presiding from her high-backed chair at the top. Round the walls family portraits by Romney and others hung in their gilded frames; we used the crested silver - I never saw any other - and stacks of silver entree dishes every day as a matter of course. Afterwards Miss P, Edith and I would cope with the mammoth washing up in the butler's pantry, and since Miss P was inevitably in charge all was rapidly and efficiently packed away in shining rows on the shelves while in the kitchen the "daily" dealt with saucepans, baking dishes, basins ("My mother will use a dozen basins to make one pan of soup;" said Zoe), and tidied up generally.

Although the setting was formal mealtimes were usually highly stimulating and amusing; we guests were rendered light-hearted by our recent escape into Penton's comparative safety; relief and relaxation helped us the more to enjoy Mrs Montagu's talk, Zoe's pungent comments, or Miss P's garrulity. It seems almost an impossibility to recapture good conversation; the pleasure of listening to Mrs Montagu derived not only from her wide-ranging interests and endless repertoire but to her impassive delivery and perfect timing, both impossible to reproduce. Her tales were apt to be long ones in the sense that she never told "funny stories" or brief anecdotes; she was always original because her perceptions were quite unstereotyped. And she had a sharp wit of her own. We followed up an article in *Time and Tide* one day with a long discussion on the role of the sexes - very unfair since Paul was the only adult male present, the boys affording him only silent support. Eventually Mrs Montagu pushed back her chair with a meditative; "Well - yes - a good *man* is a god maybe" - and then, suddenly quenching Paul's gratification as she stood, "But - *where are* the good men?" - a question destined to be long remembered and requoted.

With her mother present Zoe tended only to intervene with amusing asides and parentheses but alone with her I enjoyed many glinting moments. Her sly, always gentle humour could be penetrating and she wasn't afraid to risk embarrassing her listeners; for example she was well aware of her own peculiarities which were natural and native to herself, and she had too much innate pride and honesty to hide or disguise them. So I thought that she took special pleasure in recounting to Edith and myself the struggle of an Edwardian hostess to improve her plain daughter. After years of failure she had given it all up; "Well, well, my dear, you'll never be beautiful *so you'd better be odd*!" Her smile as she watched our laughter conveyed something over and above a shared amusement.

Our first week was difficult in spite of everyone's kindness; it rained heavily so we were often house-bound; I was much away, in the first instance because we had no clothes and I had to spend hours collecting what I could discover at Maryfield or shopping with our issues of emergency clothes coupons in Crediton. Poor Richard was often a cross and unhappy little boy and just when he most needed me I wasn't always available. Di, of whom he was very fond, had just entered upon the lethargy and sickness of her first pregnancy and sometimes found it hard to respond to his demands; nor was she comfortable in our new surroundings being very much in awe of Mrs Montagu and positively afraid of Miss P; that she struggled on for Richard's sake, not for a few weeks as anticipated but for several months, said much for her devotion and goodwill. At two years old Richard could not understand why he had been suddenly separated from his familiar home and his small friends, his story books and playthings, his beloved dog and cat. Even his clothes were not the same. Now he found himself living in the home of three adult strangers in an unfamiliar museum-like dwelling, surrounded by fascinating objects like boomerangs and spears and shields, strange masks and feathered head-dresses that he was not allowed to touch much less to handle and examine.

The playroom upstairs soon contained what little we had salvaged from the rubble of his nursery and a few new story books, but Philip and Martin rarely joined him there and never stayed for long. There were times when he would break things out of mere frustration; he cried a great deal in a loud and angry bellow not for attention or sympathy but simply to express his resentful hostility to life in general.

This unsatisfactory situation was transformed for him, and for us all, once we had visited Pound's Hill, home of Zoe's sister Ruth, where Martin and his parents were sleeping in the converted coach house at the end of the back drive. We were at once welcomed into this vital, sprawling untidy household. There were four daughters; the unpredictable elfin Susan, a dark sprite of a child aged six; Tuppy, a plump placid easy-going ten; June, fair, with her grandmother's regular rounded features enhanced by most exquisite colouring, now seventeen; and Margaret, nearly twenty-one, away in the Land Army. There was a pony in the stable and a goat in the shed, bad-tempered old Clara Butt, also cats and dogs and poultry, mice and guinea-pigs. Philip was given the guinea-pig "Burnt Toffee" right away, and she had produced her first litter, black, orange, white and two mixed, before we left; Richard had a mouse. Both these pets had to stay at Pound's Hill, however, on Mrs Montagu's strict order; they were some consolation for the loss of Molto, languishing in boarding kennels in Exeter. The days grew warm and bright and soon everyone was living out of doors, exploring the neglected grounds, walking in the entirely unknown countryside, and especially sharing the teeming life up at Pound's Hill. The mice and guinea-pigs proliferated, baby chicks ran peeping in coops watched by ever-anxious hens, and even Clara Butt produced two kids. We all went up to see these last arrivals and found the unwanted male had been at once separated from his mother and laid under a hawthorn hedge to die. He did not seem to suffer but lay relaxed and gentle as if about to sleep, with dainty unused hooves, like acorn cups, among the buttercups and daisies. "A shame he'll never play in the paddock with the other one," was Philip's characteristic comment, but none of the children showed distress, just took the situation for granted.

Martin and Philip were given special permission to play duets on the grand piano in the drawing-room. They also listened to the radio. They discovered Lord Haw-Haw, broadcasting propaganda on behalf of the enemy:- "Chairmany calling, Chairmany calling" - and secretly listened to many broadcasts with fascination and some fear until Martin had such nightmares as a result that Lord Haw-Haw was forbidden - a relief to them both as Philip confessed to me afterwards though neither had cared to suggest giving up listening to the other.

These absorbing new interests made it easier for me to work at my time-consuming tasks. FG urgently required the complete list of our total losses for the insurance claim and this, with the willing help of Philip, Edith and Di took many hours to complete as we mentally went through the contents of every room and of every drawer and cupboard and shelf in every room; and there were curtains, carpets, pictures, fittings, as well as cleaning, gardening and other equipment. We must have forgotten or overlooked a lot, and Philip in the end felt that Lear's "Yonghy Bonghy Bo" had been a wiser householder; "Two old chairs and half a candle/One jug without a handle/These were all the worldly goods/Of the Yonghy Bonghy Bo."! Eventually I posted off several sheets of foolscap and turned to the final disposal of what remained in the shell of Maryfield. This, an exhausting business, entailed bus journeys to and from Exeter and the long walk up and down Pennsylvania Hill before I could even begin on my miserable labours in the rubble; when the inventory was finished I ruled the whole thing off and engaged a local carter to move the salvaged goods to a large empty barn that I managed to rent at a farm near Copplestone village; I went out there twice to check and organise but the barn was so full that I had to leave things as they were - temporarily, I hoped, but they were stacked up there for the next four years.

So next I turned to house-hunting in good earnest. Our names remained on the house agents' lists, and in addition I advertised and answered advertisements and travelled scores of miles on Di's bicycle inspecting furnished "rooms", houses, cottages. I was offered a property where I found that I must hire a boy every morning to pump the day's water supply, another offered me a pony and trap as the only means of reaching the nearest shop. Often I returned late from a fruitless expedition to find Di waiting for her bicycle in the courtyard and Richard already bathed and awaiting me in his crib. After three months I began answering advertisements in the national press, considering the Lake District, Northumberland, even the Welsh non-industrial valleys.

In mid-August our Exeter agent sent an order to view "Berrydown", a furnished cottage on a remote part of Dartmoor between Chagford and Okehampton. FG was on summer leave so we hired a car and took both children with us on a rare family outing. The roads were good until we left Chagford then we found ourselves bumping along narrow winding lanes, rutted and stony, and when we sometimes emerged from behind their steep banks and high hedges our road was flanked by empty moorland wastes extending to the horizon; the last half mile was very difficult indeed as we lurched along our rock-strewn winding way, so narrow that we brushed the grassy banks; eventually we reached a fine stone farmhouse at right angles to the lane which was blue with fruit from a stockade of damson trees. A few yards further along and the granite and thatched cottage that we sought stood behind a loose drystone wall with two red-berried rowans screening it from the road.

Within half an hour I knew that our quest was at an end. The cottage had grass and trees on three sides and two massive beeches at the back where a second gate led into half an acre of paddock just now let for grazing. Indoors the cupboards and shelves were generously stocked with tableware, silver and linen; the owner, a Sussex businessman, had equipped the place as a holiday cottage hence the well-sprung beds with Jaegar blankets, the good upholstery and covers, the coloured Italian tiling, the simple blue and white china, the sturdy unpretentious farmhouse furniture. A "Cook-and-Heat" stove with cool and hot ovens provided hot water for sink, bath and basin and supplied an unexpectedly large airing cupboard, the water being filtered and tapped from the leat. All six rooms were well lit -

possibly the original cottage windows had been enlarged; when I looked through those in the big bedroom from the one stretched a coloured patchwork of fields to the skyline, from the other I looked across the lane to where a stream ran beside the road to cascade into a ferny pool. The cottage seemed situated on a cultivated shelf of the moor below the bleak uplands.

At first, remembering our journey, we were primarily concerned about the isolation. There was no post office, no baker, no butcher, and no doctor nearer than Chagford town; FG, our friends on visits, must travel by bus and then hire a car for the last, worst part of their journey. We then discovered that a telephone was available at the neighbouring farm where we could also buy our rations of milk, butter and eggs; a butcher, a grocer, a laundry, called weekly for orders and deliveries. Just beyond the cottage the lane became wider, more open, with a reasonably smooth surface; here it divided, one road leading up to Scorhill the other down to Throwleigh; on either side of both roads stood a few modern houses in cultivated gardens and in two of these families with young children had taken up residence for "the duration". Finally a small boys' school evacuated here agreed to accept Philip as a day boy in the autumn term.

For me the area, the very isolation, meant peace and security for the children. We discussed the pros and cons on the long way back, and Richard was excited, Philip quietly satisfied, when we decided we could not do better.

We left Penton when the agreement was signed. Just before we left I took a snapshot of our little group on the seat beside the front door. Mrs Montagu sits a little sideways to that she can look benevolently across at the two boys. Philip looks forward smiling at some joke which Zoe is making, while she stands beside the seated party perhaps hoping not to be included, laughing without restraint, her hands for once not clasped but hanging loosely at her sides. On the other side stands Richard, in pullover and dungarees, looking extremely serious as well he may, for not only is this the great removal morning but he is being firmly clasped round the middle by the seated Miss P, characteristically with someone under her control to the end.

Both Mrs Montagu's sons had perished in the First World War; both had been friends of Rupert Brooke at Cambridge. It was while staying as guest at Penton that Brooke had written *Dining Room Tea* of the room where we had assembled round the table three times a day. Far more memorably than does my fading photo print the poet has caught a brief moment and held it forever:

> I saw the marble cup; the tea
> Hung on the air, an amber stream
> I saw the fire's unglittering gleam,
> The painted flame, the frozen smoke...
> And lips and laughter stayed and deathless,
> And words on which no silence grew.

Chapter Seven

Arcadian

The first month at Berrydown I worked single-handed, glad to prove to myself - and therefore to FG - that I really was physically capable of my undertaking. Those four weeks I learned to toil like any peasant from early morning until bedtime as though I had never known any other way of life. I chopped wood in the big shed and carried in coal and logs for the fires, cleaned and filled the oil lamps, prepared meals and cleared up after them, swept and dusted, washed in the tiny scullery and ironed with heavy flat irons heated on the stove, daily collected our cans of milk from the beautiful seventeenth century farm down the lane. Horned sheep gazed gravely over the paddock wall as, flanked by the Primus stove, of which at first I had been very nervous, I worked at the kitchen sink under the open window. I shared a newspaper twice a week with a neighbour, my real link with affairs being the radio of which the precious batteries were changed fortnightly; as expected, butcher, grocer and laundry called for weekly orders and deliveries.

Every day Mr Border, the country postman, came in his little red van to collect the hamlet's mail from a letter-box built into the granite wall between our cottage and the farm. With or without letters to deliver he called daily at isolated dwellings on the moor so that no mishap or domestic accident should go undiscovered. He was also an important link with the world of paved streets and shops and other amenities; if in emergency we telephoned from the farm to the Chagford chemist he would hand over to Mr Border a package of medicaments to deliver; and he was invaluable in carrying messages from one household to another for we were widely scattered sometimes over considerable distances and I don't think one of us had a telephone. Mr Border was everyone's good friend and presently our friend too.

When eventually FG arrived for a long weekend he brought with him Molto the Sealyham in a state of rapture of reunion after five months in Exeter kennels; he and Philip's kitten luckily made friends so that we were once again a complete household. It must have been our most carefree weekend since the beginning of the war; home and possessions seemed to me well lost if the result was this haven of peace and safety for us all, while FG's weekends and holidays would give him, as Exeter never had, a complete respite from "Alerts" and air-raid sirens. Now he could let himself really go to sleep at night. By special request he had brought with him two stout notebooks in one of which Philip proposed to record Richard's *Sayings and Doings*, the other was simply a *War Diary* in which he noted major events from now until, three years on, he set down the words "unconditional surrender" and ruled a line across the page.

That weekend FG's ingenuity solved a lot of problems, he fixed the radio on a high shelf safe from Richard's meddling fingers; he also bought a big oil-container which most conveniently fitted exactly the wooden seat of the old earth closet in its sentry box beyond the shed, so that the carrier could now bring me a month's supply at a time. I think he went back to London feeling we had been right to come.

Philip was now at school all day, and I wished at first that little Richard, now three years old, might have had playfellows of his own age as well as his mother, dog and cat, and of course his brother in the evenings, but his life could not have been more full than it turned out to be. I had carefully stored away all the unnecessary or fragile or more valuable contents of the cottage, and, since there were high brackets in every room for the oil lamps, he was free of the whole place indoors and out and could explore to the top of his bent. His was a lively questing nature, and he used to their utmost capacity his senses of sight, hearing, smelling, tasting, touching. A twisted stick called his "Buzzard" - why we never found out though the birds were familiar to him in the sky - with Molto accompanied him everywhere. The garden's trees and plants, lichens on the wall, toadstools in crannies, birds, worms and insects; the peewits, horned sheep and long-tailed ponies of the moor; the farmyard hens, cows, pigs and horses; the colour, shape and patterns of stones and pebbles; in the kitchen, flour and rice grains, sugar and salt - which looked so alike and tasted so different; to all these things he gave his entire attention, desiring not merely to note appearances but also to discover and experience the "whatness" of things. I was at pains always to answer his questions as well as I knew how and to use the right words - my reward being that one day he confided to a tea-party his famous discovery; "Philip and I've only got nipples - Mummy's got udders too!"

He had a fellow-feeling for the creatures he discovered - for the snail on the twig ("the poor thing's got no legs"); the ladybird on the leaf that he couldn't bear to desert at bedtime, running back from the porch to bid it farewell - "Goodnight, ladybird," waving his fat hand over its back as though it could see and hear him; he who was tirelessly active could remain whole seconds attentive to a bee in a snapdragon flower; "He's a very long time! When will he come bumbling out?" He not only talked to things animate and inanimate, but he seemed to listen to them as well. How often I saw him, firm and stocky and still, blue eyes fixed and unblinking as he stared at his latest discovery, almost as if a message awaited him. Perhaps it did.

Maybe because all was so fresh and new he never seemed bored or lonely. He played with the clean gravel and pebbles and running water outside the gate using a large iron spoon to fashion his mud pies; a whole afternoon he spent heaving up the largest stones he could find and building them into a great cairn under the rowan trees - his "castle"; Molto, in constant attendance, though not unnaturally highly nervous whenever Richard was "busy", watched operations from a safe distance, panting with anxiety and eagerness to join in, but afraid to. Or he might be occupied indoors; having mastered the opening of cupboards he explored everything within his reach in the kitchen, examining every utensil and on one occasion, to Molto's huge delight spilling the cat's biscuits all over the floor (both sampled them). Standing on a chair on baking days he would make himself a gingerbread man or roll a bit of pastry until it was grimy from his hot hands when given to me to bake; he ate the result with relish and gave a taste to the dog who gratefully swallowed it, and to the cat, who disdained even to sniff so lucky Molto had her piece too. On a wet morning he would himself get out his "rain-y boots" and sky-blue waterproof cloak and sou'wester in great anxiety lest, because of the rain, I might suggest going to get the milk from the farm without him. He stared at his blue reflection in a pool, then quickly jumped in and fragmented it, his dark-lashed forget-me-not eyes and downy pink cheeks suddenly splashed with water drops. Happily we returned with full cans, hung our wet clothes up to dry and perhaps sat by the fire while he had his morning drink of government-supplied orange juice before we started again, I with an array of all the lamps to clean, polish and refill at one end of the table, and he with his model farm or plasticine or paints at the other. His own special picture books, toys and games had gone, but others had been sent to him, and like most children he liked to hear his favourite stories over and over again - and not stories only - James Fisher's *Book of Birds* was a great favourite, and the chapter on "The Great-Crested Grebe" Philip and I read to him countless times.

Living with this eager questing little boy I was often startled into seeing things as he did - freshly and spontaneously as though for the very first time. Like a poet or a painter his perceptions were sharp and true, direct and unadulterated. What then had been happening to my own? Were they become stereotyped by the familiarity of repeated experiences? Or dimmed by later preoccupations? Or - more likely I feared - blunted by disuse? Perhaps a bit of my edge and shine had been rubbed off by long currency while he was still mint-new and bright. And perhaps it is only briefly as little children that most of us have known the sense of timelessness that now pervaded Richard's days and gave him freedom to perceive, freedom to take all life into himself, to realise his kinship with all things. He was in his Arcady; and most of us have lived there once and know ourselves exiled from our one time "visionary gleam".

Philip had taken the change in our lives in his stride and his time was largely taken up by his new school fellows and his lessons. A useful relationship with him began after we had established ourselves on the moor remote from all our old contacts. In his father's absence - he was already in Exeter - I had begun to seek help in all my practical and mechanical problems - when the chain stuck on my bicycle, or I had to repair a fuse, or replace the driving belt on the Hoover I would usually go to Philip for advice. What FG called my "mechanical illiteracy" amused and shocked him; incredulous and tolerant as his father, he had always helped me out - first a characteristic sideways cock of the head and grin, then the patient explanation or demonstration. Now that we were many miles away from help for household emergencies his practical, intelligent bent - which eventually Richard also evinced - came to my aid over the flues in the chimney, the oven dampers or the clogged water pipes. From this, isolated as were now were, it grew to be the most natural thing in the world for us to discuss every plan or project together; our letters to FG show this. I would write; "We think Richard would like ropes and a seat to make him a swing for his Christmas present," or he would say, "We are now giving Molto a very necessary clipping; you'll be glad to hear that we've successfully done his tail - a very delicate operation."

During the winter he took his bath before Richard and sat in pyjamas and dressing gown by the log fire (writing up his war diary or his letter to FG or preparing for post the next move for his chess correspondent or recording Richard's latest exploits) while the latter had his noisy ablutions and departed - always protesting no matter how drowsy he was - upstairs to his crib where he would prolong his "sleepy-songs" as long as he possibly could, stretching his day to the utmost. At last I could descend and join Philip by the fire. We'd been busy all day, apart for most of it, and now his "prep" done and satchel packed, his journals written up and my domesticity finished till morning, we were together for an hour of sewing, reading, talking or listening to the radio.

Sometimes he'd give me his letter to enclose with mine to FG, or hand over his journals for me to read his entries. Here are four typical notes made at various times over the first six months; "The pony of the bearded old farmer who jogs down the lane is so small that the old boy's feet almost touch the ground. His woollen balaclava turns him into a helmeted knight, so we call him the Crusader. Today he brought to show us a beautiful soft creamy-feathered buzzard that had died caught in a rat trap - its drooping head, cruel beak and talons, immense wing span." "We've called the skirted goat 'Joad' after one of Daddy's brainstrusters". "Today after a story about lost treasure Richard rushed up to Mummy and hugged her knees and said; '*You* are my treasure, *you* are my gold,' and ran away laughing." "The farmer's wife calls unwanted odds and ends *confloptions*. Richard calls buttons, braces, shoelaces, etc., his *flapperty-baps*. If he made it up I think it's very good." (Typical this caution!) Mostly we talked - of FG and Richard and school, events in my day and his, of the war and plans for our future, or for next day or weekend. One night we found ourselves discussing the idea of colour - did *blue* mean to me exactly what it meant to him, and if so, why? After a school "pi-jaw" he spoke of willpower, not as a personal problem which wasn't his way at all, but as a practical one. By willing sensibly ("it's silly to hope by willing it to fly to the top of a tree") or by using will as driving power very difficult objectives may be attained. Will resided in specific action, not in vague desire; the will to attain a skill appears only when we begin to work to attain it. This was probably his memory of the "pi-jaw" and if so I am sure he said so for he was never pretentious.

But we were not often so serious. The dog and cat asleep together in one basket yawned and stretched and basked in the heat from the hissing logs, and we'd laugh and talk and exchange news and views, like Richard prolonging the last hour of our day. Our hour was good and we looked forward to it; it became routine and we expected it. So simple, so inevitable were the beginnings of our eventual intimacy, something beyond the mother and son relationship, not born out of Freudian attachment but out of comradeship, a bonus conferred by life on us both; even regarded in today's long perspective as one of my life's best goods.

We were come to live close to land spaces as yet uncontrolled and unchanged by man, though as Bronze Age monuments and hut circles testified, humanly occupied for millennia. In central Europe and especially in the USA I had traversed more spectacular landscape but had never known the present exhilaration of daily living close to and surrounded by vista. In these remote areas drystone walls enclose fields and settlements and prevent stock from wandering, but at the top of the steep hill between the cottage and Scorhill the road simply stops; and after passing through the heavy gate to the moor a very short clamber over rough grass reveals the vast panorama, the land planing away on all sides to the horizons a bit like the sea in mid-ocean. There are no enclosures here; Nattadon, Meldon, Cawsand Beacon and other hills are curving grass-covered heights and no granite tors interrupt the smooth contours of the skyline; in the long perspectives colours merge and blur - brown bracken and purple heather; red ploughland and golden stubble, woodlands blackberry-blue; over all the slow-moving cloud shadows change the tones all day. The very arch of the sky, soft, deep and immense, seems larger here than anywhere else, and under it peewit turn and cry plaintively, and kestrels and buzzards float unmoving. The air is fragrant with a pure cool scent, speaking with continual soft whisper as it sifts through the short fine grasses and tiny flowerlets blooming on thread-like stems. And the whole gold and purple landscape is laced through and through with brown peaty streams running down to Dart and Teign so that the trickling tinkle of water sounds everywhere. We had our own amber runnel descending from the moor clear over coloured pebbles; opposite our wicket gate it cascaded musically into a ferny pool where the hart's tongue ever dripped and trembled.

Last thing at night, children and dog and cat asleep, I would sit awhile in the window alcove. The sky reflected the glow of sunset against which each leaf of rowan and beech hung its dark silhouette, the trees rustled, a wakeful bird twittered, the stream plashed. When the last glow was succeeded by a dome of stars over the hill I would take my lamp and go upstairs.

Over the weeks we gradually became acquainted with the neighbourhood - of "native" Devonians in widely scattered cottages and farmsteads, of families from bomb-vulnerable areas renting safety "for the duration", and involuntary refugees like ourselves - a French war widow and her two little girls, an exiled Austrian musicologist with his wife and small son. But for us at Berrydown during the early autumn the exploration of our undiscovered natural surroundings absorbed most of our weekends' leisure. Our plans were conditioned, as would have seemed inconceivable to us in Exeter, by the day's weather indications - we would notice the wind direction, the shape and movement of the cloud formations, perhaps get a word of advice from Farmer Bowsher or Mr Border. Once or twice, with all our precautions, a cloud crept up treacherously from behind a hill to blot out the sun and fall in a brief tempest of rain the while we sheltered under a tree, or the lee of a stone wall or a handy barn. We normally packed the tricycle basket with our wet weather garments however bright the day, the sight of them rousing Molto to the wildest anticipatory excitement. Though our weeks were quiet and uneventful our weekends seemed crammed with happenings. We might call at Ensworthy Farm where the striped sow, we had heard, had just farrowed; there a late clutch of goose eggs was hatching out and the boys listened to the taps coming from inside the shells with wonder, presently seeing the curled damp fuzz of a gosling furiously freeing himself, soon running about with scraps of shell adhering to his fluffy back. In the kitchen close to the steely glow of a peat fire sat the great-grandmother, ancient brown face wrinkled as a loft-ripened old apple, keeping her old bones warm.

On windy days we'd take out home-made kites, exultant when they soared on a long taut string, disconsolate when they fell suddenly and tangled long-laboured - over paper tails in the prickles of a gorse bush. One kite would never do well and his rather lugubrious face rarely rose more than a few yards before he sunk to earth; eventually he went out no more but hung on the wall in disgrace. He was christened Pestimographes and he became the boys' scapegoat, blamed for every mishap and disappointment even if it rained on a picnic; his long tail grew full of knots. Richard's tone of reproach matched his look as he turned "Pesti" face to wall as cause of one of his own lapses from grace.

We went up to watch the annual "swaling" - burning the bracken high on the moor. This was exciting - the furze bushes were dry as tinder and a few blown sparks sent them crackling up in a roar of orange flame; an eddy of wind would set hot air fanning our faces, the moor, seen through a heat haze, wavered and undulated like a sea of fire, and I told of Beowulf's dragon who lived on a bleak moorland waste and "burning flew folded in flame".

We returned from our expeditions saturated in sunlight and fresh air - a snapshot captures the instant before one such returning; Philip's beautiful young face so strikingly handsome turned to me half smiling, Richard, challenging and eager, holding a willow wand and taking the afternoon sun in eyes and hair, looks as though about to take flight. Through the little gate and under the thatched porch we entered the cool cottage, blue and white cups on the table ready for tea, kettle on the hob and cat on the rug. Molto was usually exhausted, his initial enthusiastic caperings having covered twice the ground we'd covered, and after noisily lapping from his bowl he flopped panting into his basket; the children and I weren't tired but bright and refreshed as we sat around the table under the open window.

We were to discover, however, that life on Dartmoor wasn't always idyllic. After a mild and pleasant Christmas I was awakened one January morning by the tearing and roaring sound of our two giant beeches straining in a gale. We breakfasted to the sound of tempest rushing over the roof and the hiss of rain sluicing down the windows. Sheltered as we were by trees, and well below the open moorland heights, I discovered our storm to be as nothing compared with the screaming hurricane up the hill; I returned from the farm with the milk cans, dishevelled, crimson faced, streaming wet and gasping, for the wind actually seemed to snatch my breath clean away. And though the roar in the tree tops was continuous and steady, in the lane I was buffeted by powerful gusts and eddies of wind that twisted my wet clothes round my legs and made me lurch and stumble over the loose stones. Our little stream was become a torrent. Poor Molto, out for a brief run, rapidly became a sopping wet mat who had to be dried by the fire. However the cob and thatch cottage was completely waterproof, dry and warm, and since I had my week's supply of edibles in stock we prepared to be marooned. I built up a peat fire to last all day in the big sitting room and got out my sewing arrears; Molto groaned and grunted with the heat he inflicted on himself by sleeping too near to the fender, and the children played all manner of games or built with bricks or Meccano, or made and mended with needles, hammers, screwdrivers, paints and scissors, or Richard clambered around in the contraptions he contrived from chairs, cushions, hassocks and the inverted fireguard.

But this snug comfort lasted only twenty-four hours. The wind changed and the kitchen fire refused to "draw" and began to expel its smoke down instead of up, and to seep from every crack and cranny in the fireplace. Opening all dampers, closing every aperture made no difference whatsoever, the smoke increasing to volumes with each angry gust until I could scarcely breathe or see. The kitchen looked and smelt like a foundry. When sooty particles and fumes began to percolate into the rest of the house I let the fire out and began to experiment with the small Primus stove. In a few days my neighbours came to the rescue by loaning me small quantities of oil until my next ration should arrive - indeed they sometimes cooked our rations of meat together with vegetables so that some meals I had only to heat through. They were generous and kind, at the same time *knowing* - "us wondered when that old chimney would start to play you up," and "once the wind's set in this quarter 'er may go on for days." Although we managed to eat something hot every day the rest of the house without the benefit of constant hot water circulating in the pipes soon became very cold indeed, yet always bone dry. Every drop of hot water for toilet purposes, for washing dishes or clothes had to be heated in meagre

129

kettlefuls on the Primus; baths and the evening rituals disappeared. We were virtually housebound "stuck and confined to the cottage as Noah to the Ark", as Philip wrote to FG, our great comfort the smokeless hot peat fire in the big sitting-room.

On the third day we had barely a trickle of water from the taps and much mystified I consulted Mrs Bowsher at the farm who smiled at my innocence; "The rain's washed grit from the filter bed into the water pipe. I expect you'll be able to scrape it clear with a stick." So I rolled up my waterproof sleeves and, having managed to raise the granite blocks covering the filter in the paddock, I attempted with a long stick to poke out the blocked pipe. Naturally my stirring clouded everything up so I poked away blindly; arms plunged in icy water while the rain cascaded and the malign wind blew as though it would never cease. For all my efforts on this and other occasions only a slow trickle emerged from our taps, so jugs stood in bathroom basin and kitchen sink conserving every precious drop, while for household purposes I planted bowls and even saucepans outside to catch what fell so bountifully out of the sky. Surprisingly this never seemed to amount to much. The climax was a violent thunder and hail storm which, Mrs Bowsher averred, killed one of her hens. A worse disaster for us was that Ben, the farm dog, always afraid of electrical storms, ran to hide in the cow shed where he so alarmed one of the cows that a whole container of milk was kicked over and we and everyone else went short all day.

The fierce gale ended as suddenly as it had begun; we went to bed one night to the sound of a hurricane and woke next day to accustomed moorland airs moving softly under mild clear skies.

On my birthday in February we had tea with windows wide open to the spring; violets and periwinkle had already appeared in the crevices of the beech roots and gorse flowered golden all over the common. FG was unable to be with us, but his letter together with Eliot's recently published *East Coker* lay on my bureau. The dark-eyed schoolboy, then almost in his fourteenth year, in his school blazer and tie, and his small brother nine years his junior, so fair of colouring, clad in his usual jersey and blue dungarees, sang "Happy birthday to you," and Richard turned me a perfect somersault. On the table was a home-made cake of which Molto was given a taste, and the cat's saucer was filled with top-of-the-milk. Nine months before how differently we had anticipated our future, how widely scattered now were Susan and Carola, Kathleen, Pamela and Seeta, Kaye and her three children with whose lot ours then had seemed so closely linked!

But I rarely regretted beautiful Maryfield, now an empty shell, but rather sought to share our haven of security with all who cared to make the journey, especially Edith who came several times, and Martin during holidays. When FG had leave we could explore more widely afield than we usually managed. One day we spent in the trackless emptiness surrounding the Scorhill hut circles, curlews calling, larks singing as we ate our picnic with our backs against the ancient stones.

For Richard, as I recall, the vistas of land and sky meant nothing that afternoon because he was engrossed in his new toy kaleidoscope from which he refused to be parted. He sat apart shaking the small cylinder and staring into the spyhole, entranced as the coloured particles within combined and recombined with their mirrored reflections to make endlessly varied patterns with the symmetry of crystals. He concentrated, as usual, on one thing at a time. On Philip's birthday in June we were driven in a hired car to Bovey exploring very different country as we walked and wandered for a long sunny day beside open heathlands, plantations of trees, the river under Bovey bridge; the car returned to drive us back in the early evening. After bath-time Philip sat on the couch with Richard perched on the arm beside him and they re-lived their happy day. They looked fresh and vital sitting there in blue pyjamas, their damp hair smooth and shining, their eyes bright and lively. The evening light slanted in through the rowans, golden like the ripening grasses in the lane, and I recognised that here was a rare moment of such significance that in memory it would remain intact for always. They chattered away gaily rejoicing in a sense of achievement and of well-being; two human creatures happy in themselves and their good hour and with no thought beyond that hour, and I gloried in them - *for* them, too, because they

131

were unaware. Something precious, something unrepeatable was being enacted and I could not interrupt it. Not until the sun had gone down and the light faded did I ordain bedtime and did so unwillingly even then.

PART TWO

*A Time of Dedication and
Endeavour*

CHAPTER EIGHT

Year of Vicissitudes

Midsummer came and went and at the end of July Philip's school broke up for the long holiday. In mid-August the Tiverton doctor (introduced to us more than two years before, at the beginning of the vitamin therapy) made the long journey out to Gidleigh to see Philip again. Since before he was eight we had conscientiously carried out all instructions given on his behalf, encouraged since his eleventh year by the belief that eventually all would be well. He was now thirteen and, while she found that he had grown and put on weight and that his appearance, good spirits and general well-being left nothing to be desired, she was disquieted to find him unable to extend knee and ankle joints to the full. She assigned three reasons: constant use of the two tricycles never demanded in full the extension of these joints; my daily stretching, although regularly performed both night and morning, had been "too gentle" to be effective; and undoubtedly there was some shrinkage of muscle fibre. She felt the need of expert advice and treatment, strongly advising a second consultation with Mr Capener in Exeter, he being "one of the foremost orthopaedists not only in this country but in the world."

That evening FG and I had a talk over the farm telephone and next morning I set about fixing an appointment and then arranging transport - both to and from Exeter with a two hour wait midday. At first this seemed difficult but neighbourliness and goodwill were always forthcoming among the scattered inhabitants of the moor, and within a few days a Mrs Walpole who lived some miles away and whom I hardly knew cycled over to see me with a plan. Her car in full working order stood idle in her garage; on medical grounds she would apply for the necessary allowance of petrol and would herself drive us into Exeter and back. Richard was invited to spend the day with a family of friends close by; we ourselves had gratefully accepted the offer of lunch and brief rest at "Barnburgh" with Mr and Mrs Read, Edith and Paul, before leaving for the consultation at two o'clock.

The night before the journey I sat as I so often did in the window alcove; as usual boys, dog and cat were all fast asleep, I had taken my bath and was ready for bed but remained below attempting to summarise our situation but in reality girding myself for an interview to which I would go as reluctantly as - judging from the curtness of his note - the consultant would come to it.

Next day Mr Capener and Philip had a brief friendly chat mainly exchanging their experiences of the air-raid in which his previous consulting rooms with many of his invaluable files and records had been gutted. He then had a talk with me alone. I could perceive little change in him since our last meeting - five years ago - his head and face foursquare and strong suggesting the very mould of an eminent scientist, alert, observant, and behind the undoubted goodwill, the detached and clinical objectivity.

With regard to contracture he agreed that treatment was feasible, even describing the procedure by manipulation which I could not at the time really understand. But, he added, this was only worth doing "on those whose muscular future promises that they will be able to retain and use the benefits conferred." This brought us immediately to the question of vitamin therapy. On this he was unequivocal. However convinced researchers might have been at the time of writing their reports long-term experience had not borne out their conclusions. He thought it "imperative" that I should no longer cling to belief in their findings, and one by one he loosened my hold on all recent

136

expectations. He was not rough but stern and most certainly inflexible; a humane surgeon, he regretted the infliction of pain, but thought it necessary and did what he had to. I did not flinch but was terribly shaken when at last the interview was over; and had only a few moments for self-adjustment in the hallway before joining Philip and Mrs Walpole already seated together in the car.

They greeted me eagerly and I told them that nothing had been decided but that contracture could certainly be treated which news seemed to please both; I got into the back seat and we drove off immediately. I was speechless, my mind in a turmoil for most of the long drive home, while the words I had just heard sank into and seemed almost to burn my brain. Phrases repeated themselves over and over in my mind; "the findings you describe are totally unacceptable and are based on gross simplifications of complex processes;" "I know of no case in this country or elsewhere that has been arrested let alone permanently cured;" "your recent advisers, the whole medical profession - and emphatically here I include myself - can claim in this regard only a profound and abysmal ignorance;' and finally, "Yours is a fine boy; he deserves a better lot."

Back at the cottage, since she refused - considerately perhaps? - to come in for tea, I thanked Mrs Walpole for her great kindness and trouble, saw Philip settled with a book beside the open window, then set off up the hill to collect Richard.

I stood a moment in the lane, irresolute, then I walked round to the back of the cottage and pushed open the door of the big shed. Inside was cool darkness and most welcome solitude. I leant against the big upright post in the middle then turned and clung to it pressing its hardness against my body which seemed at that moment to share in my almost unbearable agony of mind. It was not only the future prospect that then seemed so terrible, but the thought that the years of hopeful labour had been based on nothing more substantial than my own deluded hopes and desires, and that all we had done, all we might do, had scant validity. Certainly I had known moments of concern of late, seeing no positive results from the new approach so gladly welcomed more than two years ago; but I had been totally unprepared for being so abruptly parted, and with such overwhelming certitude, from all faith in some ultimate success. After the first interview Mr Capener's words, although their meaning had been the same as today's, had given rise to very different reactions - numbed acceptance, torpor, and, at first, despair. This was not despair but desperation, not torpor but struggle, the anguish of accepting what all my most powerful instincts urged me to repudiate, all that for so long it had been life's endeavour to prevent.

Presently I tidied myself up and went for Richard, then leaving the boys together telephoned to FG from the farm, telling him of the possibility of treatment, hinting that the specialist's attitude was still negative. I wrote and posted a brief letter to Tiverton. During the next few days my private pain could rise to an almost unbearable dimension. I might be upstairs making the beds, or cooking in the kitchen, or washing the clothes, when perforce I laid down the sheets, turned off the heat under pans, left dusters and brooms, cottage and children, and almost ran out to the shed. Sometimes I would merely stand there in the dim light absolutely motionless, waiting for the pain to ebb; and sometimes it grew so excruciating that I had to cling with all my strength to the wooden post until the crisis passed and I could return to my work.

Eventually this ended and I could concentrate on present problems. As usual Philip was splendid and in his usual cheerful contented humour, glad to know that contracture was treatable, though with no idea of what this might entail for him, while Mr Capener's doubts and reluctance made me sceptical of the gains if any. In spite of this a letter from Tiverton urged no delay in hospital treatment but since I knew very well the effects of even brief periods of lying-up I had good reason to fear the effects of surgery and hospitalisation. Therefore I replied saying that I needed time to consider further, and about now I also wrote to the London dispensary to discover what changes, if any, had been made in vitamin therapy - it seemed strange that we had heard nothing whatever about this since I felt certain that Mr Capener had been sure of his facts; the reply made it very clear that further discussion would be useless; the writer had obviously been deeply disturbed by the invalidation of his theories. All the same his help and encouragement had meant much over the years just past, and I thought it only right to tell him that and to thank him; this letter was briefly and formally acknowledged, no more, and there our contact ended. So now we asked our always helpful Chagford doctor for his advice and he drew us diagrams to illustrate the lengthening of the ankle (Achilles) tendon which procedure I could understand better than Mr Capener's talk of manipulations and of plasters; seeing us still hesitant he next offered to arrange a consultation with Lord Horder in London and before FG left we had agreed to this.

Once the appointment was made and we had been granted the necessary petrol allowance we drove in a hired car to a guest house in Virginia Water staying there to avoid the risk of subjecting the children to another air-raid. We managed the long journey from Gidleigh in a day, and after twenty-four hours in the quiet Surrey countryside we were rested and fit next morning for our brief drive to London. In Harley Street a man servant showed us into a long vestibule with carpeted stairs at the far end, which led through double doors to a smaller room where Lord Horder awaited us; he was pouring water from a ewer into a flowered china bowl on a mahogany stand in order to wash his hands and talked to us cheerfully as he dried them on a towel. We all warmed to his cordiality and instant kindness; he was dressed even more formally than Mr Roper in morning coat and (I think) striped trousers but there the resemblance ended for his face was lively and dynamic where RER's was reserved and non-committal, and his speech and manner bristly and rapid whereas RER was almost excessively speculative and deliberate. His room was mellow and Victorian rather than clinical with a chaise longue and comfortable chairs. Presently he indicated to the boys a shelf of books and took FG and me out to discuss our problems in the hallway.

He complimented us on the boys' appearance - "their general health seems excellent, they look extremely fit to me." He added that he was, "all for having the contractures dealt with surgically - the boy should only be in hospital a couple of weeks." He smiled tolerantly at some of our questions - "when we know the answer to that we shall be close to the secret of life itself." A man walking with a stick emerged from another room and passed us on his way to the main entrance. Horder waved to him genially as the servant opened the door, and as he departed expressed joy at the surgery which had made a helpless polio victim into a walking man. He explained how the remaining muscle in the legs could now be utilised and how disuse equally with disease might soon have rendered them impotent. He identified himself with this wonderful result, he glowed with goodwill, enthusiasm and hope. "More hope for a polio victim than for a dystrophic," I ventured to suggest. Characteristically he rejoined that I must continue to work exactly as though a breakthrough could happen tomorrow. "It could, you know! Why not?" I indicated the difficulty of dismissing Mr Capener's twice uttered prognosis but he refused to be daunted; "You must work to postpone that day as long as possible." I clutched at this common-sense observation tossed to me almost offhandedly and so gained at least one asset of value from an otherwise fruitless exercise - namely a limited but possible objective.

Back home I wrote again to our adviser in Tiverton not telling her of the London consultation but plying her with still more questions. This time she replied with some displeasure adding, "If you still feel unhappy about letting him go into hospital the only thing is to cancel everything - however I hope that you will not do this as in my opinion you could not put the boy into better hands...far be it from me to discourage you in any way but I am sure nothing can be gained by seeking more advice...I think the treatment I propose is the best that can be done for him." After this I began to wonder if my reluctance meant that I was opposing Philip's best interest and therefore arranged for his admittance into hospital.

The authorities informed me that at Mr Capener's request I should be allowed to visit Philip as often as ever I liked without regard to official "visiting hours" for which consideration I was most grateful, and decided that Richard and I would move into Exeter in order to avail myself of it. I telephoned to Edith who with some difficulty booked us a small bedroom and use of a dining-cum-sitting room shared with four middle-aged residents in a guest-house a few minutes walk down the hill from "Barnburgh". Since Martin was now away at boarding school she also offered to take complete charge of Richard whenever I should be away. And in the event she companioned him tirelessly, playing with him, reading him stories, taking him out; and then, quite out of the blue, old Mr and Mrs Read invited us both to stay permanently up at Barnburgh in what, after the somewhat primitive "digs" and the hard labour of life in the cottage was a life of comfort and even of luxury. Here was a debt of kindness impossible to measure or repay which with Edith's supporting encouragement enabled me to come through an exhausting trial of stamina. For the contractures were treated not, as we expected, by a simple cutting and rejoining of tendons but by forcible stretching of the joints under anaesthesia, after which the torn ligaments were kept at full tension inside rigid plaster casts until they had healed in their new position. Philip entered hospital hopefully and cheerfully, a lively zestful boy with good colour, bright eyes and an air of happy well-being. The effects of prolonged and sometimes severe pain and three months' immobilisation in a hospital ward were predictably disastrous and it would be futile to record his ordeals or my own on his behalf.

After his third manipulation Edith and I realised he had reached his limit of endurance; he had by then come through the first agonising return to consciousness and was under strong sedation; during the following days he lay in a state of lethargy; his gay and cheerful spirit seemingly crushed by pain and weakness. He seemed not to heed what was said to him. I found Mr Capener and asked him how Philip did. "Not well, of course. Yes, when he's fit to be moved you may take him home." I returned to his bedside and told him this, told him there would be no more operations and that the moment he was strong enough we would all return to the cottage. His wan expressionless face indicated little interest - merely tired scepticism. However, on my next visit he told me that "the *hospital*" - by now for him arbiter of his destiny - had told him that he should be home before Christmas Eve, and with that official promise and with that hope and prospect before him he rallied all his forces so that presently I felt able to leave Exeter with Richard to prepare for Philip's return and convalescence.

I was relieved to find the cottage bone-dry, and blazing fires and ventilation soon got rid of the first stale fustiness of the rooms. Active labour on his behalf replaced the sickening anxieties and utter helplessness of the three months past, all was clean and bright and the larder stocked, a fire in his room and a hot drink ready when he was brought by ambulance the long journey from Exeter. He was a stretcher case enclosed in his now "bivalved" casts from toe to thigh but he seemed to be pain-free, his aspect no longer inert, his eyes bright, and, though naturally he was very pale, his features looked somehow firmer and conveyed a grasp on life very good to see. When Richard presently arrived from the farm although well prepared by me in advance he was at first taken aback by the change in his brother and was silent and wide-eyed, but very soon they were plainly exceedingly happy at reunion and I hoped familiar company would do Philip good.

His room was on the ground floor between kitchen and big sitting room and from his bed through the open window he could see the garden and the lane and hear the waterfall; from this cosy homely room, so different in sights and sounds from the big hospital ward, I hoped he might enjoy watching family activities until well enough to join in them himself.

I was thankful next morning to find him no worse for the journey. He called me at eight o'clock and I went to him. "What time is it?" he asked in rather a dispirited voice, and when I told him a look of astonished delight lit up face. "*Eight o'clock? You mean it's morning? It's day?*" I assured him that it was; a warm bright day. "Mummy! I've slept all night! I *must* have done. *I've slept all night!*" He seemed for the moment unable to believe his good fortune; he hadn't slept a night through in the ward - characteristically it was only now that he told me this - and so his good sleep seemed like a miracle. I was moved that he should be feeling such extremity of joy merely because he'd had a good night's sleep; a year ago that we should have celebrated such an event would have been unthinkable. Now we were happy to have him at home even as he now was; I didn't realise that he must have been dead-tired after being got up at five the previous morning, still less that this was to be the last unbroken night we would ever know.

After breakfast I performed with him all that the Ward Sister had so carefully explained and demonstrated to us both in hospital - not easy, for to move his straightened joints an inch caused sweating pain; then he rested while Richard and I got milk, butter and eggs from the farm. He managed to look at some of his books and even to read aloud to Richard before lunch after which we all had a siesta. Around teatime I built up a glorious log fire, and after tea I lined a big armchair with cushions, fixed footstools and leg rests, and with the utmost care succeeded in getting him seated beside the fire - the big plasters, which seemed to double his weight, at least prevented any disturbance of knees or ankles. There he was when the taxi drew away down the lane and FG came into the bright room for his Christmas holiday. Philip was triumphant. "I'm up, I'm up!" he shouted. "Daddy, I'm up!"

I was downstairs several times that night trying to ease his limbs fastened in their rigid casts and he looked tired all next day, only wanting to rest; it was Christmas Eve and he lay watching Richard and his father decorating his room and planting an ornamented pine bough in a tub at the bottom of the stairs where he could see it. Next day his strength and spirits were poor; Mrs Endacott of the farm gave us as a present a beautifully cooked chicken which she herself carried to us piping hot and placed inside our oven; another friend called with a Christmas pudding before going on to church with her four lively children, and I recall how quickly our festive laughter was quenched when we closed the door and turned within. After this our situation seemed daily to worsen. FG and I shared the endless taskings - carrying fuel for fires and tending them, filling the oil lamp, bed bathing, bed making, bed exercises, cooking, cleaning, day and night nursing; nor did we neglect Richard's walks and games and stories. (He was now four.) Philip seemed withdrawn into his hospital apathy and was very quiet and unresponsive when his good friend Dr P of Chagford came out to see him; afterward the doctor warned us that "for him the prospect is not rosy." He said he would try to get hold of a trained nurse and meanwhile FG's leave was extended on "compassionate" grounds and he

143

and Richard scoured the neighbourhood seeking a more suitable place for us to live if and when Philip could be moved.

We heard eventually that a nurse was prepared to come out next day and I emptied drawers and cupboards in the spare room and put a bowl of fresh heather on the dressing table; I did extra baking, planned meals with the rations I had in stock, and gave FG all available food coupons with special instructions when next day he hired a car and went himself to fetch her from Exeter.

The two children were expectant, the table laid and the kettle simmering when the taxi drew up in the lane. FG ushered in a gaunt woman with a face as cold as a stone who almost disregarded my words of welcome and taking no notice whatever of the boys followed me upstairs and looked round the charming bedroom without appreciation. During tea she was taciturn and somehow conveyed disapproval of our whole set-up, said she would not undertake any duties till morning and withdrew to her room where she stayed until supper time. After this FG put Richard to bed and I settled Philip for the night while she sat and smoked by the sitting-room fire.

During the next hour she talked to us about herself and her experiences with the obvious intention of showing that she did not intend to be exploited, and some of her stories, I thought, made her appear a callous if not a cruel woman. On retiring she told us she would exercise Philip "tomorrow, and no nonsense about it," and her tone of voice made me feel very uneasy on his behalf. I was up as usual several times in the night being careful to be specially quiet. I was first up in the morning and when Nurse appeared I asked her if she would attend her patient before or after breakfast and was told that she never undertook any duties before having her early tea. I immediately made tea which she drank with me standing beside the fire and then departed upstairs, so FG and I tended the children both of whom were now awake; breakfast ready I went to call Nurse but she was nowhere to be found. At almost eleven o'clock she reappeared telling us that she had been out to the farm telephone and that the taxi she had ordered to take her away would arrive at any moment. I was first astounded, then angry, then *glad*; FG, always articulate even in moments of crisis, had

144

words to say and said them, but I felt that I would prefer to work myself to a standstill before entrusting either of the children to her ministrations.

We returned to our labours. Philip's condition fluctuated and there were days when I didn't try to get him into a chair but he was holding his own, learning with the pain each day to bend his knees and ankles a little more, able to read, to enjoy the view of the garden and the companionship of Richard (who was his tireless messenger). He and his father one morning arrived from one of their daily excursions with news of a guest-house in a neighbouring hamlet and I cycled over at once to see it. I found a house in several acres of grounds where two good bedrooms, a private bathroom and a very tiny sitting room were available; the owner, a red-faced voluble and energetic Devonian, a middle-aged widow, would light and clear fires and do all the cooking and the dishes afterwards; I would make beds, keep our rooms clean and do all our washing and ironing and for the rest of the time be free.

With this booked for us in February FG returned to London in the middle of the month. Immediately Philip had an unaccountable relapse and a young woman doctor took charge; the isolation of the cottage was forcibly brought home to me when at ten o'clock one night the scarlet thread of mercury told me that his temperature was 105 degrees Fahrenheit, the highest I had ever read; I had to leave him unattended while I hurried with my lantern down the lane to the farm to telephone for medical advice. There was nothing to do but watch all night with glucose drinks and warm blankets in case of a sudden collapse when the temperature came down; happily before daylight the crisis was past and from then on Philip began progressively to improve; in a few days, to my joy and astonishment, he grew able and willing to sit in his chair for longer and longer sessions and eventually to allow his knees to be supported at the back with a cushion, to bend without support of plaster.

Edith now wrote telling me of a voluntary organisation in Exeter which, in those days of labour shortage, provided "lay" help for cases such as ours; a "lady" was now available - would I like Edith to interview Miss Addams for me? When the letter came I went to the farm with recent experience tempting me to say no - and what a mistake that would have been! - but on the telephone Edith pointed out how glad I might be of help when it came to the sorting and packing away of unwanted goods and preparing ourselves for removal. I agreed with her that the risk was worth taking and that if Edith thought her suitable I should be glad for her to come. I was not especially pleased when I knew that she was coming, simply felt that two pairs of hands would be better than one.

I cannot be sure that there were flowers in the bedroom awaiting Miss Adams but I hope that there were. Dulled by work and vigil, yet when the Chagford taxi had again lumbered from the wicket and a small figure stood in the porch I knew instinctively that doubts and defences were unnecessary. The look on her face was of goodwill manifest and she was accepted by us all with joy. It was especially good for Philip that she arrived just when she did, now that he had slowly begun to emerge from weeks of pain either doggedly endured hoping for relief, or sometimes with despair that relief would never come. (During all this time we never asked for and were never given opiates or pain killers.) Now that he knew daily periods of comparative comfort he was ready for the companionship I couldn't always give when doing essential cleaning, cooking or our laundry, whereas Miss Addams could give hours of unstinted company; sitting with him, she reminisced with him, gossiped, told him stories that made him laugh aloud. Slowly (as I thought) his faith in the future returned together with his essential gaiety of spirit. He was convulsed at her attempt to teach Richard to say:

> Betty took a bit of butter
> For to make a bit of batter
> But the butter it was bitter
> And it made the batter bitter
> So she took some better butter
> Which made the bitter batter better.

With Richard she went for long walks into the open country from which he returned with bright cheeks and news of all that they had seen and heard. For all this - and she was probably ten or twenty years older than I was - she found time to help me with the endless sorting and packing, deciding what to take and what to store and I remember these sessions as always easy and often hilarious. Quiet and unobtrusive, gentle and never hurried, her industry and cheerfulness raised and strengthened us all.

We always had a splendid fire in Philip's room and all lived our leisure hours there with him until the boys' bedtime. After supper the first evening Miss Addams went upstairs returning with a slim cylindrical case of violet velvet with ribbon ties on which the eyes of both children were instantly riveted. She seated herself in the big chair opposite Philip and untied the ribbons - to take out her recorder! Every evening she sat piping old tunes in the firelight, Richard standing entranced at her knee, blue eyes wide and rapt, Philip and I often half asleep, but apprehension lifting and hope returning to us both.

Thanks to our careful planning all was in good order on the day of departure, the plates and cups of our last meal clean on the shelves, unwanted furniture docketed for storage, unused oil and food stores given to our neighbours. Miss Addams accompanied us on the short drive by hired car to our new quarters, and when she had seen Philip safely installed by the fire in the little room she went on in the car back to Chagford town and so to Exeter. I walked with her from the house up the drive, reluctant to part company. The rhododendron leaves shone in clear sunlight, the air was bland and windless, and I went back to the children bearing the glad news that spring was come to Devon.

The house stood on a broad ledge of cultivated land and from the drive one saw a wide pillared portico with a big door in the middle and windows either side. This aspect from the gravelled courtyard was usually dark and rather austere and the house very properly turned its back on it; the other side, the front, overlooked open lawns and flower beds whence azalea plantations sloped down to the water gardens; beyond the land rose steadily to the open moor and Cawsand Beacon (1799 ft). Our living room unluckily was on the courtyard side but I hoped we would spend most of our time out of doors.

I gave Philip the small single bedroom hoping he might sleep more soundly alone, and myself shared a very large room with windows on three sides with Richard. Both these rooms were bright and airy and with the adjoining bathroom gave us half the upstairs accommodation; another wing, exactly similar, awaited Mrs D's summer guests.

In spite of many advantages in the beginning I found life extremely difficult because of the broken nights. Uncomfortable and heavy though they were Philip went regularly to bed encased thigh to toe in his plaster casts. So easy not to have done so! - but to risk losing all that had been gained at such heavy cost was unthinkable, though our resolve meant that he was completely immobilised and had therefore to call me - never less than thrice nightly and sometimes more often - to ease and move him into a new position. This of course was more to his benefit than had he lain heavily inert for seven or eight hours at a stretch. Philip was exceedingly thoughtful for me and would sometimes lie awake a considerable time before calling; he made up for lost hours by sleeping late in the morning, but unfortunately for me Richard woke regularly at his normal time and Mrs D expected us down for breakfast together, often some time before Philip roused. Sometimes I felt almost light-headed with fatigue, and when eventually FG got down to pay us a visit I was in rather a bad way. Characteristically he set about improving the organisation. He made me take the single room where I slept better alone and there I was to take a siesta every afternoon while the boys amused themselves for an hour indoors. He fixed a small electric buzzer under my pillow attached to a bell push attached to Philip's; this not only meant that no one in the house was disturbed - important when Mrs D's other visitors should begin to arrive - but that after a call I didn't lie awake listening and waiting for the next but could go to sleep again with an easy mind. At this time too we arranged a loan of a wheelchair from the Red Cross. As soon as Philip had begun freely and without pain to move his uncontracted joints and could take the weight of his legs from bent knees we used the chair, though in the beginning he was apprehensive of being moved in it; as soon as he had confidence I got him out into the sun on the big central porch and eventually, after nearly six months indoors, out into the open.

The days of tricycle riding were over - but what cared we? To have him restored, to see him gain strength, colour, energy, no longer to see the wary defensive look on his face - for these things my happiness was intense, and I felt elation, not regret, when for the first time I pushed the chair up the steep gravel drive and brought him safely back. (Extraordinary my happiness in a situation that a few months before would have horrified.) At first we stayed inside the big drive gates content to sun ourselves on the grassy verges with their primroses and thick clumps of daffodils while Richard chased off by himself returning at intervals with news of his discoveries - Mrs D's big hen run, her bee hives, sheep, lambs and cows at pasture beyond the iron railings. Daily we explored further; at first we wandered in the lane, then, keeping on the level, we found a farm behind tremendous sycamores wherefrom the lane bent and rose steeply between high banks to attain a metalled road skirting the open moor; painted wagons, a tractor and farming gear were kept in sheds outside the farmyard endlessly examined and admired by the boys the while I stared up into the unfathomable world of the trees. If from the drive gates we walked in the opposite direction the lane was lined on one side by almost a score of small detached stone houses with fanciful names like "Nuthatch", "Sweet Briar", and "Ragged Robin".

Presently we had new acquaintances; a retired banker and his wife, a professional musician; a widow with two young daughters; three maiden ladies, lively and talkative, their walls hung with horse brasses and samplers and patchwork kettle-holders; an elderly bearded church organist and his pretty young wife - a gay creature whose brightening eyes and deepening colour said in advance that she was about to tell us something amusing; a dogmatic and loudly self-confident lady who lived in a larger house with a husband we rarely saw. My first meeting with her, at the post box in the lane, had been painful; she questioned me closely about Philip's condition and when under pressure I had hinted at the slowness of cure and the need for patience she had exclaimed; "My word, I'd not be satisfied with that! If he were my son I'd give all the doctors in the world no peace until they'd found the way to put him right - and quickly too." As if, I thought, feeling wretched for a moment as I walked back, as if it were not one's helplessness, one's seeming acquiescence that made the situation so hard to endure, so hard to create good in. (Before we left the husband of "The Masterful Woman", as Philip had christened her, died very suddenly at work in his garden and Mrs D's comment, "She'm had life her own way long enough," perhaps expressed the countryman's sense of the fate awaiting the hubristic.) I don't think many of these were Devonians (they called themselves "residents") and it was at some distance from their houses that the lane plunged abruptly down to the real village - a few cottages, a smithy, a beautiful towered church, a shop or two, a post office and the pond. On certain days a bus passed through to pick up passengers for Okehampton, for here we were aligned on a different axis and no longer looked to Chagford for our business.

By now Philip had a chess correspondent and "conversation" with me in the company of a French war widow, we borrowed books for ourselves, and others to read to Richard; when the days grew longer other visitors began to arrive, some of them with children. We were especially enlivened when a Captain Houghton arrived with three fine healthy teenage boys whose education had been interrupted by various accidents and for whom Philip's chair was by no means a novelty to be stared at (Ian - one of the boys - had suffered a broken hip which had laid him low for nearly two years). In the absence of their parents overseas they had been put in charge of the Captain, recently retired from the navy; he was helping them to catch up with their lessons before they returned to their respective schools. All seven of us usually met in the big hall or porch before lunch or after tea when I was astonished to find how Philip shared their knowledge of the conduct of the land war, air and naval strategy, Germany's new secret weapon, the allied invasion of

150

Normandy in June. They had a long discussion one evening on the exploration of outer space when the Captain stated categorically that there existed no substance able to withstand the immense friction and heat generated, so that all attempts were bound to fail. Philip commented quietly; "I am sure you are right that this is so *now*, but so many strange things are invented that I think, though I can't imagine how, that some day we shall certainly be able to do it." This was felt to be visionary thinking by the others, not argument at all, but Philip wasn't shaken. He repeated, "Because a thing is impossible today it may not always be so," convincing me if nobody else. I wonder if any of them recalled this discussion when his belief was proved well-founded?

In June came Philip's birthday. Mrs D and the Captain arranged that we should use theirs, the big sitting room, and she made a cake with fresh eggs and butter decorated with fourteen candles. From the village Mrs Baker toiled up the hill in the blazing afternoon with strawberries from her garden and the long table was laid with a fine repast for our guests - Captain and boys, a neighbour and her daughters. After tea the elder ones performed, or rather read from behind a screen, the play for radio that Philip and I had written in 1941, *The Great Toytown Sale,* to a most appreciative audience, the curly fleece of a lamb discovered on the moor hanging up on the screen the only stage property. At the end of their month's holiday Captain Houghton and boys departed and the regret was mutual; I was moved when they said that they had known more fun with us than they had ever known - it meant at least that we were making a success of our lives.

After this our place in the menage became unsatisfactory. In the early days Mrs D had been kind and helpful, constantly applying to us the adjective "little" - with her a mild form of endearment - but, even then, background noises from the kitchen told us of a very different relationship with her son, and I soon wearied of hearing the pair cursing and abusing each other, though Philip was amused by the banging about which made him think of the Duchess in *Alice*. When the rooms of both wings had been let we thought that she must sleep in the kitchen and after some speculation we found that poor Jim was established in a cupboard, probably unventilated, under the stairs. We were never quite sure of this but we certainly did see him being hauled forth thence one morning in shirt and trousers, unbrushed and unshaven, a yawning shambling young man, looking - and no wonder - thoroughly unrested and miserable. His mother neither noticed that or our presence; "Will ye get up or won't ye? Ye lazy good-for-nothing faggot, ye'll be losing the tractor and yer job if ye don't get off to Bowsher's - he's been on the phone twice already." She pushed him into the kitchen and banged the door.

With all her efforts it was often eleven o'clock before he started off on the tractor which was the delight of Richard's life. Why Jim wasn't called up I never understood but believed he worked for the County Agricultural Committee taking his tractor from farm to farm, transferring equipment, or collecting gear for repair; probably he was young and overworked and neglected. With him to galvanise, her bees and hens and large garden to care for, and often six guests to cook and cater for in addition, Mrs D must have been put hard to it and after five months I think she had begun to tire of us. Usually she meant well but all depended on her mood; she would cut off the electric current; she gradually moved all the covers from our rooms; waited on us in black and thunderous silence after one of her fights with Jim. I had brought with me two good mattresses rescued from Maryfield for the boys' beds and myself slept on one of hers; presently I found myself presented with a lumpy flock affair. She was volubly and noisily angry when I asked about this. "Let Richard have the flock bed then - it's *ridickerless* you giving them mattresses to children, why should they have them I'd like to know?" "They are both growing. I want them to lie with straight backs." "All right then! Please yourself," and with a toss and a flounce and a red face she was gone before an answer could be made. The can of hot water regularly brought to my room every morning for many months suddenly ceased to arrive and when I asked about this - "Plenty of hot water on the kitchen stove - you can always come and get it" - and this indeed is what I had to do from then on. Since I knew of no alternative in sight I accepted the service and shelter we had and made the best of it.

Yet sometimes she was exceedingly kind. One evening, depressed after twenty-four hours of malaise and headache I expressed to Philip my feeling that she wanted to drive us away - and then next morning she brought my breakfast to me in bed and declared her intention of taking Richard off my hands for the day; after a Saturday when even the children had been resented she ceremoniously and all without precedent brought me a glass of port on a tray after Sunday dinner!

Such friendly gestures grew infrequent, signs of antipathy increased, and when a guest arrived from Chagford town for a holiday I drew her aside on her last morning and asked her to let me know at once if she heard of furnished accommodation to let. Philip's condition had stabilised, and although I would no longer agree to live again remote from medical and other facilities I could readily cope again with a household of my own. She promised to do her best, at the same time saying that Mrs D notoriously could not be happy with long-term visitors. Talking things over that evening, Philip and I decided that she had grown sick and tired of our daily presence, she wanted to change us for fresh people and felt us like a continual burden that she wanted to get off her back. For a woman of her impatient, irascible temperament to endure without vent was impossible and the explosion came at the end of the month.

Mrs D was up the drive and we had just finished lunch when the hall telephone rang and I answered it; it was FG in London calling with the happy news (the city then at the mercy of the flying bombs, Hitler's latest weapon) that he would shortly be taking twelve days' leave. Out of my delight I smiled, receiver in hand, at Mrs D as she passed under window and received in return a look, a glare rather, that at any other moment might have startled me. But I didn't worry, I felt gay at heart as I hastened back to tell the boys the good news.

"I saw Mrs D," I said to Philip "She *did* look cross about something."

"She was probably thought you were telephoning to Daddy while she was out - stealing a trunk call," he said astutely. "Better tell her who rang up when she comes in."

She came in then and there with her tray so I began at once. "My husband has just called us and he would like to take his annual leave here if possible at the end of the month."

"How long for?"

"Ten or twelve days he hopes."

"That's more than a weekend."

"Yes, but this is his *annual* leave - he'll be glad to get away from the doodlebugs."

"Shouldn't wonder."

"Well now, is it convenient? May I tell him it's OK?"

"You can't have another room. Manage same as weekends and he can."

She was clearing noisily; I took the boys from the table and stood beside them, back to the window.

"Do you think we could save the meat rations that week and have the joint on Sunday? He'll not arrive in time for it the day before."

Mrs D stopped in the act of folding the tablecloth and lifted her head. Colour rushed up and mantled her face and neck like an angry turkey, she glared again and when she spoke her voice was thick. "Mr Thomas'll get no cooked dinner here on a Sunday so you can stop thinking about that straight away."

I had unluckily supplied the pretext she had been seeking for weeks and she now put the cloth under her arm and faced me squarely.

"I'm not putting myself out for you nor for no Londoners and that includes Mr Thomas, so now you know," and she launched into one of her passions so far only heard, not seen by us, holding forth at the top of her voice without pausing for breath, bubbles in the corners of her mouth, head shaking. I wondered as I stood there what might be the effective way of dealing with her - FG now, always so equal to emergency - what would *he* have done? Since reasoning was impossible and I could not desert the boys I heard her out to the end, tongue-tied by my absolute dependence on her for the roof over our heads,

154

until eventually she took cloth and tray and stalked wrathfully out. I sat down and looked at the children.

Richard looked wooden, Philip sympathetic. "Don't worry Mummy," he said, "Don't worry. She'll get over it by teatime."

"Worry!" I said. "Did I look worried?" I knew that my face was hot not with indignation but at my impotence, my humiliation in front of the children.

"No, not worried," he replied, thoughtfully and slowly. "But you looked appalled, simply appalled. You looked shocked. That's it. Shocked," he repeated.

"I suppose I was. Living with you and Richard and Daddy hasn't given me much practice in dealing with this sort of thing," and now he looked at me with head cocked and laughed suddenly.

"You sound as though you wish it had! Come on, let's cut our lessons and go out - the room smells of brimstone."

My own smile was probably a bit stiff but how glad I was of this, my comrade who offered me humour with his sympathy, and comprehended even Mrs D in his quiet understanding. When FG eventually did arrive and we told him for the first time of our problems I rejoiced that his reaction was to endorse what I had decided; "We must get you out - we must find an alternative - in her own house she's absolute mistress and naturally controls everything."

During his holiday FG halved my duties, thereby doubling my energies. With him we greatly extended the range of our expeditions; we got up the steep bank to walk aloft on the so-called "Mariners' Way", the ancient track I had so often looked at with longing; we had an exciting afternoon at a local gymkhana; sometimes he and I left the children for odd half hours of cycling together on the high moorland road - all was renewal and refreshment. We were living apart, FG in the insecurities of the London of 1944, his family where we were accepted only on sufferance; we had lost house and home; we had forfeited our hopes for the children's future; yet such is the resilience, the almost indestructibility of the will to enjoy life on almost any terms, that we laid care aside and had one of our best holidays ever.

FG was delighted with Richard's progress. He had arrived in the early evening, Philip still up, Richard bathed and in bed urgently hoping to see his father before he went to sleep so we went upstairs right away. Richard instantly sat bolt upright in his crib and plunged at once into a long and detailed list of his holiday plans, all pell-mell. When he had finished, as FG stooped to kiss him goodnight he whispered shyly; "Daddy!" "Yes?" "Daddy did you know which," (he still said *which* for *that* sometimes) "which I have a shirt and a tie?" He nodded towards his chair and FG inspected the new garments gravely and looked approval. For a week now Richard had discarded the jersey tops and dungarees he'd worn the past two years and though nothing had been said I saw how important the little shirts and trousers were - the toddler was become a little boy. Downstairs FG was pleased to find Philip now using an ordinary chair and presented him with a beautiful old French set of chessmen made with pegged bases to fit into the slotted wooden board so that games could be left safely unfinished; the pair of them used it often - out of doors at my insistence - greatly mystifying Richard by their sessions. Philip now stayed up to hear the latest war news on the radio, and he and FG were in great spirits at the way the French campaign was going and discussed it endlessly. My elder brother had been flown into France on some administrative commission, and wrote of his evenings hobnobbing and drinking cider in Normandy villages.

We really began to anticipate the liberation of all France and eventually peace in havocked Europe - though it wasn't peace but victory that they talked about.

Three weeks after this I was writing to FG:-

"I have just heard that a bungalow in Chagford is likely to fall free; Philip and I are trying not to build on this but I have written to ask for the first refusal.

"Richard is perched on the arm of my chair demanding paper to write to you. No - sorry to disappoint, but he will only write with a fountain pen, mine or Philip's, since neither of us will take the risk he refuses to write at all.

"New guests today; then, after them, four more; then we'll be alone here for the winter - but hope not.

"Fortunately Mrs D is as kindly disposed to us now as in the beginning - positively invites Richard into her kitchen, takes him with her to inspect the gardens, the new chicks, even the *tractor*. It's done him good not to feel unwanted any more. She's offered to make me plum jam with her surplus fruit (and *sugar*) and has bottled me six jars of tomatoes. And last week when she was free of guests she suggested that I leave her to give the boys lunch, and spend a few hours in Exeter. (Visited the house agents who didn't think it worth while to take my name).

"I found a silver thread in my hair next morning and Richard, who cannot bear to think that I shall ever be old, consoled my by saying; 'Never mind, Mummy, you *look* old but really you aren't really!' I tried to look pleased.

"'Yes, I agree with you. Acceptance is the thing. If one accepts one's material, one can hew a life out of that medium - it's no use to repine that you'd hoped for easier material to work in.'

"A month now since you started your holiday. Dear, dearest FG what a happy time. It's hazy, warm weather, harvest time, and they'll soon think of swaling the moor, so come again soon and stay as long as they'll spare you."

How innocent I was not to guess that the new dispensation resulted from Mrs D's knowledge of my intention to move! - for of course all Chagford must have heard of my enquiries. Nevertheless I kept my counsel till I knew for certain that the bungalow would really be available but Philip and I talked of it every single night until at last we heard that it was actually vacant, that I had first refusal, and the key was at my disposal. I arranged to leave the boys for a few hours and cycled out that afternoon to inspect.

CHAPTER NINE

Halcyon Days

I could not pedal road fast enough on my return for I had found the little place ideal for all our requirements. I pushed the bike hard at the hills, rode awhile on the bare sun-baked uplands then descended at rushing speed down to the wooded valleys and narrow winding lanes where foxglove bells hung over wild strawberries under the hedgerows. Once I dismounted and picked several handfuls into my basket for the children.

I found them in our little room. Though the westering sun shone full on one side of the house their room facing the gravel courtyard was dark; my heart contracted to see them waiting patiently, so confined. But not for long I felt. "It's lovely," I said at once. "It's really perfect. I'm going to do my utmost to take it the moment I possibly can." Their faces lit up and they plied me with questions. Yes, it was all on one floor; yes, it was quite large enough - two sitting rooms with big sunny windows, three bedrooms, bathroom with airing cupboard, kitchen with fitted sink, cabinets and best of all a gas cooking stove; we would also have electric light, an "Ideal" boiler to heat the water and a big shed for all unwanted things. What was it like? Well, it stood a fair way back from the road whence only a blank white wall could be seen because it stood at right angles to it; access was by a gravelled driveway protected by stout wire-meshed gates so that - yes, certainly! - it would be perfectly safe to have Molto there - much jubilation. Its supreme value in my eyes was the site, a little shelf of land which fell away from the side of the tiny garden down to the steep lane leading to Padley Common, while the main windows faced fields which sloped down to the invisible Teign which could be heard rushing under its stone bridge a quarter of a mile away. A high holly hedge would protect us from the prevailing wind and screen us from the fields now under grass; it was therefore, without being unduly exposed, both light and airy with windows on three sides. And it was only a few minutes walk from the little township (for Chagford is not a village but an original "stannary town" where once the miners brought their tin to be weighed and stamped). We would enjoy smooth pavements and street lighting, the services of doctor, dentist and chemist, banks and shops, even a newsagent's delivery service - many of the advantages of Exeter with none of the wartime hazards. Next to having Maryfield and our lost possessions restored this was the best thing that could have happened to us and we rejoiced accordingly.

FG managed to come down to assist and we were all fit and well when, on a sunny October morning five of us including the driver somehow packed ourselves with our cases, and boxes of books, and Molto's basket, and Philip's chair, to say nothing of Molto and a little black kitten, Mrs D's parting gift to Richard, into a hired car bound for our third home in less than two and a half years. It was a very full load and a week later Philip wrote of our extraordinary departure in his French exercise (I cannot vouch for the French):

Le jour avant le déménagement nous etions très excités. Nous attendions l'arrivée de papa ce soir là, et le jour suivant etait le déménagement. Il y a avait dans l'automobile une quantite énorme de bagage, et pauvre papa ne pouvait pas trouver une place pour ses pieds. Moi, j'avais un matelas et aussi Samedi (la chatte noir) dans un carton sur mes genoux. Avec Molto aussi nous étions tres serrés - presque écrasés...

That weekend we all worked like beavers, I as always seeking to contrive the maximum of uncluttered space. I had the dining table and chairs moved out from the larger room into the square vestibule where stood the "Ideal" boiler and airing cupboard, so making a small permanently heated annexe for our meals. Instead of the tiny sitting-cum-dining room that we had just left we now had a room of which virtually the whole of one side was window, containing only armchairs and a cupboard for toys and games - free for the goings and comings of two adults, two children, two cats (for Philip had been given a golden kitten to companion Richard's black one) and the ever present Molto. The smaller room contained my writing bureau and the boys' big working table so that they should not have to dismantle or put away their projects before they needed to. Every single unwanted object was stored inside the clean dry shed.

In this, our own home, we found ourselves freed from many irksome restrictions - we could eat what we chose, when we chose, where we chose; use the plentiful hot water in the taps without stint, could switch on the lights, the electric iron and kettle at will; I had now far less to do than at the guest-house because a young woman, pleasant, intelligent and kind, came in twice daily and did almost all the work. In the morning Edna washed up and prepared the day's vegetables, emptied the ashes and brought in fuel, dusted and swept; in the afternoon she came in to clear and tidy after our midday meal. She had a husband on active service and a little boy, Walter, who sometimes played with Richard in the tiny garden.

Almost at once we evolved a happy regular way of life. Nights continued broken for Philip and me, so he was asleep when Richard came along to my room around 7.30 and got into bed beside me while I made and drank my tea. We had breakfast by ourselves leaving Philip to have his sleep out and then have his breakfast in bed so that we could do all the exercises before he dressed. At about eleven o'clock we would set out with Molto for our first walk, leaving the little cats asleep by the fire.

The boys loved the typical village shops - butcher, baker, greengrocer, hardware, dairy, grocer, not forgetting the blacksmith. Both always came inside with me whenever practicable; commodities in themselves fascinate little children and Richard watched the weighing of our rations of tea, sugars, fats, bacon and cheese quite overcome at seeing these articles in quantity for the first time in his life. Indeed for a while he was almost demoralised by all that he saw; with a bank exchanging cash for Mummy's signature and price tags on articles, he could not understand why we didn't exchange inert money for mechanical toys and story books. Molto, Philip and I chafed impatiently while he stood immovable, nose glued to a window; eventually, as there was little traffic and there were no roads for him to cross, we would push on and leave him to catch us up. There and back we met more folk in a morning's outing than in a month on the moor and almost always they would hold us in talk so that it was usually time for me to prepare our meal when we got back.

Then came my siesta; since Philip had slept late in the morning he would read to Richard or they would play together; Edna would come and go unseen by me; and at the appointed time Richard would call me (once with a note they had typed on the old "Underwood" portable for my benefit; "Dear Mummy - come, rise shine and be lovely - it's 2.30!"). It was part of the ritual to lay the table and put the full kettle at the side of the "Ideal" boiler before our departure - not to save time but because it was so cheering to return to the glowing eye of fire, to see the shining cups and saucers, the little cakes we had bought in the morning, the dish of jam or honey, the children's eggs all ready to boil. This time we set out for a country walk and for many days to come every walk was an exploration; we had become over-familiar with the limited excursions possible at Throwleigh but now every radiating road had its enticing lanes and byways leading away into the unknown with its possibility of endless discoveries more. We must have covered scores of miles during the ensuing months, Richard indefatigable though Molto did less well - he always set forth enthusiastically and had a thoroughly good time chasing smells and suspected rabbits and a few stray hens; but on long walks he was sometimes done up before we got back and had to ride part of the way home.

After tea the animals were fed. Horse-flesh was delivered for them twice a week; three plates of cooked meat duly cut up with some suitable vegetables were carried outside - until the day when Richard saw two unhappy cats sitting beside two empty plates and we all saw Molto slinking guiltily behind the shed, the very picture of a sneaking felon. Thereafter he ate shut up in the kitchen, the cats as before outside, re-entering the house sleek from post-prandial grooming, purring and well-pleased to sit with the children until Richard's bath-time, while I finished off my day's work and prepared for the next.

The boys were always busy and it was good that we had at last some of our salvaged equipment - the "Matador", the two tricycles, games and few books; both had inherited their father's mechanical bent and they made a great Meccano crane - a real working model more than two and a half feet high in their workshop; I also remember with less respect and much more affection two cardboard aircraft models, Philip's a monoplane in red and yellow, the "Sun", Richard's a flying boat in green and gold, the "Moon". And after Richard was abed we two again enjoyed the companionable hours of two years ago though now we had a second session of massage and exercises to perform and we worked faithfully through our nightly routine sharing an unspoken joy in this restoration of a way of life withheld since the dire experiences of twelve months before.

So went the days, and soon we were preparing for Christmas with decorations and secrets, anticipating FG's coming. The boys ordered for their father a small cask of draught beer complete with spiggot, and attached a scrap of verse thereto; "When Dartmoor storms blow loud and drear/And Chagford pubs seem far from near/Come, take a cup of Christmas cheer/From your two sons who love you dear!" FG and Philip played chess again to Richard's mystification but he was presently consoled by seeing his first real snow with which he was enchanted, and later we all trudged up into the village which looked as unreal and insubstantial as a fairy town, the shadows violet-blue on smooth white hills. I telephoned Exeter, and Edith and Paul and Martin, home for his holiday, came out for a day and with their help we all reached the top of a slope above the village, almost an Alpine vista which Philip would have missed without their help. The next day all had melted away to Richard's keen regret; however he was cheered by the prospect of a village Christmas party in the afternoon; especially exciting was the prospect of a conjuror.

It was quite a large party with most of the local children there, and after a wonderful tea with crackers and balloons the chairs

162

were ranged in rows for the conjuror to perform. Toward the end he asked for six boys and girls to join him on the platform and quietly, in the most matter of fact way imaginable, Richard got up from his chair and without look or word to us he mounted the steps, Philip and myself naturally astonished and I for a moment almost anxious for him. I need not have worried. When he got up five others followed, and he looked not in the least nervous though perhaps impressed with the importance of the occasion - eyes enormous, pink face serious as he was grouped with the other children and then listened attentively to the conjuror's instructions. A small model house, "the house that Jack built", was produced and out of its seeming emptiness were conjured in turn the malt, the rat, the cat, the dog, the cow with the crumpled horn and so on, each small model being given, as it appeared, to one of the children who held it forth and named it each time it came round in the conjuror's solemn recitation of the rhyme. All went without a hitch as the children followed the simple instructions. Up aloft, one in each hand, Richard held his two bags of malt, standing very straight, speaking loudly and clearly his, the final sentence, that came at the end of each verse "the malt that lay in the house that Jack built." He alone had to repeat more than two words and to speak at every repetition from the first to the last one, but he spoke out every time directly and quite naturally to the audience; he seemed quite oblivious of the applause. At the end he came back to his place as quietly as he had left it, sat down, and awaited the next item. When all was over the great mound of whirling paper streamers of the finale was solemnly presented to him by the conjuror, probably as the youngest and smallest performer.

By common consent we didn't speak of his part in the proceedings then or later; the boys disentangled the streamers and wound them into coloured rings and I made a note in my journal with feelings that would have been absurd in a mother whose children's independence could simply be taken for granted as their natural right. He had looked so very *ordinary*! - just a bright-eyed little boy in a white shirt with blue silk tie matching his blue velvet corduroys, and with all my heart I trusted that his future might be "ordinary" too...

163

When we met our hostess next day she said to him; "You *did* do well!" and he thanked her in the low gruff voice that he used when pleased. Later he made his only allusion to the performance; "Do you know how the malt and such a lot of things were got inside that little house? *Springs*! They were all pressed down quite flat but when they were picked out they sprang out big! I could feel the springs in the bags all the time." Philip advised him "not to tell" and so far as I know he never did.

Came spring time and in March and April we sent boxes of violets and primroses from the lanes to FG in London, going further afield and taking picnics as the days grew longer and warmer. All changes in growth and colour of plants and trees, every fresh flower, every bird nesting or in flight or song we'd note and share. Going and coming we continued to meet old and new friends and acquaintances in the village, often stopping for a natter before going further. One of these was a rather formidable eighty-five year old lady; with her witch-like appearance, her cracked voice and rather abrupt manner she wasn't at first attractive to any of us, yet her imaginative goodness of heart was once more to show that first impressions may be deceiving. She stopped us after her greeting one morning to say that she would be glad to have us walk in her garden and grounds whenever we chose. I cannot think that she ever guessed - though I am glad to think that more than once we tried to tell her - how many happy hours she gave us that spring and summer, and the facility was to be of the utmost value during the ensuing autumn. Every walk we took without exception entailed steep climbs up the hills or descents into the valleys that rose and fell on every side from Chagford's central square; "Millholme" was on our level, so that we could slip over in the interval between two showers, or enjoy fresh air and wide vistas when not feeling equal to more strenuous outings. We didn't go too frequently - rarely more than once a week - entering unobtrusively by the back drive between the old grey walls studded with pennywort and topped with valerian, and beginning by wandering along the paths of the large walled kitchen garden. All was kept in tip-top order - vegetables in neat rows, budding raspberry canes and greening gooseberry bushes flanked healthy cabbages and thin young lettuces, backed by pears and peaches trained up the red brick. We inspected everything and noted progress before proceeding through the tall screening hedge and beyond the flowering trees and shrubs to reach the long sloping lawns below the frontal terrace. We kept to the path flanked by its banks of splendid scented wallflowers already humming with the first bees and with beds of the finest polyanthus that I have ever seen - huge brilliant clusters on thick sturdy stems - under the trees down the hill lay flocks of daffodils and narcissi. Such was "Mrs Fleming's Garden" - and the words are numinous for me still.

My only cause of discontent during this time was the erotic activity of the neighbouring male cat population and I grew heartily tired of our little cats' espousals and accouchements and the need to dispose of the unwanted ones. Molto, egged on by both the boys, loved chasing the toms and would break my plantlings with joyous abandon as he plunged after their escape route through the holly hedge. Brownie brought forth one litter in a corner of the sitting room with Richard an absorbed witness, very excited and pleased as he hailed me with news of four new arrivals for her private kitten box. The corner where delivery had occurred was spotless. Unluckily for me FG was not in Devon, so leaving the cat one kitten to suckle I removed three skinny, blind and naked creatures, tied them into a small weighted linen bag and dropped them into a pail of water. I stayed to make sure that it would remain well sunken, and was horrified to hear the kittens mewing for I had thought they would die at once from shock; I closed the kitchen door and an hour later buried a sodden silent bag at the bottom of the garden.

That same evening Blackie, the older cat, decided that her kitten no longer required her help to get of the wooden box where she groomed and nursed him. Usually she jumped out carrying him in her mouth for him to nuzzle her side where she lay prone on the rug. But tonight despite the outraged squallings from the box Blackie sat unmoved by the fire and washed her face, so perforce the little kitchen had to scale the straight wooden walls for himself. He was very tiny, and when by great effort he had got his two front paws and piteous little face over the edge he could only mew loudly at sight of his unresponsive parent so very far removed. His little back legs and minute triangular tail trembled as he strove, only to fall back, whimpering and wailing to his cold and empty bed. But he never gave up. Again and again he reached his vantage point, tiny claws scraping, and again he rolled flat on his back and cried for the help that never came. His mother sat and awaited him as though she knew that he could reach her and had no intention of rendering assistance. But she was by no means indifferent; she didn't go to sleep as usual but sat upright alert to his every effort and outcry. The children and I watched breathlessly - tender-hearted Richard would like to have lifted the kitten out but a stern look from Philip forbade it. Eventually with a superlative effort the kitten's hind legs propelled him over the top so suddenly and unexpectantly that he fell headlong to the floor, and instantly righting himself he hurled himself at his mother at full speed. Benevolently she rolled on her side and while the kitten drank frenziedly the sound of her triumphant purring filled the room.

And now the war in Europe drew near its end; with the crumbling of German resistance came the over-running of the "extermination" and other camps to taint and temper joy in victory. Relief was universal, of course, but Belsen and the rest filled us with horror. Philip and I talked long of this after Richard had gone to bed; many of our friends that day, in their first revulsion, had execrated the whole German nation as innately disposed to crude bestiality, as inherently an evil people. Privately I could not go along with this, since after all the first sufferers from Nazi atrocities had been Germans themselves, and (again privately) I could not accept that the dismay and astonishment with which the Germans shown the camps by the allies had reacted was proof merely of collective and gross hypocrisy. Certainly I thought it necessary that they should see these enormities if only to forestall an idealisation of "the Party" by patriotic but misguided historians in the future. Philip thought that German shock was probably often genuine; as usual he was quietly realistic; "How could everyone have known what went on behind the wire? Supposing such terrible things had been going on for years in Princeton prison, how could we in Chagford or Moretonhampstead, though we live so near, have got to know about it? And if we had known, how could we have stopped it? I'm sure lots of Germans had no idea." Considering all that he had heard said that day it was good that he thought as he did; many of his generation must have been thinking on similar lines and that generation - not the one that had fought twice for survival against the German military machine - would ultimately be responsible for the shaping of post-war society.

Events moved fast. It was presently announced that the German Luftwaffe had virtually ceased to exist, that at last our country was safe from air attack. Finally, on May second, 1945, in large widely spaced capital letters Philip recorded in his War Diary the German surrender and closed the book and put it away, his record completed; and though events of great moment occurred in the ensuing months he annotated no longer but left the rest of his notebook blank. Our local celebrations had been thought out in advance of the day, and on a cloudless hot afternoon a feast was held in the little town at which old and young, residents and refugees, rich and poor, the butcher, the baker, the candlestick maker, sat together at long tables set out in the square. The children and I were sad that FG was unable to join us; when later in the month he did so we knew that we could positively count on eventual reunion, although since peace now presented him and his colleagues with almost as many problems as war we would have to wait awhile - as it turned out for more than a year.

During the following weeks our small community grew diminished as many congenial acquaintances quickly returned to their own homes, their wartime sojourn over. Roosevelt died suddenly and Truman succeeded him; Churchill's long leadership was abruptly terminated; and in early August came the atom bombs on Hiroshima and Nagasaki, dropped without warning to the Japanese or the horrified world. We were shocked as at the extermination camps of May; when "VJ" day came we felt no gladness as on "VE" day, rather a sombre feeling almost of fear at the forces at the disposal of fallible humanity; however extenuated it seemed impossible to *celebrate* such an enormity. With the end of global warfare came a sense almost of anticlimax which the sunless overcast weather did nothing to dispel.

Chapter Ten

Declension

When we had celebrated Philip's birthday in June I had somehow found it hard to sustain the usual mood of festivity. All four of us, that glorious afternoon, had managed to get to the top of Nattadon Hill where we had baked ourselves in the sun and identified tors, river valleys and villages, returning for the birthday tea prepared before we left. Philip had stood the long trip well; yet alone, making adjustments to the candles on the cake, I had to scold and exhort myself - a year ago he'd only just emerged from convalescence, surely I should now be rejoicing that we had enjoyed a whole year without setbacks? Yet a fleeting uneasiness that I couldn't pin down or define had that afternoon floated up into consciousness; I felt rather than heard a whisper that all was not well - perhaps I was so closely attuned to him that invisible changes were perceptible to me or perhaps the afternoon's effort had shown up the ground lost since two years ago. Certainly this wasn't knowledge, merely a sense of being less glad than usual on a birthday; but it seemed almost like knowledge.

Anyway we had a gay birthday celebration, especially glad because we could begin to look forward to a future as a united family even with no idea of where. My strange concern evaporated and was soon forgotten, our regular ways continued until, early in August, having been unusually quiet for two or three days, Philip seemed unwell after our afternoon outing and went early to bed to rest. There followed two days and two nights of nausea, sickness and fasting, succeeded during the next twenty-four hours by long periods of exhausted torpor, so severe that the doctor warned me of a general deterioration. But he slowly emerged, and by the end of a week was up and dressed again. But he had not recovered. Three weeks of semi-starvation caused by what seemed an inexplicable revulsion from food and drink by the end of the month had brought about a startling change in powers and physical appearance; he grew pale, tired, thin and terribly frail-looking, with blue veins showing up in his temples and dark eyes huge in his somehow smaller face. Weakened by this prolonged ordeal the most poignant effect of all was the lowering of spirits, his facial expression often anxious, he so rarely daunted, so essentially blithe of heart. We were mystified and helpless until at my despairful insistence our doctor carried out some chemical tests which disclosed a severe acidosis for which condition he prescribed glucose.

The effect was almost immediate. Nausea ceased and, eating daily a little more, Philip gradually normalised the processes upset by under-eating, and very soon it was no trial to sit at table again with Richard and me. It was astonishing how rapidly he changed facially - his cheeks filled out, the bones of his face were hidden again, his colour normal and his eyes clear and bright. His voice returned, his usual animation; he awoke with his usual cheerfulness every morning, went to bed as he always had, in confident hope of his morrow. We understood how glucose worked and the thought that we could control and even prevent further attacks raised our spirits tremendously; I hoped he might enjoy life as much as before, even wondered whether by neutralising acid in the system we might assist the muscular tissues. With buoyant hope of restarting, believing these past miseries best forgotten, we worked hard at our old routines and even instituted new ones, though now I began to balance activity with periods of rest for recuperation.

My relief at his response to treatment, his delight at well-being restored each morning that he awoke happy and confident in a recurrent miracle, endowed me with a strength I never dreamed I possessed. During September and October the bright skies and warmth of an Indian summer blessed my enterprise and we took long country walks thrice instead of twice daily, often carrying picnics, and I walked away into the hills or distant villages as though I stepped on air. After six hours in the sunshine the boys' ruddy brown faces and Philip's good spirits made me almost exultant with my happiness. He had come through, was well at ease and happy, and each day's plans and projects gave the illusion (for such it was) of present security.

In truth, although for some weeks there were no clouds on his horizon, his sun now shone lower in his sky and when the days grew cooler and shorter he had become less and less able to share as before in our family life. While Richard played with Molto, cats and "Tiger" his special kitten, his swing and tub of water with little Walter from next door, I would take Philip to wander quietly around Mrs Fleming's garden or simply to sit peaceably together in her little summer house, watching the white clouds move over the high skies from east to west, saying little, glad to be there. "Horas non numero nisi serenas," said the sundial.

There was no more illness, but brief periods of headache and lassitude, which always responded to rest and glucose, suggested that without this therapy it might perhaps recur. Faithfully we worked at all our routines but other activities were gradually curtailed by the need for frequent rest. Underneath his brave front, his good spirits, the foundations of his existence were truly eroded and his grasp on life had weakened. Slowly - so slowly that I scarcely perceived it from one day to the next, only by comparing one week with another - he was steadily losing ground. Presently it tired him to sit in a chair for long periods of time and we gradually increased his times of lying prone, seeking on my part to spare him unnecessary effort, on his, to avoid it. From trying to increase his strength my aim changed to an attempt to hold the position stable, and then it seemed that I was to fail in this too. Hope and determination were not enough, the tide against us was too strong and we had begun helplessly drifting. Truly I had been warned of the outcome seven years ago and had lived eventually in the hope that it was not to be yet and might well be a long way off. Now and visibly it drew near. My concern was never to betray my deep misgiving, to

171

behave as though every setback was temporary and to continue unaltered all our accustomed rituals. There was within me a confusion of contradictory feelings but alone I surrendered sometimes to my secret despair, and at night fear clutched my heart.

One autumn afternoon when FG was again on leave we walked with the boys up the Nattadon road. Secret grief weighed me down, a heavy burden, and I lagged behind the others and presently wandered into an empty field and sat down under a tall bank. In unaccustomed solitude I faced the future and at first it seemed very terrible. The long struggle to preserve him had made him precious and in the process my identity had become so closely bound up with his that I could foresee no future at all beyond the span of his life. There could only be emptiness. It was a still afternoon and over the quiet trees the eternal sky enclosed the ancient outlines of the land, and these things, perceived almost unconsciously, helped me towards a new attitude of mind arrived at, it seemed, without use of thought or will. I knew that what I had striven to avert would come and perhaps come soon and our long struggle end in defeat, but the bitterness of this thought was suddenly submerged in a rush of tenderness for him. For of him I would think now. Even if I must relinquish the finite hope which had so long sustained me I knew that I would strive just as hard without it to ease his burden and to smooth his way. Fear left me then and love now took its place.

But this new way of facing reality didn't mean passive acquiescence. I realised now, and our doctor agreed, that the acidosis had been the result of some fundamental failure, its nature at present unknown. So now by day while he rested and Richard was at play, and at nights when both had gone to bed I sat studying reports and text books, often astonished at the frank confessions of ignorance - of muscle physiology and its tie-up with other functions - made by the apparently learned. After some weeks I set about summarising all I had discovered in a reasoned memorandum, sending a copy to FG in London while telling him at the same time, "I feel that if something can be done it must be soon." Since today my brief paper will certainly be outdated, irrelevant, and the data on which it was based very probably erroneous, the only point in referring to it now is to show how intelligence as well as feeling was mobilised, how total my involvement, how hard I was trying.

Nevertheless at the very least this work led to a consultation between our co-operative Chagford doctor and a specialist in medical biology whereby a helpful therapy was devised to supplement the glucose intake, and happily the illness of early autumn was never to recur. This was much. But still there remained the problem, at which I worked by devising diets and little treats at meal times, of helping him to absorb any but minute amounts of nourishment, the truth being that the whole organism was exhausted and almost too tired to function so that to eat and digest food was simply too much trouble for it. Seemingly we had re-started the engine even though it was only ticking over - taking in sufficient fuel for the day-to-day requirements of an undemanding life but not enough to replace used tissues and depleted energies, still less to build a reserve.

Nevertheless he ceased to slip down the slope and for a while he seemed to hold his own though he didn't regain what he had lost. Regular, varied and minute meals, fresh air and changes of scene (always now preceded and followed by a rest recumbent), careful observance of necessary supplements, glucose always available, scrupulous care that he never got over-tired, such was the regime now - almost invalidism - and we all soon took it for granted, relieved and thankful for our easement.

When he felt well, as he always did when rested, then he looked animated and bright, frail perhaps but certainly not ill with his fresh clear colour, lively eyes and general air of interest and intense vitality. He hated to admit to tiredness, but unnaturally wide eyes and a tight mouth would betray him and I would then make some excuse for suggesting a rest, without stating my real reason. Only once did he ever ask to rest himself, and went to bed early instead of spending his usual hour with me after Richard's bath. He lay in his room, to my deep disquiet,

173

alone in the dark, not asleep but quiescent and seemingly content. This episode was never repeated and never explained.

During the days when he had been rapidly losing ground, when his clear intelligence must have seen whither he was tending, I think he didn't realise it as actuality though certainly as possibility. Once or twice when I spoke cheerfully as I made him comfortable for one of his enforced rests he looked up at me almost *wisely*, as if he knew far more than I seemed to. Once he interrupted as I was planning some project for the future; "We must try to be happy with all that we have *now*. Because perhaps in the future we may not be able to be so happy." Only once did he speak specifically of his condition and then without any show of feeling; "Well, somebody had to have it, and you see it was me."

I was startled at the assumptions underlying such words, assumptions that were then, and remain now, to me entirely unacceptable. But I didn't comment or probe into his reasoning; enough at fifteen years old he had so stoically explained his life to himself - remarkable and honourable and brave. Not for the first time his unflinching fortitude called forth my pride and admiration. He was still only in the first half of his sixteenth year, but I saw him not as child but as a fellow mortal for whom I hoped that while he yet lived his days might be easeful; as I look back now it was a sad declension from the ardent anticipations of fifteen years before.

On his part inevitably he turned himself more and more towards me, and always with unselfishness, understanding and affection; "You looked sad - I noticed while I was reading to Richard. You mustn't be sad - things are certain to get easier for you." Once or twice, in his room at night, he broke his reserve to express other feelings; "You know, when you come to me at night with your hair all down your back, you are exactly my idea of a goddess," and his face evinced such devotion that it was hard to laugh and tease him as once I would have done. And another time the convinced assertion; "Had I not been as I am, I should have missed the best thing in my life which has been the knowing of you." And while transfixed in my deepest self at such a tribute yet passionately I regretted the price he had paid in recent dependence for an intimacy as precious to me as to himself. I would have given all up for him to have known length of years in which his capacity for ardent living, his warmth and discrimination of response, his mental powers, might have been fully deployed, and found wider opportunities for fulfilment.

Every night, Richard bathed and asleep in bed, came the day's anticipated climax when, cats curled up together basking in the heat of the log fire, dog yawning, blinking and stretching until his basket creaked, we did a second session of massage and exercise. These sessions we both regarded as purposive work and we gave them all that we had. No enterprise could more have deserved success; even although when we seemed to have gained ground we presently found ourselves to have slipped a little further back we never ceased to try; for my part to acquiesce in accepting an end to endeavour was so impossible that thereby came strength to fight the hopeless odds. His courage, my pertinacity, the reticence and self-control of us both - for each never shared misgiving with the other - these held us up. I would assert to myself privately, "if hopes were dupes fears may be liars," but really, I think, I had ceased to be concerned with eventualities, the endeavour was to do what we must and to do it well. Life wasn't based on expectations.

Afterwards we usually sat together and talked. Disability didn't exist as we discussed life and the world as we knew it, the day's happenings and encounters, remembered times past - homes, holidays and school-days - books and reading, imagined ourselves reunited as a family, sometime, somewhere. We forgot our fears, voiced our resolves, were never sated, never dull, always sorry when bedtime came. This hour so punctual and so peaceful, in its regularity and continuity gave a reassuring stability to our days, and in it disappointments, anxieties and frustrations were

175

dissolved. For a long while words had not always been necessary to us; a gesture, a speechless exchange of looks, an unspoken sense of sympathy in a group of strangers - these had for so long been a part of our intercourse that they were unconscious and taken for granted. Reactions and responses were implicitly recognised without being expressed, as though we communicated directly without translating thoughts into speech; so now as our eyes met, each understood the other's thought almost before, certainly just as it was uttered. Our intimacy seemed as complete as human separateness allowed.

I had no time to record these weeks of life running more smoothly and without immediate anxieties except in letters to FG:

> "If only it can *last*! His rounder contours, clear good colour, ability to do so much more and not so quickly tire! This afternoon they worked at Meccano and though Philip's voice is still quiet I could hear them talking through the wall. They are playing a new game now - here comes Richard to tell me the score. It all seems nearly miraculous..."

In December we despatched a large box containing seventy separately packed gifts, one for each year of her age, for my mother's birthday, the devising of which had taken many weeks. Philip himself selected and paid the sum of ten shillings (very extravagant in those days) for a silk tie for his father's birthday, and on another occasion at the antique shop he earmarked an old lustre jug for mine - two months ahead; about now he projected for himself a programme of reading. To our usual Christmas preparations of tree, puddings and pies and FG's small barrel of beer in the pantry, at Philip's insistence we added a turkey for the first time since Exeter. He and I re-read *A Christmas Carol* together, and having discovered a copy of *Alice Through the Looking Glass*, Philip read it to Richard while I prepared delicacies in the kitchen. With FG's good help Christmas Day was a quiet but real celebration with Philip sharing in everything - stockings and tree, feast and exchanging gifts. With my gift he enclosed a note expressing such modest and loving hopes that it shook FG to read it. Not a "Happy" New Year, but a "happier" one was his desire for us all, and the comparative said much.

Early in January, having gone early to bed, he died soon after sleeping with a typical tranquil and gentle acquiescence. All morning he had been drowsy and during the day had grown more and more withdrawn, speaking to Richard and me quite normally sometimes, sometimes murmuring to himself; we remained all three together until after Richard's bath and they bade one another goodnight as usual. I knew from our doctor what his strange day had portended yet all was as usual when he kissed me goodnight and asked me, as he did sometimes, to repeat the de la Mare poem beginning, "Softly along the road of evening". Except for the early hour all was as routine, but now instead of leaving him I stayed beside him while he slept. Of those hours I made no written record, yet when today, scores of years later, I look back at that time I see events happening in the present's instancy, and I do not seem to be remembering at all.

I seem to know that the end has come and rise stiffly to my feet. The placid face on the pillow lies calmly unchanged and yet I lay my hand over the heart with almost certain pre-knowledge of what is to come. Heavily and with interminable pauses between, the heart beats once, twice, perhaps three times, then ceases its beating, lies silent, and all is very still. His aspect does not change, he looks exactly as when, with closed eyes, he had last spoken, murmuring my name. With an intense searching gaze I lock my eyes upon that unresponsive still face as if by the very force of my desire I might yet hold him longer. This urgent scrutiny is followed by a look of incredulity presently succeeded by one of certainty and conviction. Of what? I am not sure. Perhaps even then the knowledge that in a moment of time an irreversible barrier has been imposed, that a line has been ruled right across a chapter ended, that nothing can ever be the same again.

Next I look preoccupied because although I had never seen death come, I knew about the changes that death may bring. So next I reassure myself that the eyes are closed, the inert limbs straight, and I fold his hands but will not cover his face for that would not, I feel, be seemly for one so young. His sixteenth year - but what do years mean now? From now on and forever, time for him will be irrelevant. At first I show no pain, seemingly feel no sorrow, my aspect is grave as though I feel awe rather than grief. I walk mechanically, move a chair, pull back the curtains, open the window wider. I see myself stand in a cool current of air, watch the trees stir, a single cloud pass slowly by.

It is after I have left his room that realisation begins to flood consciousness, a grief and despair obliterative of all else, a sorrow so intense that it nearly forgets the cause of its existence. I cannot stand, but sink into a chair where I remain motionless and nothing is real but pain, its endurance and its continuance, and while this lasts I seemingly can neither think nor act.

When I emerged I bestirred myself. I closed the bedroom door and locked it; Richard was sleeping soundly down the corridor but I hated to leave him and hurried out to use a telephone returning very relieved that he had not awakened in my absence. At the end of his brief visit the doctor offered to telephone a message for FG in London so that I didn't have to leave him alone in the house again. There was nothing to be done until morning. I sat quietly by the fire and waited for day; I did not stay with Philip though I went in to him several times. Remote and calm he looked, lashes laid on cold cheeks, hair softly brushed up from his brow, yet I did not touch those silky strands nor spoke to express endearments for his complete unresponsiveness to my presence was the surest possible proof that our long companionship had gone forever.

Richard came along as soon as he awoke as was his custom, to find me not in my bedroom drinking tea and awaiting him, but up and dressed in the little sitting room. He was very content to dress himself in front of the fire "as a treat" and I then told him that we were going to have breakfast by kind invitation with our friends across the way in half an hour. "But Philip!" he exclaimed. "What about Philip?" I told him at once, as gently as I could, that Philip had died in the night and that Daddy would be with us soon, and at this he simply crept up into my arms where he remained speechlessly, his head buried into my shoulder. For nearly fifteen minutes we sat quietly together while I stroked his hair and held him close. He did not speak nor had I words to say. At last I said we must get ready to go out for breakfast and he got up quietly, brought his coat and we set off. When we returned FG had arrived by the overnight train.

I now asked our doctor to arrange for an autopsy - for if Philip's body could further knowledge of the rare condition by which he had been afflicted I knew he would have agreed with me in desiring that it should - and the body was therefore removed to Exeter for that purpose quite soon. (The result led nowhere.) While this was done I took Richard for a customary walk to exercise the dog on the common, for I did not wish to impose upon him unnecessary or abrupt changes in his usual way of life. Richard certainly knew what death meant to cats and kittens and animals on the farm; and for him and for us all this death meant absence, in his case of his constant companion from earliest infancy until they had bidden one another an affectionate goodnight the previous evening. But now he said nothing and I never knew what his deprivation meant to him for I respected his silence then and afterwards and thought it best to allow him to adjust to what he had been told in his own way and in his own time. The presence of his father, to whom he had always been devoted, may have helped.

That afternoon I wrote in my journal a thanksgiving for our good days together - a farewell and renunciation as I thought, but renunciation was not so easily come by and not to be found for a very long time had I but known it. But for the next days I was living in an unreality where grief and love were inextricably mingled in a strange almost ecstasy of feeling; at the crematorium (there was no religious "service") I repeated Ben Jonson's classic lines on the beauty of brief living, felt Philip to have been indeed a "flower of light", really believed then that "in short measure life may perfect be". Such uplifted thoughts proved transient.

CHAPTER ELEVEN

Exile

No sooner had we emerged into the cold January light than strength began to seep away and during the long drive back from the crematorium my very will seemed to disintegrate. It almost seemed that during the four days that Philip's physical body though lifeless had remained still in existence I could live and act according to the standards we had maintained together; now that the long endeavour had ended, the spirit that had sustained me suddenly failed and inertia paralysed my faculties.

It had been decided that Richard and I would accompany FG when he returned to London and there were barely two days in which to prepare. With Edna's good help I emptied larder and store cupboards and packed away household goods; she and her little boy Walter would be happy to look after Molto and the kitten, but I had to arrange for the two grown cats to be "put to sleep" the day after our departure. At these and many such tasks I worked mechanically and steadily in a seemingly numbed state of mind but from time to time my dormant faculties were pierced by sudden anguished *realisations* when perforce I hastened to my room, closed the door and there endured what seemingly had to be undergone, the pain would ebb, I would emerge and work again. To apathy, intermittent crises of suffering, automatic activity, the ache of deprivation in place of satisfaction and endeavour - to each in turn I submitted without even an attempt to achieve the gallantry that Philip most certainly would have hoped of me, and that for a short while perhaps I had hoped of myself.

In this state of mind I had not been rationally persuaded into the error of uprooting myself and Richard from our familiar countrified surroundings to live among strangers in the world of post-war London. I had merely surrendered myself to any arrangement that might be devised. Of course removal from daily reminders of recent happenings, a period of respite from domesticity, a chance to assimilate sorrow and to devote myself to the needs of FG and Richard were all things to be desired and, had I not allowed myself to be sunk into torpor, I could have seen to it that we obtained them all - but in some quiet place in the country or near the great parks and commons of London's green belt.

But seemingly decisions were not then in my power and according to plan we were driven to the nearest station to catch the London express. It was very cold under a grey sky, the icy wind blew dead leaves and old tickets and paper wrappers into miniature whirlwinds which then fell to drift with the dust up the long platform where we paced to keep warm.

In retrospect the next three months seem strangely off-key mainly because myself was out of tune; memories are sometimes vivid, often blurred, and I gave up the journal for weeks at a time, making a mere four entries between mid-January and April, mainly because inarticulate though also chances to be alone were few. On the first night FG offered to put Richard to bed having in advance arranged for one of his colleagues to take me out to dinner. I must have made a poor companion, sitting opposite my probably embarrassed host; try as I would to be interested in the brightly-lit restaurant, in the food and conversation, my mind would keep wandering off to keep tryst with recent memory - at this hour a week ago, sitting with cats and dog beside a bright fire we had happily argued over the plot of a story that Philip intended to write, both deluded (as I saw now) by our recent sense of security.

Next day FG returned to his office duties and Richard and I began our new life. We were installed in a pleasantly secluded small residential hotel near Kensington Gardens. He had his bed in my room (unthinkable then that he should sleep by himself down the corridor); and daily we descended for meals of wholesome simple food with choice enough to make them quite suitable for a little boy of six; there weren't any other children but the other guests were quiet and friendly and Richard soon at his ease with them. Whenever the frost and fog relented we would go out - wandering hand in hand through Kensington Gardens, watching the birds, looking for green signs of snowdrops or buds on the trees, getting sometimes as far as the Round Pond. For me all this was a kind of banishment seeing it all with an exile's eyes, but I think that Richard often enjoyed it very much, returning with bright cheeks and frosty eyelashes to listen to stories or play floor games in the bedroom. He asked questions and showed intense interest in everything he saw and heard and evinced no sign of unhappiness nor ever spoke of his brother. Yet he was now without the companion and playmate of almost every day he could remember, and he must have found me sometimes absent-minded and preoccupied. At first I found this reserve strange and had he shown signs of disturbance I might have talked with him about what had happened so that he might perhaps unburden his mind. But he showed no such signs and it seemed best to leave things alone.

I concluded that his reaction might resemble his father's with whose temperament Richard had so much in common. Deeply as FG had felt the loss of his son he had accepted it stoically, saying farewell once and for all to the boy and the great hopes he had once entertained for him; now his eyes were bravely fixed on a future of happier endeavour for us all. His own situation too must have been helpful in this time of trial, or so I felt; because his way of life continued unchanged, and his place of work, his colleagues, his daily duties and assignments remained exactly as before. Not in any way a compensation but certainly at least assuagement.

182

With surprise I presently realised that both FG and Richard were adjusted. After his bath followed by his usual rituals Richard went to bed, and at first I would run upstairs from the lounge three or four times to see how he did; I invariably found him placidly asleep, and although I felt mystified I was very thankful for his adaptability. I am afraid that I could not emulate either of them. I had to come to terms with the knowledge that a worthy endeavour prolonged over many years had ended, its objective never to be attained; and that at a stroke I had been bereft of a beloved companion and an all-absorbing way of life. I think that I needed occasional privacy and at this time I was never alone by day or night. Yet Richard's lively presence was often solace and FG's always strengthening - like a hand put forth to raise me up to his side which was where I needed to be; but we met only after his long day's work at the office and then seldom alone. Several evenings a week we passed with FG's friends of the past six years; they were a lively group of able and successful people, and I was sensible that, except that I happened to be FG's wife, they had no reason whatever for welcoming a complete stranger into their midst. And of course for them Philip had never existed. So I exerted myself to do better than on my first evening and, since FG once said they thought me "simply marvellous", I imagine that perhaps I succeeded. So it was stupid of me privately to accuse myself of "putting on an act" and despising myself for it, because the effort and the company were respites and I should have been thankful. Yet because I was living in a state of near despair to which I awoke each morning, in which I lay down each night, the contrast between outward behaviour and inner feeling created a cruel impasse from which there seemed no escape. I seemed quite incapable of rational thought.

The wife of FG's most valued London friend twice invited us to visit her home deep in the Kentish countryside. Although not far from a small town and equipped with gas, electricity and telephone, her home seemed as isolated and remote as our first

Dartmoor cottage for it stood quite alone at the end of a sloping trackway that climbed away from a long country lane, a wintry wood behind and bare trees and bushes in front. Here in normal times she ran a household of herself, husband, two grown sons, and a daughter and son in their teens, but only the younger two children were there just now. J herself was small and slight and in spite of her bright eyes and good colour she seemed at first delicate; but really she was tough and wiry and managed her high-spirited family, together with dogs, cats, rabbits and hens, with ease.

But we saw little of the real country because all was smothered under the deepest snowfall I had seen since America. Roads, fields and hedge-tops were become one level expanse, the brown distant woods and our own trees were burdened by great wads of frozen snow, under a monotonous grey sky there stretched a monotonous sterile desert marked only by a few animal footprints or the seals of the birds that came daily for food. The trans-Atlantic snowscapes that I remembered had been brilliant with colour, the glittering world under the cobalt blue sky being diversified by evergreens and brown buildings each casting its own long violet shadow. In Kent the purity and the unbroken levels of the snow at first seemed very lovely but presently the uniformity and the silence suggested a suspension of the world's life; as day followed day without sunrise or sunset, it merely grew lighter or darker; blurred tree shapes stood inertly hard-clamped in frost; from the starving birds a subdued chirping and fluttering in the bushes told us that they survived. Down one side of the house hung a thick icicle, black and rigid, which Richard examined constantly - the first he'd ever seen - looking vainly every day for the merest drop of water at the tip. Sometimes we were restricted to a twice daily trudge round the house on the sand-strewn track that we had trodden to the rustling rabbits in their steamy straw-filled boxes, as warm, or warmer, as J once said, than we were in the house. I was touched at Richard's interest and care for the rabbits and birds, and seeing this J promised him one of the baby bunnies she was expecting and a house to keep it in as soon as his parents had a "house of their own". Here J made it possible for me to deal with the pile of correspondence I had with me, and she also often talked with me of her own family; at night she would build a huge log furnace and all five of us made a big semi-circle (and till then we two had been strangers to them all) to bask in the warmth of her fire and loving kindness. She did us both much good. By nature a fostering person - of plants, birds and animals, family and friends - dear J, even in the few short days I knew you, as mellow and sound to the core as one of your own russet apples!

Towards the end of month my mother invited us to visit her in Yorkshire and FG came with us on the long rail journey. It was almost ten years since I had seen the industrial north but the revolving wheels of the first pit shaft, always sinister I used to feel, were significant of what was to come, and on the slow branch line from Sheffield we travelled through the black heart of it. Here were the miles of chimneys belching thick smoke, the polluted rivers sluggishly flowing with filthy scrap and junk littering the banks, here the monstrous shapes of foundry and bessemer, the sterile hills of slag, the rags stuffing broken windows of steel mills with flame-lit interiors, the coal barges creeping along canals, the lines of trucks clanking to corrugated sheds on railway sidings. Close to it all, monotonous rows of grimy houses clambered the hillsides with lines of washing hanging in backyards. It seemed as though the endless litter of industry had created such universal disorder that it was beyond men's power to cope with it, and they had long since given up the attempt. A thought that had often occurred to me in girlhood now struck me afresh, that had we taken from Sheffield a train going in another direction, in the same space of time we might now have been passing through Derbyshire looking at green-grassed villages, cottages with gardens, sturdy stone farmhouses, and clean rivers curving by woods and pastures. The contrast between two ways of living, two worlds, the green and pleasant land so near the satanic world of industry seemed unendurably unfair and never to be justified.

My elder brother was waiting on the platform as our train drew in though at first I scarcely recognised in the grave figure in dark winter coat and trilby hat the tanned bareheaded brother of the summer holidays before the war. Well - I hadn't seen him since his early thirties and now I supposed he would soon be forty-two; he had done war service; and the serious look on his face was probably concern for all our sakes. He and FG sat talking in front of the car as we drove up the long hill away from the town; at the back Richard sat sleepily on my knee and I leaned forward staring at the houses that streamed past my window behind their old grey walls. They had built their mansions to last, the men who had prospered on coal, brass, iron and steel in the valleys of Don and Rother, and so far as I could see they remained exactly the same as in my childhood. Eventually we turned aside to descend the familiar tree-arched grove to alight at the red brick house with the big garden at the bottom.

Here my mother and sister welcomed us into a house where again nothing had changed. The rooms seemed large, the panelled doors substantial, stairs and landings lengthy after the little house in Devon; carpets were thick and curtains too, now drawn across the windows concealing the cold garden. Richard gazed at it all wide-eyed, speechless with tiredness, and while FG unpacked I put him at once to bed in the dressing-room where I had slept as a child; he seemed delighted to lie "in the bed Mummy had when she was small"; we left the communicating door open for him to see where we should be sleeping quite near to him all night, and he was fast asleep himself when we went below.

A roaring coal fire blazed in the dining room and as soon as we were assembled round the table my mother announced her plans for the morrow: "We are all invited by Leslie and Joan to spend the day with them and the children and to meet Joan's parents as well." This was my younger brother whose wife, small daughter and two baby sons we were now to meet for the first time. "The little boys were born one year apart *to the very day* - we shall be a real family party!" exclaimed mother all in one breath. "The first time I shall have had all my four children together since before the war when Peg was only twenty-three! It must be nearly nine years since you were here with Philip in 1937 - but that was in September, of course, so it would be eight years and five months ago, to be exact." Mother was just seventy, active, robust, and lively as ever; she lost no time in conveying the sort of visit this was to be - a sort of jolly family reunion with everything kept on a convivial footing. I understood at once her intention and except on one occasion when some careless reference brought the tears to my eyes, I was careful during our visit to keep my sorrows to myself. (She hated to see emotion though capable of very strong feelings herself; on that one occasion she had looked at me hard, exclaimed; "Now please don't go upsetting me!" and departed quickly to another room.)

She now continued her survey of the years since our last visit; the war had been "declared" and "won"; both her sons had held commissions overseas; her younger daughter had trained and qualified as a nurse; three more grandsons and a granddaughter had been born; and she had throughout tended her large house and garden virtually single-handed. How indomitable she is, was my thought (and in the event she had nearly another twenty years of activity ahead of her); what she and none of them could realise was what exactly we had lost in Philip for they saw him still as a child of seven and could not be expected to visualise him differently.

Richard had felt quite at home with J and her family in Kent but at first he felt strange in his grandmother's house. No question of it, my mother was a formidable woman, and her almost aggressive vitality he didn't quite know how to cope with except by retreat, though later on he was able to appreciate and enjoy her company. At breakfast the first morning I noticed that it was to his quiet and genial Uncle Roland that he turned when he wanted to ply questions about this unfamiliar house and garden; he looked forward, I imagine, to a good "explore" presently, but before he had got his bearings he was sitting on his father's knee being driven to yet another establishment. This was altogether too much; he became silent and watchful and remained so after our arrival. His baby boy-cousins were too young - one and two years old - for him to play with them while little Linda at first seemed as shy of Richard as he of her, a motherly, plump and pretty child in a velvet frock who presently was showing him where she kept her toys and picture books. Then we sat around the table, nine adults and four children including the bibbed infants in two high chairs, and things became even livelier, my mother in great form - "If only I could eat!" as she tackled her first course. Presently Richard wriggled down from his chair and retreated to the other room and after a few minutes I followed him when he grunted merely that he wasn't hungry and refused to return. I didn't try to persuade him, merely let him perch himself on my knee where I sat on a chair; he was calm and collected but took and held my hand. Eventually I left him playing on the hearth rug with a mechanical toy and told the company on my return that he had probably had, in less than a month, to make far too many adjustments.

Next day my brother and sister went back to work and FG left for London while Richard and I remained with "Gran" to share her life for a time. He and she were quickly good friends; a quiet domestic life without stimulation from strangers was just what he needed and we soon settled down into regular ways. "Yes," I told him, "this is where I lived when I was a little girl," and the fact in itself seemed to make him feel at home. Gran listened very attentively whenever I spoke to him of my childhood, always ready to supplement my recollections with her own.

The Grove was still the grove I remembered, as lovely with its inter-arching tree tracery in winter as in summer; it had no pavements - though there were gas lamps - so that the road seemed broader than it actually was, cars and delivery vans could get up and down but it was barely wide enough for them to pass one another. Hence, since it led nowhere, it remained as peaceful and secluded as it had always been. Regretfully Gran reminded me of the hedged fields with narrow footpaths that used to lie just over the garden wall now turned into allotments - and very forlorn they looked with their little sheds and shanties in their unkempt winter bareness; she was thankful that when her trees were in full summer leaf they were completely screened from her sight.

Yet to me things seemed little altered even to the chirrup-chirrup of the house sparrows in the ivy and the banshee wail of the wind in the bathroom drain; and the furniture - satin walnut upstairs, mahogany down - was old and familiar too. A few pictures had been replaced - where, for instance, I wondered was that portrait of Ellen Terry in her scarlet judge's robe with a scroll in her hand? - like a child who resents the least change in a story being told I was aggrieved at memory's disturbance. To one important change mother drew our attention - the atmosphere was very much clearer and cleaner than it had been in 1901, and since at that time neither Richard nor I had been born, we could not dispute the point. Even so, it was only when the sky flared red at night as a blast furnace was tapped, or when fog laid dank fingers on our hair and we breathed an acrid hint of factory fumes that we were reminded of the world of industry.

Although all the windows were permanently closed, the Victorian house, away from the warmth and comfort of the two good fires downstairs, seemed to me shivering cold especially along the passages and stairways, and though I believe there were new gas fires in the bedrooms they were only for occasional use - certainly never for bed-making and dusting sessions and these, my duties, I performed with all speed. True that except for a brief schooling at Harrow-on-the-Hill I had lived my first eighteen years in the climate of this same house, but since my only visits since had been in the summer I had forgotten the rigours of wintering in it. Ever since as a young woman on a visit to the south west I had seen for the first time white-painted houses with pillared porticoes and broad southern facades I had known myself not to be a tough and hardy "Northerner" no matter where I had been born. And fortunately it has been my lot to live my life in the warmer sunnier south with which I have always felt akin, though not for many years did I discover that my great-grandmother had been born in Bristol.

Even so I have never shared my mother's almost violent hatred of wintertime; she awoke one morning to tell me with real horror that there had been a heavy snowfall in the night: "It came down softly when I wasn't looking and now the drifts are as high as the garden wall and pressing up against the back door. Horrible!" Luckily there was a speedy thaw; when asked to explain why she couldn't accept what was surely after seventy years a necessary fact of life she spoke of bare trees, colourless flower beds, no sight or sound of bees, birds or butterflies, her own physical discomforts. "It drives me to despair! What a pity it isn't summer now and Richard could live with me outdoors and help me in the garden." Truly enough in the warm weather, all doors and windows wide, the old place always took on a fresh dimension. "Do you remember, D, the big bunches of flowers we used to take on visits to Granny Lee? In May?" (Mother now looked happy as she took a long breath.) "There'd be lilac, irises, Solomon's Seal, peony buds, lilies-of-the-valley, pyrethrums, pinks, London Pride, mock orange, even pansies—" and I said, "Yes, of course I remember. And how when we got there they would always take in flowers and family with a triumphant "*Here* they are!" Never, from anyone or anywhere, have I been given a warmer or more heart-cheering welcome." My saying this pleased my mother very much.

Every morning I would hear her moving downstairs very early and join her at six to drink tea and talk - often until we all sat down to breakfast at eight. After the day's plans were made and some household tasks completed I might go into the town with a shopping list; Richard came with me only once because the noisy jostling crowd at the trolley-bus stop and outside the shop windows made it impossible for him to examine and admire the goods in peaceful leisure as in the village. So he remained at home with Gran and they usually told me that they had been "very busy" when I got back; all the same I was concerned that he had been so long indoors and whenever possible would contrive that at least we walked to the top of the Grove and back before the midday meal. This was rarely later than twelve noon which made a very short morning - my mother had always liked to be what she called "forward", though even she for once looked taken aback on noticing that we were sitting at table at just after half past eleven one morning. And then, with fires banked up and "all done for the day", she would retire upstairs, and Richard and I would have our daily expedition.

With him I sought to discover the old pathways and places of my childhood, both of us well wrapped up against the cruel wind, his knitted-gloved hand in mine. The "fields by the White Gate" were all built over, but we could walk the same road to our old milestone where he could wonder at the square cavity built in the wall of the grange to accommodate an enormous tree root - for years a marvel to my brothers and me. We might walk another half mile down to the village with its grey church on the hill and a bridge over the stream with its waddling ducks scurrying for scraps. To go further we went by bus to "Worry Goose Lane" and since nobody could tell us why it was so called we invented a story of a marauding fox based on an old ballad of which I could remember only the refrain: "For the fox has been through the town, e'oh!" One afternoon we went to see his great-grandmother's house of happy memory, going by train to Sheffield, and taking the Fulwood bus (it used to be a tram) from the station. The house still looked over a close of large grey stone houses built round a grassy green, but to reach it we had traversed a long, noisy, dirty area of industrial chaos, and returned to Gran both exhausted and filthy.

We were frequently housebound and I imagine that it was in her desire to divert my mind that mother so frequently suggested "turning things out"; so we discovered that the contents of cupboards and drawers were, as she averred, in some cases preserved as she had inherited them from my grandmother's day. In the kitchen dresser the big wool cupboard was still crammed with coloured skeins and balls; here was the tape bag, here in the buttons bag beautiful Victorian buttons, some more than a hundred years old ("they must have belonged to Grandma's mother"); in the long top drawer lay cork mats and kitchen cloths and underneath everything I think she was as surprised as me to find a "very valuable" set of carved ivory spillikins tied up with ribbon; the recipe drawer still contained small notebooks of yellowed paper covered with copper-plate hand-writing ("take eight eggs and a pint of cream"). Far from feeling the modern housewife's urge to be "up-to-date" she proudly displayed the ancient jars of glazed earthenware in the corner cupboard each still containing a big cockle shell for scooping up sugars, cereals and pulses; in this same cupboard Grandma's old brown coffee-pot with the long spout stood dustily surviving in the corner. We emptied and cleaned several bookcases, tackled all the arrears of sewing in the mending baskets, took out her wedding silver from its green baize covers and polished it all. Each piece of silver and many of the books reminded her of people and occasions in the far past, and Richard and I loved it when she would gravely begin, "Now when I was a little girl," or, "How well I remember." Nor was Richard left out of these sortings and tidyings for she had innumerable boxes and containers that she had not looked at "*for I can't think how long,*" and he made discoveries as he "worked" at his end of the table that astonished everyone.

These were not of interest or of value, simply things hoarded lest they might one day "come in handy" - bunches of rusty keys, scraps of ribbon and tape, packets of pins, old door knobs, finger-stalls and sticking plaster, a baby's mitten, a toy whistle, two or three broken stubs of pencil, half a dozen cigarette cards depicting "British Flora", a pair of dividers, half-empty packets of flower seeds, many assorted screws and on one happy occasion a silver-wrapped oblong of Doncaster butterscotch. How right was her instinct to keep us so often busied on neutral ground with *things*: on cold and foggy mornings - and they came far too often - we sat, three generations, in an oasis of warmth and light, useful and "*deedy* "as mother would call it.

We spent our evenings cosily round the fire; for awhile Richard was busied over stitching on cardboard with woollen threads a "secret" picture of a tractor which he had drawn himself for my birthday - he thought that if he turned his back I wouldn't see it however openly he worked at it. After his bedtime Gran would take out her playing cards and either teach me to play two-handed bridge or cribbage, or play alone several games of patience before retiring upstairs with whichever Trollope novel she was currently reading. Since she often departed before nine o'clock I would read by the fire or examine the book shelves which were as confused and surprising as Richard's boxes - Herbert's *Poems* next to Baroness Orczsy, John Evelyn's *Diary* beside *Mr Verdant Green*, Voltaire's *Candide* next to *A Yankee at the Court of King Arthur* and Ruskin's *King of the Golden River*.

One evening I brought my neglected journal downstairs and read incredulously of the days of endeavour a mere six weeks ago - how worthy had life seemed then! In those days I had willingly accepted and carried a great responsibility - perhaps the insignificance of the present might be due to the lack of it, that I had allowed decisions to be made for me and had weakly surrendered to drift. Husband, mother, brothers, sister, being usefully employed integrated their powers in just the same purposeful way as I so recently could - why could I not use the positives of those days to reinforce my will today?

I could not then imagine why not, my disintegration too complete for me to sort myself out; only for Richard could I rouse myself and I miserably thought that he had jollier times with his gran than with me. It was as though the pain of loss was so unrelenting, so continual, that it created a barrier between myself and reality; I could perceive the need to act but responded automatically and could never become absorbed in what I was doing. Even my perceptions lacked focus. The remains of the old tree trunk where we had played as children still lay on its green cushion of moss; the school where thirty years ago I had been enlarged and enfranchised looked exactly the same; that very afternoon I had been up to the attic to the window corner that had once held my books and chair and deal table, the "summer study" of my girlhood, looking into and over the old chestnut tree. Almost with contempt, certainly with disdain, I thought of the dreamer I had been. Barely nine years ago I had stood there as today, when my hopes and anticipations for Philip had seemed to open vistas as wide as the fantasies of my girlhood - now equally remote. That window, tree, the smell of white-washed walls, the afternoon sky seen through the bare branches; the old books, pictures and furniture surrounding me tonight - these things had nothing to do with me any more. Past and present seemed cut asunder - what link was there between? Most certainly I had associations with these things but they had no present meaning and I closed my journal unused for I could have recorded nothing but bewilderment.

Thereafter I gave my evenings to the books though at first I could not concentrate enough to read systematically, would sit idly furling the pages, reading now here now there, until the night I took down the big folio, Boswell's *Life of Johnson*, the same from which my father had read to his children. From now on I became absorbed in this volume night after night, and it was Johnson's sensitivity of insight and understanding, not his powers of intellect or conversation, that held me fast; I copied some extracts into my journal.

The bleak northern winter was loosing its grip when early in April we said goodbye to those who had so generously shared with us their active busy life. I do not blame myself today and hope they did not blame me then that I could not enter more fully into it. I had not been purposely withdrawn but unwillingly adrift. On the day of our departure crates of racing pigeons awaited the train, and while I explained to an attentive Richard why these birds were boxed up and about to make a railway journey I experienced a quiet sense of assuagement, for, as the birds without desiring it were removed from their familiar world, so we should presently find our way back whence we had come.

When next morning we again wandered in Kensington Gardens how green and clean the grass seemed, how much warmer the sunshine! Whereas only a few timid buds had peered forth in the north here the spring bulbs were already in flower; in a few days a brighter colour returned to Richard's cheeks as he sailed his boat on the Round Pond. By now I knew, to my then regret, that FG intended to give up his pre-war work in Exeter and to accept the permanent appointment now offered him by the National Dock Labour Board. Already he had begun looking for a home for us all, near but not too near to London, while once back in Chagford I would prepare for our removal. Soon we two would be living again with one who had shared our past, who could feel for our present and plan for our future, and in the outflow of love for him and for Richard frozen apathy began to melt and the springs of life to flow.

Chapter Twelve

Salvage

With obvious pleasure Richard assisted in preparing for our return to Devon, and one morning said quietly; "And you know, Mummy, when we get back, we shall find Philip waiting for us asleep on his bed." Thus he revealed at last his private explanation of recent events although from the very first he had been told the truth - had we been mistaken not to have discussed it with him at much greater length? I felt a moment's disquiet, but thought it best, gently and with no show of feeling except that I put my arm about him, to tell him at once why this could not be so, and then that many other things would await us both, that we would, I was certain, be very happy to return. Perhaps his statement had been really a question, anyway he accepted all that I said with composure and without comment and I decided to let the matter rest. All the same I hoped that he would not be distressed or greatly disappointed when he got back; I arranged that the little house should be thoroughly cleaned and aired with fires and open windows and later, when the day was fixed I asked that Molto and "Tiger" the kitten, now almost a cat, should be installed in their basket in the little room, hoping that a pleasant arrival with familiar things in place might help him to take up his life almost as he had left it.

All went well, and on the first night he snuggled happily into his "own" bed, and in his "own" room whence he could "still"

195

see, so he said, the top of Nattadon Hill. If he really had imagined that his lost brother would be restored he showed no disturbance then or later, and eventually would speak quite freely and naturally of him - "Oh, yes, I know that - Philip told me all about it." His thoughts and memories seemed unshadowed by pain and we hoped that they might remain so.

It did us both good to find ourselves part of a small intimate congregating-together of people absorbed and concerned one with another. Naturally we had been anonymous strangers in the endless streets of London as in the spaces of Kensington Gardens; here we were everywhere known and greeted by name, welcomed with warm pleasure and even affection; everyone had time to pause and pass the time of day; here there were no petrol fumes or roar of traffic but instead the sound of quiet footfalls and human voices, a clank-clank-a-clank from the smithy, and the clop-clop and jangle of horses with empty saddlebags to be filled with a morning's shopping.

We had work to do, Richard and I. Such of our possessions as had been rescued from the ruins of Maryfield had been carted into Chagford from the farm outhouse where they had lain tightly jumbled and stacked up together for almost four years; they were now accessibly distributed over the wide floor space of the big shed at the bottom of the garden. Beds, tables, chairs, chests, cupboards, drawers, all bursting with miscellaneous goods and chattels; clocks, curtains, cushions, bedding, items of clothing, toys and games, hundreds of books, even a few pictures in broken frames - I had about three months to sort through and organise it all and we worked at it every morning. I say "we", for the little boy who since he was two had lived in other people's houses among other people's furnishings and gear, now delighted to discover in the muddle toys and picture books and games that he had completely forgotten. For him the shed was an endless Christmas stocking, an inexhaustible Aladdin's cave. He liked to explore the possibilities of one discovery before looking for another, retiring with Molto from the scene of action into the ramshackle "tent" he had made from a bundle of ancient umbrellas where he painstakingly examined it.

The smell of bomb dust still permeated everything, and a wickedly jagged piece of shrapnel was embedded in what had been the linen cupboard. As I already knew the contents of the cupboard had survived the raid intact only to be stolen by looters who had visited the ruins and removed many items that we had noted as retrievable but had been too busy to rescue during that first difficult week. I discovered no glass, china or silver but was astounded to find that the unknown packers had taken down curtains from the empty window frames and folded them neatly into drawers. Some items had been nibbled by mice. Books and papers and files were cleaned as they turned up, then packed into boxes given to us by the local shopkeepers; damaged furniture was removed by the local cabinet maker and returned one piece at a time after restoration; from his wife who ran an antique shop I was able to buy second-hand many essential replacements which she kept on her premises until we should be ready to move. Richard's baby crib with bedding survived intact and I gave it to her for her new granddaughter; a week later she presented to me as her gift the beautiful old lustre jug that she recollected Philip had selected in December as his intended present for me in February.

After our morning's labour, in the afternoons we slipped back into our old familiar routines. After lunch and a brief rest, reunited with Molto, the dear old Sealyham, we would all wander down to Padley Common to the level grassy space where a thin trickle of brown water moved sedately over its pebbles. The terrier loved this because the turf was kinder than the road to his paw pads and there were rabbit holes under the hedge sides wherein he would dig violently and then explore with his nose. He never started anything but his enthusiasm and expectancy never seemed to diminish. Or we might descend the steep road down to the Teign bridge; the hedged declivity opened out at the bottom to pastures where eager ponies, hooves pounding, manes and tails wildly windblown, galloped to meet us at the gate. Or a stream of hounds might fan out from the kennels across their open green. Best of all we clambered up the lower slopes of the hills that surrounded the cosy little village with their bare broad contours.

For awhile I felt an extremity of relief at the change from the sullen black looks of northern winter to the pristine loveliness of Devon in early spring. Here no bitter winds were blowing, and the blasted industrial landscapes, with their smoke, vile noise and chaos of rubbish tips, slag heaps and tangles of rusting metal, seemed like an evil dream. Fair-haired and hatless under the warm sun, Richard gathered violets and primroses, peered into nests of naked fledgelings, the while I noted the green hooks of bracken pushing through last year's dead stalks. A heron hunched himself motionless over his pool then rose to flap slowly away, long legs lifting and extending behind. A buzzard quartered the sky. High on the hills the air whispered through the new grass soft as swansdown. Again we heard the lambs crying, cuckoos, curlews and larksong.

Too beautiful to bear. When Robert Burns wrote, "Thou'llt break my heart, thou bonny bird," he expressed that sense so overwhelming that the outside world is wholly indifferent to individual loss and pain, and things that once gave me delight now became cause of poignant regret. The exultant song of the blackbird no longer thrilled my heart, Isobel Baillie singing, "I know that my Redeemer liveth," was unbearable. All things remained as they had been in days of happiness, and therefore now I began to know finality, to find out what "never" meant. "The rest is silence," and almost austerely into that silence my beloved had now departed.

During some painful weeks the journal became my standby and into it I scribbled my bewildered and sometimes incoherent reactions fumbling my way towards some understanding, seeking first to discover the actuality of this present situation and then accommodate to it. Seemingly I couldn't let be, simply endure my pain, live it out, get on with my living until eventually it faded away. Merely as outlet my scribbling must have led to some easement though it wasn't outlet I was seeking but comprehension; feeling was the driving force maybe, but I sought assuagement through understanding. And sometimes I sat motionless before an empty page, when the sense of absence, of emptiness, had become as impossible to express in words as the idea of nothingness.

Unable to think out my problem, I did receive a few enlightenments;

"For the past weeks I have managed to do all I should, especially to share long open-air hours with Richard

198

while all the time aching not with sorrow so much as
with solicitude, regret.

"It is cruel to realise what *he* is missing now, all he must
miss in the future. To mourn premature ending - and
I realise this isn't only a parental suffering - is to feel
an overwhelming *pity* - for gifts of mind and character
unused, joys untasted, potentials unrealised.
Deprivation is hard enough to endure for the mature,
much harder to bear for the young and innocent.
Sometimes I seem to see him as an invisible wistful
presence looking with longing eyes at what he desires to
share and cannot. Bitter to know that for one with such a
capacity for living all experience is now forever denied.

"Suddenly today I see this as my refusal to face the
truth, a sentimental fallacy that I nourish to my hurt.
My feeling him deprived of this springtime and of all
the other springtimes that I feel should have been his,
deprived indeed of a lifetime's fulfilment, is to imagine
him alive and so able to be deprived; let me deny myself
this illusion. He is gone out of life and so no more
deprived of this than of all the lovely seasons that were
before he was born and that will follow his ending. He
is not missing, cannot miss anything. For there *is* no
Philip to miss anything."

A few days later I added:

"This is to deny myself comfort of a kind - but surely
one painful and delusive."

Unfortunately there were other ways in which my living
consciousness tried to identify with one that had ceased to be. I
had sometimes a compulsion, strange as it seemed, to live his
death, to share and experience it with him:

"The sheer incredulity with which on the previous
evening, both of us happy after our recent good weeks,

he would have contemplated the sudden ending of our years of faithful effort - that pain I seem to undergo ... His death sometimes seems like a little mistake on his part - his back was turned and while he was off guard and unaware he ceased - suddenly. Almost as though it should not have happened.

"This is very foolish and wasteful. It did happen; as his life had a beginning so also it had an end, and all thought of him must now include his end as well as all the rest. So it was. And such he was. To embrace this actuality will be to see him whole and entire, perhaps to give his life a kind of symmetry."

Years later, in *Elegy for Margaret,* I was to read Stephen Spender's so much closer expression of this feeling;

So to be honest, I must wear your death
Next to my heart, where others wear their love.

All this, written as thought, doesn't mean that because with my mind I had reached certain conclusions I had thereby found emotional easement. His fate seemed to me so outrageous that it was almost wrong to condone it by acceptance and out of this followed an even more engrossing preoccupation. During the months preceding our idyllically happy last three weeks, although, as I have said, we neither of us uttered our misgiving, we had both begun to realise that our struggle might end in defeat. During that time I had more than once seen a look on his face enjoining me - rightly or wrongly so I interpreted it - that I should always remember. Not necessarily himself perhaps, but the goods that we had known. So that remembrance seemed bound on me like a promise, unspoken perhaps but binding. For a while it seemed treachery to forsake him in thought, because thereby I failed to keep tryst with memory impregnated with our shared past.

"The desire to be remembered is as universal as oblivion is inevitable - how futile and inexpressibly sad seems to me the assertion over hundreds of First World War memorials that 'Their Name Liveth for Evermore' followed by the list (in alphabetical order) of Sassoon's 'intolerably nameless names'. And now the Second World War's names will doubtless be added. To accept oblivion as an abstract necessity is one thing; to accept it for oneself is another; to accept it for the ardent young and their surely legitimate hope of some attainment *first* is hard, exceedingly hard."

Now therefore I resented time's passing, for time would, I knew, tarnish the image that I wished to keep so bright; and worse, lengthened the distance between us, so that I wished the hours might stand still and cease to separate me from a precious past that daily receded further. Strangely enough I was sometimes at this time praised by outsiders for all that I did with Richard by way of continuing usual customs and contacts in addition to coping single-handed with the mountain of our bombed possessions in the shed - "so busy and good," said an acquaintance looking at me with incredulous and most undeserved admiration. For in truth all activity seemed a tiresome interruption of the absorbing compulsion to hold on to my recollections so at the very least to postpone the inevitable relinquishing. The rest of life lacked lustre - except for hours of despairful realisation when I knew in my heart that I could hold nothing in permanency. Sometimes I tried to admonish myself:

"I am stupid as a miser infatuated with his treasure, staring at it, fondling it, starving himself of living experience for the sake of a satisfaction sterile and useless. I suppose it's only human weakness to cling to memory as though it were the beloved himself, and after the long years I cannot expect in only three months to do better, maybe; but I ought to *try* to do better and I don't believe I want to - 'Ceasing to grieve will grieve me more than all the grief endured before,' I wrote yesterday but maybe that's only evasive; oblivion will be his lot as it is everyone's, and all this remembering is delusive surely. But my whole being

201

cries out at the pain of knowing no good can come of it (having an irrational notion that pain ought to be useful, productive)."

For several weeks I was swamped by this futility, and eventually found more positive perceptions and values. Bringing back into the closest possible focus my memories of the voice, the eye, the patterns of life, the whole image of a once familiar presence, was ultimately a poor expedient because these things in themselves were only valuable, even while he lived, as expressive of his unique quality. That transcended any accumulated details that I might consciously recall by an effort of will; his integrity.

And so eventually I saw something less specific and more meaningful;

"Coming he enriched me, going he made me poor, but his living has influenced all my past life just as his death has changed my present. I am permeated and for always. And through me, shaped by his influence, others will also be changed.

"It seems, perhaps, that in death as in life we signify in so far as we participate in the general stream. Merely by existing at all we affect those about us, and the effects, trivial or momentous, are permanent. Whether we will it or not, whether we know it or not, we all work upon others and are wrought upon in our turn, so that an endless chain reaction is set up in which nothing is lost, ever. T E Lawrence said truly that, 'the circles of influence are infinite.' And this alone, however anonymously, confers some immortality."

Frequently I gave up trying to "understand" anything. I believe it was Sartre who said that "remembrance is the only Paradise from which we cannot be driven", and since every evening when Richard was bathed and in bed I had before me twelve hours of solitude I would sometimes wander in my paradise, in reverie, or by reading in old notebooks. It would be easy and at the same time superficial and unreal for me to dismiss those sessions as self-indulgence, because while not sentimentalising my memories I will not deny them either. It would be untrue to say that the years I now recalled had been my "happiest", yet it would be treachery not to affirm that more moments of real joy had then come to me than ever in my life before or since.

In point of fact the notebooks disclosed a life so concerned with practicalities and activity that it would have been difficult to sentimentalise it. Since the loss of Maryfield and our arrival on Dartmoor we had certainly lived in greater isolation and in closer proximity one with another than is usual, a life perhaps not "normal", but the boys' endless curiosity, delight in their natural surroundings, zestful search for understanding, had made their lives as full of interest as that of "ordinary" humanity - few of our acquaintances found life more absorbing. Something must have been lost to us by this isolation and also by our not contributing to groupings external to ourselves. Yet most certainly we had not lived enclosed in self-absorption, on the contrary the firm basis of our lives was engrossment in relished external activity - observation, exploration, doing things, making things; and although during our walks, in the house, at our meals, we talked tremendously, life being "a continual conversation", yet we weren't exchanging ourselves but rather discussing our continued activities equally with the world outside ourselves, and of course Philip and I often talked of happenings outside our present time and place.

It had seemingly always been accepted that both were more adept than I should ever be with technical and mechanical matters and they were constantly explaining to me "how things worked", on which occasions I acknowledged their all too obvious superiority. In one notebook I had recorded a birthday - it must have been Richard's for I spoke of autumn crocus and dwarf cyclamen erect on mottled leaves - and seemingly after leaving the boys alone while I fed Molto and the cats I had returned to find the celebration balloons strangely dispersed - green ones clinging unsupported to the lintel of the door, blue ones clustering on the ceiling, and a great crimson globule with no means of support impinging on the window pane. I then heard for the first time about "static electricity". But I had never been ashamed to consult Philip's judgement on any matter when my own had seemed inadequate. If, as certainly happened sometimes, I persisted in doing something he thought unwise he would refrain from argument and let me go my way; he may have thought me foolish or merely refusing to act reasonably, but he quietly *gave me up*, looking affectionately the while with a rare ironic tenderness. His comments and judgements, implied rather than stated, had evidently been shrewd and penetrating. I used to complain that I was forever forgetting and losing ideas I wished to remember under pressure of the endless household duties of life in the Dartmoor cottage. Yet I would indulge in unnecessary activities like arranging flowers, improving the garden, experimenting with the rations, all innocent enough pastimes, but all *passing* the time that I might have *used* differently; to be honest I wasn't hindered by but rather over-absorbed by the domestic round - so easy on the mind! As a gift Philip had one day presented me with a small sturdily-backed notebook with pencil attached that I might keep in my pocket or handy on my bedside table. "Here you are! Mummy's book of happy thoughts - or a thousand ways of cooking cabbages!" He shouted his laughter, his face alight with fun and affection, but though I laughed too the scales then fell from my eyes. (He would have been amused, I now reflected, reading the entry for the first time since scribbling it down, that I had cheered myself with the thought that Martha and Mary had been two different women and that I was trying to be both; and in truth his booklet *had* been used for the double purpose he had foreseen.)

The notebooks also seemed to confirm my belief that most children come into the world with a predisposition to be "good", not in the sense of being law-abiding or clean-and-tidy or obedient, the criteria of my childhood, but as a quality of the whole person. I find innate "wickedness" hard to believe, and although of course the best qualities may be displaced or eroded very early in life it is surely "natural" to desire to love and to be loved, to enjoy giving happiness, not difficult to accept obligations to other people. If it is equally just as "natural" to be wholly guided by self-interest as to vent aggression in hate, then how important it is in early life to encourage the good, not the bad strands, to dominate (I had never forgotten how a period of struggle and hostility in my early childhood had quietly melted away when the love we shared for my two small brothers had made common cause between mother and daughter.) It is true that for my boys and myself circumstances had been favourable so that among us there had been an absence of envy or emulation, we didn't try to dilute one another, or to benefit from others' weakness; it always seemed safe to trust. Then again, though we might be kindred spirits we were by no means identical ones because of the differences in age, sex and experience. Our activities were often separate though with an added bonus when they were shared - the books we read, our country explorations. Through differences we had stirred one another up, refreshed and fertilised one another, each seemingly accepting the others' essence. Of course there had been no solemn self-consciousness about this, an ambience of goodwill was taken for granted as our ordinary everyday climate. I suppose we had been just good friends, natural, relaxed and at ease with another.

Since FG and I did not believe in a God-made, God-guided universe, nor in personal immortality, the children had never been given "religious guidance", though had Philip learned to accept such beliefs from other sources I certainly would not have tried to influence him the other way. We had read to them the Gospel story and parts of the Old Testament, they knew the myths behind Easter and Christmas, Philip also knew of other teachings and doctrines as I expected Richard would when he was older. FG and I had few theories of upbringing; we listened to their point of view and tried to understand it; we didn't try to impose our will on theirs as of right; we had not inflicted on them painful punishment for "naughtiness". But I did remember having said more than once, "But of course you know all about goodness and badness perfectly well by yourselves. Everyone does. Everyone knows that it's wrong to steal or hurt other people or to tell lies. Even when we do these things we still know all the time that we should not. Mostly we've just not stopped to think, or been careless or just wanted our own way." It seemed to have worked. Richard might have *done* something "bad" but he wasn't therefore "a bad boy" - a crucial difference here between my attitude and my mother's. Weakness, laziness, fear (root cause of much lying and dishonesty), muddle and hurry, these had been and still were at the bottom of my own lapses, nearly all avoidable had I listened to my own intuitive sense of what I should or should not do. Apparently then I had told the boys to trust their good feelings hoping that eventually honest self-examination would tell them how they should act; later still I supposed good intentions would need to be directed by their maturing understanding, but meantime my elementary approach had seemingly sufficed our uncomplicated lives and I hoped this might be so for Richard in the future.

Often the fire was out before I closed the books and after a last look at the sleeping Richard prepared to go to bed, where I could sometimes sleep, almost as glad for what I had known as unhappy that it had been taken away. For I hadn't been merely indulging an unproductive nostalgia; on the contrary it was with thankfulness, almost with pride that I saluted the standards we had upheld (which during the four months just past I had lacked the strength to sustain). Had I but known it, while it was to remain always for me a touchstone of excellence, the unique pattern of Philip's last months and weeks when we lived unselfishly and bravely, each strengthened by the other's fortitude, each finding it natural to be as patient, steadfast and stout-hearted as the other - or in my case as he had thought me to be - was unlikely to be evoked or restored by any future circumstance. No matter; at least now I could determine in the next months to do better than I had for the sake of us all.

CHAPTER THIRTEEN

Another Life

In June Richard and I left the little house in Chagford for the flat FG had secured for us in Richmond, Surrey. For many reasons in the beginning I much regretted the move from Devon. It is so large and richly varied a county that I think few would claim to know it all even after a lifetime, yet I could claim in eighteen years to have learned to know and greatly to love some parts of the whole - estuary country, open moorland, some agricultural valleys and their villages - all of them with many valued associations. After more than six years absence FG had weaned himself and was now almost a Home Counties man, certainly had no sense that he belonged elsewhere. He had decided that to continue in his present work in London held better opportunities for useful service than were then available to him if he returned to the university college; for myself I had always hoped to restart the acting group and membership audience for whom I had worked in Exeter before the war, and was sorry that now I must finally relinquish such hopes. Again, after six years he had made many friends in the London area, and although I knew that I should make friends too I yet felt great reluctance to leave behind so many known so long. The flat itself I found constricting - four rooms and a kitchen with its door opening on to the no-man's-land of landing and lift down to the street; the windows on one side overlooked a stretch of

207

broken waste land piled with the bricks and rubble of a big block of flats destroyed by a land mine.

After a few months I had adjusted to most of these things, even to the lack of a garden, and could be thankful for many new sources of satisfaction especially the restored continuity of life with FG, both of us working together to make a full good life for Richard.

For his life we were in a special way responsible because we had decided that he should not go to school; we had noted certain disquieting signs and since we knew that the normal infections of childhood had once had disastrous long-term after-effects we made this decision now, not without misgiving but in the end without regret. I taught him to read and write and simple arithmetic, to tell the time and use a telephone, and luckily he had a facility for drawing which I could not have taught, and was, like his father and brother, good at modelling and making mechanical things. Of course I read and shared with him all the poems and stories that Philip had enjoyed until old enough to read *Coral Island* and *Bevis* for himself - this was our custom every day before we went out after lunch. Every morning we heard and participated in certain BBC programmes, especially Ann Driver's *Music and Movement* series and all the episodes of *An Observer From the Past*, a vivid and plausible projection of the lives of two children in prehistoric days often as revealing to me as to Richard himself. In addition a very able musician, ultimately a lifelong friend to us all, came to teach him once a week. I am afraid he was not very interested in the first little pieces that he had to practise, but he learned other things from his teacher including notation and so paved the way for what eventually became, from his fifteenth up to his twentieth year, the dominant passion of his life.

Though it had not been immediately apparent we quickly discovered that the area to which we had come had many outdoor attractions which we explored endlessly. In less than a quarter of an hour we could walk to the top of Richmond Hill and thence look over the Thames Valley at what is surely one of the loveliest river prospects in the world. Sheen Common with its scrubby little oak trees and graceful silver birches, its wild and wandering paths and trackways, was only a few minutes walk from our door; there we played games in winter and in summer had picnics and read story books lying under the trees; we crept on tiptoe to watch the jays at close quarters - seldom succeeding; twice we had the rare experience of seeing a cuckoo; in early spring Richard kept frog spawn from the pond eventually returning the tadpoles. A gate led directly from the top of the common to one of the entries into Richmond Park with its wealth of bird and animal life, its expanses of water where wild fowl nested, its splendid trees. Richard could sail his boats in a pool reserved entirely for children's use, fly his kites in spaces and skies as wide as any he'd found on the moor, and for me the sense of distance more than compensated for narrow domestic horizons. In summer we went further afield - by bus to Kew Gardens, or best of all, embarked on a little boat, the *Andy*, and chugged up the Thames all the way from Richmond bridge to Teddington and back. We always tried to sit in the front (the boat took perhaps twenty passengers) to watch for waterfowl, to get first sight of the islands, here called "aits" or "eyots", and to obtain uninterrupted views of the wooded reaches and banks of the river up to Eel Pie Island and Petersham. I soon discovered that as well as inheriting FG's blue eyes, features, and colouring, Richard shared his pleasure in "messing about in boats" - later they were to spend a happy holiday near the Norfolk Broads.

Gradually we settled ourselves into the flat. Books were cleaned, repaired and shelved, we replaced lost household necessities, gave away the box of "dressing-up" clothes (to an orphanage, where they were in frequent use), sent off parcels to Oxfam, and the twenty-year accumulation of lecture notes, letters, filed papers, my own journals, I simply packed away unsorted into the recesses of the big steamer trunk. I compensated for the absence of garden by renting an allotment; a trackway led directly to the enclosure, not ten minutes walk away, and from the window we could see my small flower plantation, a splash of bright colour beyond the green of FG's vegetables. We all missed Molto but had decided that it would be cruel to keep him in a flat in the unaccustomed traffic of a town, and so had given him to Edna my helper and mother of Richard's Chagford playmate who had cared for him while we were in Yorkshire; young Walter had been overjoyed. After a disastrous experiment with a rabbit in a hutch on the verandah (returned to the donor after barely a month) Richard acquired a mischievous happy kitten that he christened Peterkin after the young rascal castaway of Ballantyne's *Coral Island*. The dear, devoted Mrs Butler who worked for me then (and who kept in touch with us for more than thirty years after we left), was very doubtful when Peterkin first arrived, but he was so meticulously clean and so endearing that she soon succumbed to his charms.

When FG was home at weekends he drove us into the surrounding country - into sandy pinewoods or heathlands, to little riverside villages like Laleham, up to Box Hill, sometimes into the Weald of Kent. We discovered on the Hampshire coast a sea-facing, sunny and secluded holiday guest-house ideally suited for families with small children, and eventually we holidayed there year after year, meeting the same young families again and again. Richard usually got on well with other children and all enjoyed the annual reunions, while with the parents - some of them friends to this day - FG and I had long evening sessions after the children were tucked up in bed.

At the end of our first twelve months in Surrey I made a rare entry in my journal:-

> "A year tomorrow we left Devon and looking back over it I find myself counting achievements - assets. This is new and very good. Richard is now seven years and eight months old (the age at which we first consulted a specialist on Philip's behalf). He is just under four feet tall and packed full of vital energy - how he capered all over the Common this afternoon! And he has been well all the time. With his music and reading, drawing and constructing, his small circle of friends and the company of Mrs Butler and Peterkin, his deep enjoyment of his father, and our daily explorations, he has had a full year, I think. I can see them now coming back from the allotment. He is carrying a posy

of flowers for me and has stepped aside to gather another one from the verge of the little pathway. Both are laughing, they look brown and fit in their shorts and their white shirts open at the neck. FG is carrying his spade and what looks like a bunch of leeks."

Only a year later the fact had to be faced that, though Richard had been a lively and strenuous infant and had shown disturbing signs much later than his brother, though so far we had managed to protect him from illness and constitutional disturbance, despite vitamin supplements from birth, with now the addition of a chemical substance to promote utilisation of the vitamin, we had seemingly only slowed down the dystrophic process, and our only hope lay in a real scientific breakthrough. We neither evaded or neglected any avenue that we might explore, any exertion that might seem necessary, any devising that might be ancillary to his well-being and happiness. All the time however and very importantly it was the promotion of activity not protection that we primarily sought with the one exception that we had not risked the hazards of normal schooling. So again the journal recorded my endeavours, and into it I copied my reports on progress, my letters to researchers and my notes as I attempted - ludicrous as it now appears - to study all that I could find on muscular metabolism, or filled pages with my queries. Later my doctor introduced me to a most helpful and intelligent biochemist who for nothing at all, over a period of some months, undertook a series of chemical tests which seemed to support a theory I was evolving; eventually I wrote a brief paper which I had duplicated and circulated to certain groups in Britain and the United States—I received acknowledgements (and replies:- "Dear Doctor Thomas," (sic) "Thank you for your profoundly interesting memorandum" - of course I had written objectively without stating my personal interest); but nothing followed, for as I can see today what I had noted and checked were merely some results not the causes of dystrophy; as in Chagford I found that the more one studied the more infinitely complex appeared the chemistry and physiology even in normal muscle behaviour. Thus we made contact with some workers in the field and at least we managed to avoid for Richard some of the side effects.

At this time too I turned to the heredity and with my mother's help listed several hundred names from among the descendants of the boys' great-great-grandparents and although I did not now communicate with any of them many years later this proved to have been, if only negatively, a useful exercise.

Although I gave my mind and thought to these endeavours (sometimes more difficult than to labour physically on his behalf) for all of forty months my life had no single coherent direction because as constant undercurrent to all my doings lay the persistent pain of loss and the ache of commiseration. It wasn't possible quickly to identify with our new life or to forge the links that might bind past with present. For it is not only undesirable, it is a kind of betrayal to think that after the physical and total severance of death the bereaved should substitute new and different aims and attitudes hoping thereby gradually to cease to care and to suffer; real love "alters not when it alteration finds"; the essential and ultimately the only valuable thing is to *canalise* the feeling into new channels, losing nothing of what the old life and love may have given but carrying it over into the new, intact, and permanently a part of the self. This may be a slow and unconscious process or it may be precipitated as though an invisible door has turned on a hinge and the old life passes through into the new.

Over three years life in the flat became increasingly happy and successful. Then, playing wildly with Peterkin one evening, Richard caught his foot in a little stool and fell heavily enough to fracture his leg between knee and ankle. There was little pain and no displacement, the bone being cracked rather than broken, so that a light elastic bandage sufficed for support during the knitting process; but he could not put full weight upon the limb and perforce we resorted to the big tricycle for outdoors and the little one without pedals for inside.

This was the first real setback of his life, and though he remained happy in the belief that his difficulties were temporary his mobility was seriously impaired and remained so after his leg was well. After this accident during some menopausal malaises I passed through another period of adjustment, during the following summer it was hard to see other children running in the long grass below the verandah, or FG returning alone along the trackway from the allotment. Young men strode under the window with tennis racquets and cricket gear home for the "long vac" from university and sometimes their mothers discussed with me their hopes and plans. They did not know, of course, that we had once had another son, but their own were Philip's contemporaries and the pang always came before I could prevent it, my only resource being refusal to dwell on it.

As soon as Richard had started getting out and about after his fall he began to keep a record of his doings; (at the beginning I did the actual writing for him). Every evening before his bedtime with very few breaks in continuity his invariable custom was to write in his notebooks, and over the following years his entries progressed from summaries of pastimes and incidents to his ruminations on events or the analysis of symphonies. And so, thanks to FG's independent courage and Richard's spirited way of life, plus my determination that he should every day live out his full potential, the old purposive and constructive way of living was restored; I had somehow been turned around on an invisible axis, no longer being hampered by division of feeling. I had known a good life once with a kindred spirit; now I was to know another with two very different beings. And all the knowledge and experience gained from that other life was now used to enlighten and reinforce everything that we did now - which was exactly what Philip would have wished.

Now I began to long with the utmost intensity to get away from the flat, to find peace, space and privacy, a house set in a garden not too far from the countryside, "Some day," I had told Richard, the previous spring, "we shall sit beneath a tree in a garden of our own - maybe it will be this very year, and somewhere even now that tree is opening green buds."

By the middle of September, after four years in the flat I had my desire. In a Thames-side village some sixteen miles from London a gardener's cottage with adjoining loft and stable - built about 1880 - had been converted into a single dwelling and after careful inventory FG decided to buy it. The gardener's living room became our kitchen, his parlour our dining room; the stable conversion we used as our music room, and the smaller room beyond became Richard's with its small cloakroom adjoining; here as well as his bed were his bookcase and workbench, cupboards for his tools, mechanical and drawing materials, and store of balsa wood for construction of model aircraft. One of the four upstairs rooms became FG's study. The house was bright, having seventeen windows and we found its general layout ideally suited to our special needs.

Outside in front four tall pines curved round a segment of a circular courtyard (where in the days of carriages the coachman gardener had turned his horse); under a superb ash tree on the other side FG had his white garage. From this courtyard a long straight drive, arched over with oaks, acacias, smaller ash trees and pink flowering cherries, led to the road which was invisible from the house and almost inaudible. This was a smaller version of my childhood's familiar "Grove" and gave us equal seclusion. The garden proper, about one third of an acre, lay on the other side of the house; outside the fencing on two sides narrow ginnels, probably old bridle paths, connected us through our small back wicket gate with the village houses and shops a few minutes walk away. We were back in a village community or at any rate at the centre of one, for there was behind the original little High Street and spreading around the Green and commons a large suburban area which we saw increase over the years. But always the old buildings remained untouched and unspoiled and it was among these that we now made our home. We had never lived for longer than four years in one place before; had never owned our home; now we settled down with no thought of uprooting. Peterkin arrived on the first day with foreboding and suspicion and after letting him out of his hamper we closed all doors and casements downstairs, but he at once betook himself to the broom cupboard where he remained for twenty-four hours in silent immobility; he then emerged perfectly happy and at home in house and garden as though he'd lived here all his life. Next day two little dead mice lay on the back porch.

When we arrived the garden consisted of a tussocky wilderness of rank weeds, the nettles and thistles standing above the stumps of ancient gooseberry bushes and thickets of straggling raspberry canes. There were two well-spaced and mature walnut trees, and in the midst the largest elm tree that any of us had ever seen stretched its great limbs over much of the whole area. Since the property had been empty for some while before conversion it had become seemingly the rubbish dump for the whole neighbourhood and mountains of junk lay everywhere, pots and pans, glass jars and bottles, empty tins, rolls of old lino and even four ancient rusty iron bedsteads. Down at the bottom lime trees grew in front of the fencing; there were also two small elms, a yew tree and a holly.

All three of us now became immersed in the problems and pleasures of making a garden. First we engaged the local council to remove the rubbish - two whole cartloads of it. Afterwards a gang of men laboured for two days, first to trim and fell, and then to exterminate the whole root system of the dominating elm tree which they swore was as tough and strong-rooted as an oak. This was perhaps sad but absolutely necessary if we were to have any garden at all. Having cleared and stubbed up the worst of the weeds and undergrowth FG then decided that it would take far too many weekends for him to *dig* his land so proceeded to hire a man and tractor who in one day ploughed the whole area twice, from north to south and then from east to west. This done we could survey a clear space, its fine mature trees now showing to advantage, and after much sketching, and pacing of distances, and arguing, deciding on and then discarding many plans, we eventually marked out our pathways and sited a long flower border. We all agreed that a sense of distance should be a prime objective and therefore decided on a wide expanse of grass all the way from the house down to the limes at the bottom and this was seeded at once before any of the paths were ready to be paved. Despite the assiduity of the birds the seed germinated quickly and thickly and before the end of October Richard was rejoicing over "green grass, *our* grass" in his notebook. When it came to plantings we chose to grow what

215

seemed appropriate to the site, in fact to make a cottage garden; and of course, for old associations or because of the donor, many specimens had for us a private significance. The white Japanese anemones were reminders of Topsham's cobbled courtyard, Edith gave us the hydrangeas, a friend of the old Drama Group days the graceful "Bridal Veil". Giant scarlet poppies had been Philip's favourites and were planted to flare with colour in contrast with the dark yew behind; my grandmother's favourite lilies-of-the-valley had a place, and from my childhood's garden that was still my mother's chief delight came boxes of seedling hollyhocks, dozens of irises to grow before the limes, the feathery tansy that she called "green ginger" and the "Lady's Mantle" with silky silver on the underside of its tiny leaves. Beyond the long path leading to what was eventually to be a rhododendron and azalea plantation underplanted with spring bulbs FG had his kitchen garden where he grew many fruit varieties very successfully but at first had a struggle with certain vegetables because of the tree roots beneath, so he gave up carrots, sprouts and cabbages for sweet corn and beans and spinach. I especially wanted to grow winter-flowering things - wintersweet, witchhazel, prunus subhirtella, hellebores, yellow jasmine, viburnum fragrans, iris stylosa as well as crocus and snowdrops and early camellias and rhododendron praecox. "Something in flower every single day of the year!" I said to FG and Richard, and today in January there may be ten or more varieties of blossom all simultaneously out in the garden many of them sweet-scented. Our first summer we ate our own strawberries sitting on the grass under the walnut tree with Peterkin asleep beside us; on the bare white walls of the house we could already see the first upward growth of wisteria, jasmines, clematis and the climbing variety of the old-fashioned rose "Caroline Testout".

At that time we had been parted from Exeter's Maryfield a mere nine years, but it seemed a very much longer while, so much had happened in the interim - our personal losses and renewals, the world's passage from the rigour of war into its uneasy peace.

During the ensuing months and years we were busy summer and winter from getting up until bedtime and far more closely related to external streams of living than had been possible either on the Moor or in Richmond; we were now accessible, and we had space. FG's parents were frequent visitors, Edith and Martin and others came from Devon, my mother from the north; we retained our friends in Kew and Richmond and by degrees made many more here. The village shops were then run for the most part by people who lived on their premises and were villagers themselves. Shopping was not a mere choosing of goods and paying for them but a significant transaction between two human beings which often fed or tantalised our well developed bump of curiosity. For example the lank, moustached elderly man in his long white apron at the grocer's - why did the others always call him "the Captain"? We never liked to ask and so we never knew. Mrs A standing behind her counter, forearms stringy with work and beetroot red with the cold, her slatternly hair straggling over her bright muddled little face, overworked and friendly, was roundly condemned by Mrs B in her well-organised shop, complacent and self-righteous, passing judgement on Mrs A for not keeping systematic accounts, on Mrs C for not paying her bills promptly. Richard commented that on the whole he thought we preferred those who were not too efficient - "I expect it's because we find them kindred spirits." But of course most of our expeditions led into our surroundings, watching always for seasonal changes by the river or in the countryside - birds, animals and natural growth. We once calculated that we could go forth twice a day for a fortnight and have a different walk each time.

Indoors Richard had studies and exercises to write for his tutor, the well-loved and gifted Michael, after his military service abroad now teaching at a local school and giving Richard three sessions a week; eventually ours became almost his adoptive home for his parents had died when he was small and we were proud that he made us his "honorary" ones. Richard's absorption and knowledge of music increased as he began to grow up and so did his collection of miniature orchestral scores (from which he made a few piano reductions for me - I think mainly as exercises as he despised most transcriptions as distortions); he planned out his record and radio concerts and of course continued to sketch and to construct model ships and aircraft. Our days were made up of similar doings daily repeated though never twice the same; the years were punctuated by the rhythmic return of observances, festivals and celebrations, each unconsciously enriched by memories of those preceding; they passed, then, with another year, they all came round again. So time slid imperceptibly along within a pattern of life securely laid down; the partnership between FG and myself, no longer broken by frequent partings after brief reunions as during the war seemed cemented by continued living in settled surroundings; perhaps the garden gave to us, as my mother's garden had given to me since the days of my first awareness, a sense of stability; and because Richard's good health and spirits were blessedly maintained our lives were uninterrupted by accident or illness or painful immediate anxieties.

Withal he lived a taut and meaningful life, sharing to the full FG's propensity to laughter, his constructive intelligence, his appreciation of others and his goodwill towards them. Philip and I had been akin and each had recognised this tacitly and sometimes even identified one with the other, while on the whole Richard and I were contrasted. Nevertheless, although so differently endowed and focused on different objectives our general styles of life had much in common and I remember no occasion of their being opposed. Even after he had matured and grown into early manhood, the tones of his voice deepening, shaving twice a week, wearing long trousers and so on, we could still enjoy our differences and grew together, so I thought, a little like Charles Lamb's Bridget and Elia. But the records in his notebooks admonish me not to idealise that life but to remember its solid reality and productivity, a life busy, practical and absorbed. While living that life, as it were enclosed within that tract of time, it seemed to be enduring indefinitely and forever. Looking back, it seems sometimes as brief as a dream.

CHAPTER FOURTEEN

Solitude

Three months before Richard's nineteenth birthday I spent four weeks in hospital and for fourteen days we didn't see one another - our longest-ever separation - during which time he sent me an entertaining illustrated letter every day. Our unspoken joy in eventual reunion and the slow restoration of our normal way of life was very great, our pleasant occupations and interests seemingly enhanced by interruption; when his birthday came we celebrated with the purchase of new recordings and orchestral scores and began to plan for the coming winter.

Less than a month later, early one afternoon with no outward sign of pain or distress Richard asked me if he might lie down for awhile, feeling, as he said, "not too good"; he looked normal and spoke calmly, so though surprised I thought perhaps he was simply over-tired. But his request was so unusual that I decided to stay with him while he rested; after saying that he felt "cold", and asking me why the sunlit room was "going dark" he quickly lapsed into unconsciousness. After doing all that I knew how and telephoning to FG and our doctor I could only wait and watch helplessly; he did not speak again but he was aware of nothing, complained of nothing, and I hoped felt nothing either. Before they arrived and in less than an hour he had died -

later we were told that probably a weakened heart muscle had gently petered out.

The sudden passing of this son - then in the third week of his twentieth year - from the world and the life he had so loved and enjoyed must have been a terribly severe shock for FG when he presently arrived home only minutes after the end. For me in those first hours pain seemed strangely - or was it inevitably? - muted by a sense of thankfulness for Richard's sake and, as the long-drawn-out brave struggle of Philip's last months came vividly back to mind, I could actually be thankful that Richard's fortitude had not been, could not now be, so cruelly tested. If medical science was then - as it would also be today - unable to prevent it, his premature death had always been certain, but at least here a life of gladness had ended quickly without illness or pain. All this I felt and knew as I laid away the score annotated for that evening's concert and brought to his room a bowl of roses he had admired that morning as they flowered beneath the window. I was even enabled to remind FG that, unlike Philip, Richard had attained early manhood, had tasted life and known some deployment of his gifts; he had never been isolated by illness or restricted to me as sole companion; truly he and I had known a relationship akin to that nearly thirteen years gone but for him this had been one among many others, and through his friendship with those young like himself and very especially through his affinities with FG had touched life at many points...

Such sense of mitigation lasted only briefly and very soon grief's pattern asserted itself; moments of piercing pain that assailed our undefended suffering spirits; surrender to inertia; yet also attending to many necessary tasks and duties performing each as faithfully and well as we could manage. For twenty-four hours Richard lay on his familiar bed until we looked at him for a last time knowing it was forever; a hard moment, and we went by common consent out into the garden; when we came back the bed was empty, and, closed by our desire, the oak coffin stood beside it and they had carved his name and age on the lid. If we imagined how he might look lying within, it was as he had looked all the time, calm and content with his lot, accepting it. But it was vain to remain there for though we knew what lay so near under the oak, that was not what we needed most; love was balked, and we went back to the garden, to the willow he had nurtured, the shady grass under the walnut tree, the bright border he had helped us to create.

After this second bereavement FG remained at home for two weeks and together we mourned our sons' passing, and albeit wordlessly, we dedicated our time and our thoughts to their memory. The autumn skies though sometimes veiled in mist remained cloudless and still; leaves scarcely turned as they floated down to rest with soft rustle on the grass; the tree tops glowed with colour and the roses still flowered as freely as the dahlias and Korean chrysanthemums in the border. We divided clumps of heleniums, cut back the lavender and lad's love, planted some bulbs for spring; drove out into the countryside and climbed over Merrow Down and Box Hill, wandered in the grounds of Richmond Park and Claremont and walked the familiar rides through the bracken of the Common. Often during this time I saw our children as afar and unreal as dreams remembered, could scarcely believe they had ever existed, seeing them as in a picture with a kind of numbness. Or again their absence seemed unreal, or perhaps only temporary; I could almost imagine reunion and arguing about books or music and having visitors; or Richard completing the scores he was studying or the unfinished aircraft model he had left behind. Then they seemed just around the corner, not remote at all. For all that they remained forever inaccessible.

The day came when FG returned to his work in London to pick up the threads he had temporarily laid down; he would for most of his waking hours live in the same world, work with the same colleagues, follow the same routines and, most important of all, concentrate his whole conscious mind on matters not remotely concerned with his sons' passing. None of these things could repair his great loss or ever console him for it, but they gave him reprieves and, I imagined, perspectives. But for me no return was possible to a way of life to which all threads had been irrevocably cut and as the sound of his departing car faded into silence my strangely emptied days and weeks loomed ahead in a vista that almost appalled me.

As I look back at this turning-point in my life I wonder that I felt no relief at the cessation of twenty years of vigilance and responsibility. But I knew that my labours had ceased only because I had been defeated, that I had fought two long battles and had lost them both. It was scarcely consolation to know that no means existed - not then, and be it added, not today, more than a score of years later - whereby the outcome might have been different; the inevitability of failure could not make it easier to endure it when it came, nor was the taste less bitter because I had experienced it before. Many questions without answers were to claim consideration in the bewildered months ahead and I was much longer this time than last in finding an adjustment. Two problems presented special difficulties; outside activities were frequently limited by the dismal ups and downs of my slow convalescence from the illness of four months before; and for the first time in my life I had no immediate and significant work to do.

I had realised very soon after Philip's death and our removal to Surrey that my sphere of usefulness was to lie chiefly in relation to Richard's need so that in the end a transference, not a change in life's purpose, had taken place. The unhampered development of our sons' gifts and aptitudes had depended on my own life becoming almost entirely invested in that objective but - let there be no mistake about it - my own life had thereby been enhanced not truncated, and had I been free to do more I should surely have experienced far less. Their self-fulfilment had been immensely fulfilling for me also. As for outside work, had we not moved twelve years before, I might then have revived my pre-war activities in Exeter out of which I once hoped that so much might grow, but I could not envisage that now in Surrey I might initiate in 1959 as in Devon in 1934. Changes in self, in circumstances and surroundings to say nothing of the lapse of a quarter of a century prevented even a hint of such an undertaking from crossing my mind. Since neither of my adult activities could avail me longer the plain truth was that the purpose as well as the structure of my life had been fragmented.

Still, I knew that I must deal with these things and apply what I could of the lessons learned before. In the first place I chose not to go away, thereby avoiding the internal disharmony created by the struggle to conceal a real state of mind from strangers while trying to share in their activities. Those previous efforts had helped very little and had perhaps even adulterated the truth of a profound experience. Distraction, I had discovered, was a palliative often followed by a painful reaction. Certainly a public parade of private feeling would have been, to put it no lower, both self-indulgent and tasteless, but the alternative was not to pretend but to seek solitude and quietude in which it might be possible to assimilate and so come to terms - only thus should I not fail myself and children too. And staying at home among familiar things and places had another advantage in that I felt more at ease; I could come and go, stay in or go out, at my own whim and desire; and even if associations were painful they were often precious too. Thus I had not merely substituted one trial of strength for another because house and garden, trees, roads and river, even the cracks in the pavement, while poignantly recalling past occasions and asserting absence where once had been presence, could by an effort of will sometimes be turned into reminders of joy.

Perspective, a sense of proportion, is hard to discover. Our experience might be bitter but it was not unusual; we had suffered the grievous loss of two young sons; after thirty years of valued parenthood we were childless in our fifties; and we must learn to live with our situation. Millions of one's fellow beings suffer situations far more grievous than one's own, in what is today called "the third world" especially; in my own limited personal experience I recalled Susan mourning for her young husband lost in the *Glorious*, Kaye for her boy Michael who had died in the *Hood*, Mrs Montagu of Penton, whose sole two sons, had perished in the First World War, and I reminded myself that Mrs Brooke, mother of their friend Rupert, had lost her second son very soon after the first. All such knowledge was sterile and led nowhere. For the whole aggregate of human suffering is not the merging but a summary of infinite numbers of individual victims and each one is unique and special. When I remembered those I had known, reminded myself of the uncountable those that I had not known, this could not and did not make my own case seem of less account.

Perhaps this was because my mind was not capable of regarding my problems dispassionately? Yet I recollected that T E Huxley (I happened at this time to be reading the Bibby *Life*) whose perspectives included the eternal spaces and the immensity of matter as well as the intricacies of the infinitely minute, yet had felt the death of his little son - "the cause of great happiness, still retaining through all my life the blessings that have sprung from that cause" - with feelings much like mine. The inevitability of grief can no more rationalised away than an unappeasable hunger; as Huxley said "even the apes, if you shoot their young, grieve their grief out and do not immediately seek distraction". One may know with the mind that repining is a wasteful exercise, that in the nature of things the restoration into life of what has forever gone out of it is an impossibility, yet there is often on the faces of the bereaved a *searching* look as though all the time they are looking for something they cannot find. Indeed the very uselessness of regret is additional source of sorrow as the Journal recorded:-

"O, my dear, dear children, how far you are, how sweet your memory!

My longing is folly, my tears are vain, and *just because* they are vain and futile so must I grieve the more."

This predicament has much in common with physical suffering which, like grief, is caused by injury to the self, palpable, very sensitive to clumsy handling, but different too, because in grief there is no hope of restoration to what had been the normal way of living. Meaningful life will certainly be, and perhaps again infinitely valuable. But certainly different. Since nothing can change this necessity, as with inevitable physical suffering there is nothing for it but stoical endurance. During the war I several times heard bereaved people use the physical analogy as when they said that they had endured an amputation - the painful removal of an irreplaceable part of themselves; though maimed they trusted to be healed...In my own case it seemed that not a peripheral attachment like a limb had been removed but a rooted part of my innermost being, and that deeply within myself not to a part of myself had injury been inflicted. Either way, as with pain, grief must be endured.

Those who are physically ill are allowed to withdraw while acutely suffering, are allowed convalescence and a slow return to normal activity. Upon the grief-stricken heavier demands are made. Before they are adjusted they attempt to live as usual, to show a normal demeanour; attempts are made to "take them out of themselves" by visits, holidays, changes of scene and similar diversions. The accidents and illnesses that frequently assail the bereaved during the first year or so after loss probably have great value in giving them excuse - through obvious physical incapacity - to betake themselves to privacy, withdrawn from day-to-day demands until they feel equal to them. Those known to me all got up after physical withdrawal mentally better adjusted, even stronger. Mourning is private and cannot be arbitrarily shortened or beguiled, therefore attempts at consolation may be resented as intrusion; myself received from two widows, two women completely different in temperament and social circumstances, the same half-shame-faced complaint; "They mean well - but if only they'd leave me alone!" - very similar to Job who rounded on his "comforters" with "How long will you vex my soul and break me in pieces with words?"

Many customs and conventions must surely have evolved to benefit society rather than the individual bereaved? These vary from the solemnity of the Christian committal to the cheerfulness of a wake, from the stoicism of "the stiff upper lip" contrasted with the wild demonstrations of simpler peoples. Then there are convenient ready-made phrases available, suitably varied according to circumstances; "He had a happy life", or the converse "He's out of misery", "a happy release"; "He died full of years" or, "Whom the gods loved die young"; there are many ways of saying "He died" such as "He passed away", "went over", "was called home", "his spirit was freed". It was often among the unsophisticated who did not attempt to express a commentary on loss that I found the most understanding - no easy philosophies, no probing curiosity (exquisite the pain of clumsiness when even a touch could hurt). Attempts at consolation for those who recognise the pain and finality of loss - whether facile in cliché or fumbling in sincerity - are realised as futile and therefore unattempted.

Society probably benefits by encouraging the bereaved to go away while the neighbourhood adjusts to the loss of a member and, more significantly, to the presence of the survivor.

Twelve years ago my three months absence had given friends a time for adaptation and they could welcome my return without constraint. This time, because I had stayed at home and because Richard's death had been sudden and unanticipated, acquaintances might ask after him and it was painful to see their suddenly horrified faces; they seemed almost frightened, almost to require my reassurances, and for a while afterwards some would avoid me when they could. As an elderly villager said with simple discernment; "I feel so sorry when people ask me about my poor baby grandson. It's them I'm sorry for - I hate to make them feel sad." It seemed that perhaps the aloneness of the bereaved is not all due to self-centredness (not the same thing as their need for solitude). Proximity with suffering which they cannot alleviate is cause of unease to many; moreover the bereaved are afflicted people, sufficient cause for avoidance by those who fear all pathological conditions. (Of course they are innocently injured and undeserving of rejection - and yet how natural it is!) The bereaved are a *momento mori* for those who live as though death does not exist, cancelling by their negative the bright affirmative of those solely concerned with the living present. Encounters are not easy for awhile:-

"I was buying fruit in the market when accosted by an acquaintance from another village and blithely asked how Richard is today. I murmur my news, pay the stall holder and hasten to the bus. Travelling home I reflected that until a moment ago for that woman Richard was alive with his living news and welfare with which she could concern herself; now his existence was extinguished for her as if in another way he died

226

once again. I walk up the drive quickly for my heart seems bursting - but why the hurry? I wash my fruit and put it away...'

Occasionally came the relief of tears. I think the tears of grief are different in kind from those of childhood which are almost invariably a purposed appeal - for attention, for aid, for sympathy. Grief's tears are not similarly directed. The ache of continual lamentation may be inwardly endured for days or for weeks on end, but somehow the weight of sorrow accumulates; it rises invisibly pent up and silent, until at last the overload topples over in an avalanche of misery and a sudden storm of weeping:- tying a shoelace, about to go out for a walk suddenly immobilised and helpless; then, composure restored, bathing my face and putting on a hat and coat; or cleaning the car upholstery, seeming absorbed in the task, suddenly clutching the Hoover nozzle, hot tears dripping into the dust. Always afterwards came a sense of some easement, of liberation perhaps from tension and stress; and maybe the knowledge that such anguish can be surmounted as well as endured gives courage to go on with the daily business of living. With a sense of a fresh start one begins again.

During these tracts of time with more than a decade separating them it seemed that my sense of reality wavered awhile. This time the journal became most valuable because the simple recording of day-to-day events made some kind of reality out of experience which otherwise lacked all semblance of actuality. The entries increased my hold upon life, like hooks that latched on to happenings. The sense of unreality was not, I think, an unconscious evasion of a painful situation, but simply that I had not had time to accustom myself to it; despite instinctive reluctance to give up the children never for a moment did I think of them as recoverable:-

"Mentally I know they are forever gone but my instincts are not adjusted or why do I feel startled when a musical cadence cannot be shared as formerly? Why feel it wrong that M should visit when Richard is not here? Perfectly well I know that I shall never again touch their hands, hear their voices, enjoy their presence, plan their future: but - incredibly - I sometimes *forget*, and then the pang of realisation startles with its intensity."

After a journey:-

"During the long drive home I ardently longed to be back and was intensely happy at sight of familiar roads and trees, delighted to see again the white walls of the cottage and eventually to push open the gate. I almost ran indoors and of course found only a silent empty house and myself, irrationally, *disappointed*...It's primitive, animal-like, and therefore natural, I suppose. Charlotte Brontë wrote on her return to Haworth after Anne's death in Scarborough: "The dogs welcomed me with special joy. I am sure they thought that if I were come the others would soon come also.""

And again:-

"In the library I was unable to resist looking through the window whence I used to see him waiting for me outside. I believe I half hoped for a hallucination."

Or:-

"As I posted my letters I thought that if they could see me R and P would watch my endeavours with love and understanding."

It seems that I never denied the reality of loss even if sometimes weak enough to imagine their solicitude or interest; always I accepted that the separation had occurred, was complete and was final. So repeatedly was the true reality of my situation forced into consciousness.

But though the loss and the pain of loss were real enough, the world unconnected with loss was unreal. I continued to visit the old familiar places beside the river, through the common and into the woods, and wherever I went and whatever I did the main preoccupation remained a part of the self and not to be evaded. So monotonously did my mind circle round and around one train of thought that there was little room left for external impressions. Pain too had power to deaden perception as I stood motionless staring at tress or at sky. The autumn weather continued benign right up to the end of November and it was almost with incredulity that I watched the seasonal changes unaltered by my private concerns. Every evening as always the gulls flew over the house in great skeins and arrowed formations homing from the distant estuary to their roosting places upriver; sometimes I imagined I could hear the beat of wings. Punctually in the garden the fragrant viburnum and autumn prunus became spangled with blossom, the sprays of yellow jasmine again embowered the goldfinch who, without doubt, would sleep another winter in the joist under the porch. All these things I saw as from a long way off, a remote witness never a participant. More than anything else I desired to build some bridge between these outside realities and that inner one that so weighed me down with its burden. I touched the trees, a physical contact, and turned from them in such despair that unshed tears stung my eyes. With unappeased aching longing I returned home; my bridges would not be built quickly. I thought that I had accepted that *nous n'irons plus au bois*. But had I accepted acceptance? That would be harder.

Winter fell suddenly in the last week of November with frost, fog and two days of dreaded "smog". The muffling vapour pressed close to doors and windows; trees and bushes loomed pallid and inert over frosty grass; all was hushed and motionless, the birds invisible and silent. Yesterday's world was dead - immobile, icy, rank with approaching decay, its very inhabitants turned into shadows of themselves, unrecognisable as they hurried by holding scarves and handkerchiefs almost up to their eyes so not to inhale the smog. The dank fume-ridden atmosphere and bone-melting cold sent me hurrying home after my trip to the pillar box back to my fire, my sewing and the cat on the rug - outside the casement of white nothingness, inside an island of warmth and light. For two days the cottage seemed like a ship at sea where the lights and life are encompassed on every side by the unfathomable mysterious enormity of ocean.

It was a relief when the storms began, the sudden roar of the wind woke us all up in the night and the rain lashed the windows as though trying to batter the house down. Next morning we found a great pine bough lying across the courtyard and the garden strewn with leaves, twigs and small branches; in the village an old elm lay prone, limbs had been wrenched from many trees; pavement pools were blown into wavelets or mushroomed up into fountains; the mud-brown water of the Thames swirled in wide sulky eddies under the bridge carrying its flotsam very rapidly downstream and piling brushwood on the side of the island. I went out again in the early evening when from ragged clouds a red sun had briefly emerged; I enjoyed submission to all this violence and turbulence, found it invigorating and releasing. From now on my life was centred on the outside world, going out and about in all weathers, walking, standing, staring, *listening* - but to what and for what I did not know. Stillness after storm brought frost, ropy cobweb trembling on the gate, wallflowers and holly with silver scalloping, wisteria stems thick and woolly, leaf studs glassed in ice, hoar frost scattering. And when January brought, as so often, a brief spell of calmer airs and skies then cloud shapes grew rounder and against them, black etched on grey, the elm tops thickened "delicate as flower of grass".

Almost imperceptibly time slipped along to spring when came a real respite from pain and incapacity; freed from such limitations I began to fill my time with modest and satisfying activities. To be occupied not preoccupied was a marvel and I found real delight in a variety of simple duties that required attention without concentration. An endeavour completed to the best of my ability not as narcotic or for pastime or distraction but for an end-product - merely to be *useful* - such seemed so worthwhile that it had for me then an intrinsic goodness and value. I took pleasure in the evening as I drew the curtains, put FG's slippers before the fire and warmed bowls ready for the soup simmering on the stove. As I sewed it was good to watch the material shaping stitch by stitch till a tangible result was attained and I hung up, carefully cut and lined, three pairs of new curtains. One evening alone in the house I took down from the shelves the worst of the war-damaged books and set to work to repair them with scissors and ruler, a pot of paste and a roll of cartridge paper - an undemanding job done without urgency, each repaired volume a little achievement. I recalled youthful hours at home studying my books downstairs when the family had gone to bed, no sound as now but the ticking clock or the drop of a cinder in the hearth. During this time I managed to work in Richard's room sorting through his possessions, many of which had once belonged to Philip. I dusted books, listed his gramophone recordings, sorted tools, orchestral scores, chessmen, sketching blocks; and, although much time, thought and workmanship had gone into them, I ruthlessly put out all but the four best of his model boats and aircraft. Of what remained I spent some days making nearly fifty individual parcels neatly tied and labelled hoping a boys' hospital might make use of them. And while glad at what I had done I felt a foolish pang when we delivered them at seeing these cherished objects carelessly handled, a piled jumble of odd packages on a trolley being wheeled into the ward.

I puzzled awhile about the value of *things*. Objects only seen and used in their good company seemed inextricably associated with memories of the happy past. But would it have been meaningful to retain them? I wrote:

> "If I hoard their things merely to keep them by me to
> look at them sometimes of what value would they be?
> It is self-distrust to imagine I need them for their power
> to recall, because if I forget, absolutely and completely

forget, all that the boys were and meant then a drawer full of bits and pieces will have no significance; and if I remember, why then I won't need them."

Of course I acknowledged that, apart from their utility, objects are legitimately cherished for their beauty or rarity or historical significance. But about private and personal associations I wasn't quite so sure. I remembered how after Richard's only serious illness when the crisis was past and myself again aware of my surroundings that I had momentarily seen with startling clarity all things stripped of their human correlations, thereby reduced to their basic physical elements. For example an open book consisted in white sheets of paper covered with black symbolic characters, Richard's pictures were pigments enclosed in wood and sheeted with glass, his little purse of money a stitched leather container of discs of metal.

Most personal possessions quickly lose intrinsic significance when separated from our use of them. Belongings that for my mother had been intimately bound up with her whole pattern of life became meaningless - almost junk - when collected together for inventory after her death - glass, china, silver, linen, stacked on tables and chairs, rolled carpets and rugs and piles of books on the floors. Upstairs in the dressing-room individual objects perhaps meant more; Father's opera hat in its calfskin case; Mother's "honeymoon" trunk with white silk lining studded with scarlet buttons recalled childhood's seaside holidays; here stood her long-handled parasol of lilac-blue silk patterned with black - with what an air she would walk beneath it, what incomparable *swank*! Truly, *sunt lacrimae rerum*, and for a moment memory gave these things a very special value. But the moment was brief; their day was over; I had no desire to possess myself of any of them but left them where they were to be what they were - a trunk, an opera hat, and a blue parasol.

It is possible to keep things for the wrong reasons and I determined to resist in myself a tendency that in others I found morbid and even dreadful, certainly so in the cases prolonged over the years. Perhaps for such people the possessions left behind when the beloved has gone seem like a last remaining link with his physical identity something of which may even have rubbed off and into them? For me, after five months, Richard's unprecedented and continued absence was proof enough that no physical token of his past existence could bring him near again; on the contrary all such objects most poignantly asserted our eternal separation; he was gone, he would not return and his mortal relics underlined it; for me to deny this would create a falsity of realisation. Surely this was true; surely today a collection of all that remained of his personal belongings would be, and could only be, themselves.

During this time reading had become unimportant, irrelevant; seemingly I didn't want life mediated to me through literature. Weeding in the kitchen garden how clear and sharp the scent of chives and parsley and newly opened apple blossom! There was a kind of innocence in such simple sensations and I took delight in laying myself open to them. Looking at the black buds on the great ash tree I took in the dull silver grey of its triple trunk, in colour like the powdery ashes sifted in the grate under a log fire. Ash-grey: ash tree! was that why it was so named? I looked up the etymologies in the N E D and was delighted to learn that the word "asche" in Old High German stood for both "tree" and "embers". My pleasure was not linguistic but in seeming to share in perhaps a very old discernment. Now that it was possible FG and I occasionally went to concerts, museums, art galleries, and the insights multiplied. And sometimes the insights illumined one another as when Stravinsky's scores on Greek themes related both to the calm half-smiling archaic heads in the Ashmolean museum and to the raw primitive excesses depicted on the vases. (As in Delphi the ineffable Tholos stands serene below a rugged gorge of savage memory.) Or in another context; the glittering little phrase with which Berlioz begins his Overture to *Beatrice and Benedict* exactly expresses in musical idiom the Shakespearean: "And a star danced and under that I was born." Such a concordance is entrancing, and for a precious instant Shakespeare, Beatrice and Berlioz coexist in one and the same world, and I am of it.

That year the warm summer days continued all through the season, each one unblemished, each beginning with first light glistering on the pine needles and ending calmly when we walked in the dark under the scented lime trees at the bottom of the garden. The village streets were quieter then than they are today and easefully small groups talked in shade-dappled corners, young mothers pushed brown babies in prams with sun-tanned children in sandals and shorts walking beside, all day long the birds sang unwearying; I could remember nothing like it since the legendary summer of 1911.

CHAPTER FIFTEEN

Through and Beyond a Tunnel

The homely occupations and the simple insights of spring and early summer had helped me to live alongside grief and not be overwhelmed by it; I had continued almost all the time to "*try*"- to be usefully employed, to refuse to give pain full attention, to attend to things and happenings outside myself. In my behaviour and also in my surface mind I appeared most contented. So whence the pain and confusion of the long weeks now ensuing?

The first reason was sheer weariness of will. My normal energy rhythm consisted in pendulum swings from activity back to rest for recuperation and back again to output, and usually the intervals were short for I wasn't a long distance performer. From the crest of my wave I sank fairly soon down to a trough there gathering momentum to rise and move onward again. But now I had been "trying" without respite for many months, and I needed to lapse and to drift for awhile.

This meant that my strength was beginning to falter just when I most needed increase of stamina. The passing of time - the "silence and stealth of days"; and of weeks, months, and now the seasons - had begun to press well home not so much the actuality of loss as its permanence. From the beginning I had known well enough and often enough that death meant separation that was not only complete, but final. Now I experienced the intrinsic reality of that knowledge, the iteration of which so pitilessly probes close to the very core and essence of bereavement.

Therefore I now increased my taskings - attempted longer hours in the garden, planned a course of reading, more sessions at the piano. Stubbornly I worked overhard at my projects, not gently but almost angrily staking and tying my plants, reading not for enlightenment but to escape my thoughts or despairfully seeking absorption. Of course this turned out badly; pleasant occupations became exhausting drudgery, and with misgiving I presently realised that occupation was no longer even palliative.

In the early days FG and I had been able to help one another but now, after nine months this was not so. He had accepted his sons' extinction and his own pain thereat and he realised that there could be no consolation for either of us, and for himself he did not seek it but withdrew into himself. On the other hand because for so many years my life with the boys had been founded upon mutuality and unfailing open responsiveness, because in days of trial we had given reassurance and support one to another, now therefore living with FG's silence seemed strange and almost unnatural. All too often I longed to speak and restrained myself because of the constraint that lay between us. Painfully once or twice I tried to emulate him but the result was icy hardness and what was for me an alien stoniness; the truth being that I must endure in my way as he did in his - "for such as we are made on such we be". I did not understand this new source of pain and turned as usual to my journal recording bewilderment or pent-up feeling or my endeavours to learn containment; I had yet to be admonished by the Buddha's last words; "Look not for refuge to anyone besides yourselves. Be ye lamps unto yourselves." Distanced by FG's self-sufficiency, once indispensable and now unnecessary, it seemed that I had been given a very rewarding part to play in life which I had performed to the best of my ability, but that now a tragedy had been played out to the finish, leaving me at a standstill, a protagonist without a play.

This certain knowledge, combined with the long asseveration of the permanency of loss created a mood of such despair that only when awake could I hold it at bay. My nights became increasingly dream-haunted. Constantly I saw myself, fear-filled, helpless, despairing, in a nightmare world wherein struggling, stumbling, gasping, I carried heavy burdens up endless slopes or steep stairways, or waded through dark water to reach the children. I knew they urgently needed me yet I could never find them although very often I moved in sunlight under a blue sky. Other situations of great plausibility presented themselves, though none remotely resembled any event in past life. For example Richard lies in a hospital bed quiet and in no distress and when I bid him goodnight he smiles brilliantly up at me from the pillow. I go, and presently return to find a bed neatly made and empty except that on the white counterpane lie his books and sheet music ready for me to bring them home. I awake in tears, then put on the light to look hopefully at the clock - only one in the morning and hours of darkness yet to go.

Or I dream of Philip: FG and I stand with him and a stranger who holds a full cup in his hands. The stranger says to Philip: "You can choose whether you drink this or not. It will make you sleep for a long while - a *very* long while - do you quite understand?" And the answer is unemotional yet heavy with complete comprehension: "Yes." Without another word he takes the cup and drains every drop while we stand by silently assenting, desperately wishing to check him and powerless to surmount the weight of inertia blocking the will. The horror of this consent is very terrible and I start up from bed in panic, drag back the curtains and stare down at the calm moon reflections in the garden below. I may take up a book and try to read.

And sometimes completely unrelated happenings would succeed one another connected only by the pervasive dread and horror with which I the spectator beheld myself caught up in them. As when I find myself at the top of a high stairway in a squalid room containing three drab beds. Three unhappy strangers lie prone and inert and watch me with their miserable eyes though I can do nothing for them. Presently I am holding a little box of soil with many stones mixed in it and dead leaves smothering the surface, and in it grass-like tendrils are attempting to grow, so I attempt to free them to make a growing space. And then I am alone with a book printed on rough white paper. The tailpiece at the end of a chapter is a black woodcut of an upright mooring-post reflected in water above which I read the words: "and now all three have long been dead and long forgotten. The chapel built and dedicated to Wilmot's memory had now crumbled away and been washed into the sea by the tide." Struggling up and shuddering cold I awake in the dark room thankfully back in the world of consciousness but still engulfed in the feeling generated - or was it expressed? - by the dream. Half-smothered I put on the light and wait for panic to fade as I know that it will, though sometimes it lingers interminably before sleep comes again. (Even today this last three-fold dream sequence with its unassociated proper name reverberates strangely in my remembrance.)

Nothing in real life had ever foreshadowed the fear-fraught foreboding of the dreams which now poisoned sleep - not occasionally but every single night for weeks on end. The shocks and emergencies of the past had rarely called forth fear but the substitution of a protective affection so powerful and pervasive that only seldom was there room in consciousness for any other feeling.

The dreams as symbols were easy enough to understand but unfortunately this was not to control them. On the rare occasions when I could not remember them I would nevertheless awake conscious of vague shadowy emotions lying just below the surface. And sometimes the feeling never quite dispersed but clouded even waking hours making it hard to cope with daily tasking; light-headed from broken nights I sometimes saw the world in a fog of unease, moving as in a resistant element more palpable than air.

Eventually physical symptoms - from which during four months I had been blissfully reprieved - began to curtail many occupations and to limit contact with the outside world wherein I might have found perspective. Yet if work was bad inaction seemed worse and I could not see how to break out of this vicious circle, bewildered at my own ineptitude.

With astonished relief I awoke one morning from a long and dreamless sleep and lived all day enveloped in utter lassitude and quiet, as though I were floating on life. Sights and sounds registered faintly as though far off, and despite the strangeness

I think that I enjoyed it. That night I slept profoundly and next morning drifted to sleep over my sewing, lay down upstairs and slept all afternoon. Otherwise all seemed as usual and I could only feel thankful for my respite. On the third morning I awoke from yet another good night not rested but profoundly exhausted, and felt wretched all day while trying to put a good face on it; when I fell into a doze in my chair after dinner FG roused me and put me to bed with a slight rise in temperature. There I slept restlessly in brief stretches - without dreams however, and with never a thought of Philip or Richard. For a few days I stayed where I had been put, resigned and not uncomfortable, looking at a horrid wet boiled egg at breakfast time, once attempting to dress but retiring back to bed with one stocking on, and waking one night in the small hours astonished to find myself sitting upright, the light still on, and my supper plate and spoon still on the bed.

I wasn't ill, simply tired out; fatigue hemmed me in and against it I rested myself as upon a pillow; laid aside upstairs and alone with no call to think or to feel I drifted through the hours, often sleeping, then staring at the steadfast trees or the ever-changing sky. Once a cock bullfinch with his hen settled on a bough, brilliant and homely, and morning and evening the gulls flew over, going to and from the estuary and their roosting place upriver.

About this time a letter arrived from the Parish Council at Chagford accepting our offer of a tree to be planted in the churchyard not as a memorial but as an anonymous thank-offering for the happiness we had all known there. We wanted an arbutus: with its bright glossy leaves, red mottled bark, its pink bells of blossom and drooping strawberry-like fruits, this is a tree good to look at all through the year and, though evergreen, not funereal like yews or cypress. Presently I was able to drive with FG down to a nursery garden in Kent to select a specimen to be sent direct to Devon. On the way down we recalled many good hours, but we were silent on the return journey; for my part feeling no thankfulness only mournful grief for two gay and hopeful creatures we had hoped to nurture and rear, now dust and ashes, unfulfilled and extinct, in a country churchyard.

Ah, stranger, breathe a sigh
For where we lie
Is but a fragment of bright beauty cast
It was: and now is past.

Walter de la Mare's words cut into Dartmoor granite would better than the tree have expressed what I felt then.

I was sorry FG felt I should not go down for the planting though perhaps he now gauged my strength - or weakness - better than myself when I begged that I should go. I gave in without argument. "However can your being there *matter*?" the boys would have said, and of course they would have been right. This was my last endeavour on their behalf; now there was nothing more to be done.

It seemed that for many people each moment's instancy added up together constituted what they called "living in the present" as opposed to time-wasting unproductive nostalgia, and perhaps some such living had temporarily been self-preservative in my case. But I could no longer be immersed in the necessary spaced-out activities which punctuated the days, could no longer find in them meaning or perspective, they seemed almost as pointless as a squirrel turning a wheel in a cage. Yet although thereby the mitigation of absorption was withheld, the confusion of thinking that the isolated act could be its own validation without the whole mind's consent now stood forth clearly as pretence; while not purposively evasive of my problems the search for absorption had certainly postponed my coming to terms with them. But - and this was much - now that real feelings were no longer denied they no longer haunted my nights, and the terrible dreams now ceased as though a key had been turned in a lock.

For a while life seemed empty reflecting the void where once two beings had happily existed; around them my life had been structured and these foundations having been removed the makeshift scaffolding I had tried to erect appeared to have been frail from the beginning. Everything had caved in and for a

240

while I ceased to strive. I no longer tried to build my bridges, utterly weary of feelings and of struggle I allowed myself to be submerged by a shameful sloth and inertia, drifting through the once precious hours between first waking and night's most welcome oblivion. Once I had used the journal seeking understanding as much as mitigation, now I merely scribbled for relief.

"All now seems new, strange, alien even. If I could imagine a new path to follow, a single step in the right direction would be a beginning."

"Why do I struggle, feel pain, horror, despair? Because I am pulling two ways at once. I know that I must accept deflection into quite new channels, and to remember how much better the old ways were can lead only to weariness. Torpor is not true acceding, but only exhaustion of the power to feel. Mitigation will be withheld until I wholeheartedly consent."

"Just now I cannot live alone the good life that once we knew. Yet I cannot picture any other. At least I can remember the positive, the full employment of all the faculties in the outside world, in the full light of day."

"Perhaps it isn't the life but myself who must change? And must the new self, like the priest in the myth, destroy the old one before he can reign in his stead? If so, it's going to be hard."

"How can I love what I know does not exist? Is grief simply the pain of recognising that truth? The truth is that I love them still; they still have my whole heart's affection. If this be wrong, how put it right?"

"Twelve years ago I thought I had realised that those who have passed into oblivion can in no sense now be suffering deprivation - yet still I feel it as they might if alive and aware of it themselves. It simply isn't true that the children were forced to relinquish all the good things of a lifetime, it is only *we* who know all that they have foregone. Free acceptance of this is still denied me; a huge compassion floods my heart whenever I think of them, and this is the very ecstasy of grief and of sorrow."

"This is to be a storm- broken ship, with broken rudder and no chart or compass. I don't know where I am or where I am going, so it's easiest to stay motionless or just drift with the tide."

"Even if my love has no significance because it has no object, yet my grief is all-commensurate with it. How can I wish that I had loved them less that I might grieve less now? What then is grief? Grief is love unavailing."

Strange to remember how I felt eased as I wrote those last four words! As though to make explicit a vague emotion, to underpin it with meaning, was somehow to make it endurable, for grief was surely the continuance in another form of the affection and joy generated among us in life.

During the long days of that wonderful summer, beside the river and in the country, hundreds of happy people disported themselves in the sunshine and I watched them with wonder. How were they enabled to be so engrossed and occupied, to forget their terrible insecurity, to believe in what they were doing? Like the ephemera, dancing in sun-suffused aggregations of themselves, they were enjoying their moment, but there seemed little meaning in it. Pleasures and pastimes, child-bearing and family life, the search for fame and worldly success, had surely about the same significance as the absorbed preoccupations of insects. And these were the happy ones; their inevitable frustrations as nothing compared with millions elsewhere, stultified by hunger, dire poverty, disease, and cruelty

242

at the hands of other humans (so called). What were *their* prospects? It was necessary to accept that dissolution is the price all living creatures pay for life: but if life isn't worth it all - what then? The love-pity that I began by feeling for two mortals now seemed to embrace that whole of life.

Thus through the weeks I groped for direction and enlightenment without finding either, for if my sole reaction was despair at contemplating what I could not alter, or if my conclusions were too painful for my temperamental or nervous structure to endure, then my attitudes were as useless as myself. And even then I felt that maybe my picture was a distorted one shadowed by the darkness of grief's pathology. So it was that gradually I came to realise that it was not for me to take thought in finding my solutions but to let go and allow a new life to grow of itself. Just as a bird ensnared and struggling in the net entangles itself the more, so perhaps my own efforts had been misguided. It might be wiser, more valid, to let passivity - not indolence but patience - take over, simply holding myself ready for whatever might come unwilled, waiting "for light or for leaven."

By mid-August the summer had gone on too long; the blue-green trees were dense with leaves hanging inertly or falling as in autumn; the flower beds grew raddled and dusty under a sky hazed over, intensifying the hot dazzle from the invisible sun; day and night the atmosphere remained close, enervating and oppressive, people as well as plants felt desiccated.

For some forgotten reason FG was obliged to go away for two days and for me they began emptily, for like the soil I felt myself sterile from drought. And then awaking before dawn on the first night I found myself lying in bed rigid as though my limbs were clamped in tight fetters and for perhaps a few seconds was unable to move; the moment I had freed myself from what had seemed like a metal trap I got up and hurried to the open window, urgent for room to expand, to escape. It helped a little to stare into the empty sky spaces but I couldn't go back to bed.

I walked awhile round the house, up and down stairs, eventually dressed and went outside to wander the empty streets between the curtained houses. A strange experience; I recall that I tried to walk without making a sound.

During the next twelve hours this momentary sense of paralysed alarm recurred at least two or three times, not seemingly triggered off by any special circumstance, nor could I - as I felt its approach - by any reasoning hold this evil at bay, or protect myself from it. Had the netted bird become enmeshed by her predicament, or had the world of dreams now invaded consciousness?

Between whiles - when I confess I felt sometimes afraid - I comforted myself with remembrance of Philip and Richard. How remote from my bewildered fumblings they seemed in life and in memory! The grace of their daily living had once illumined four lives; and in all these present troubles their image at least was inviolate. Thinking thus I went to bed for the second night in the empty house, but now I was no longer afraid, for perfect love, though only the remembrance of it, had power to cast out fear. Companioned by some vague unformulated knowledge of this I quickly fell asleep.

After long hours of deep and dreamless sleep very slowly and gradually I awoke; it was very early and I lay quietly awhile, my whole being permeated by an all-obliterative peace. In this half sleep I grew aware of pain's absence and of an increasing sense of freedom and of clarity as though all my encumbrances had very quietly been lifted and removed. The strange shackles of the day and night just past no longer bound me and I knew myself utterly liberated.

Through the open window the leaves and green berries of the hawthorn gleamed as though luminous, and incredulously I presently realised that after weeks of drought here at last was the rain. I went over and stood breathing in the freshness; a blackbird clattered and shivered his quills in a pool, with a scatter of drops the sparrows flew from the wisteria, a soft murmuration of birds filled the air, the gulls flew over as of old, wheeled slowly in a thermal air stream, then beat strongly away and out of sight. With curtains pulled back their furthest I went back to bed, my own aridity seeming laved in the cool life-giving sweetness; idly

I watched the raindrops trickle down the leaves. Thankfulness and delight for the living things rejoicing in the rain extended and expanded and I wanted life to go on forever and forever.

Rain fell all day lancing deep into the ground, slaking the parched earth, laying the dust, cooling and softening the air, washing away old stains and traces; the smell of wet leaves mingled with scent of the tobacco plants by the open door invaded the house. When in the early evening the skies cleared and a pale moon appeared lying flat on her back all the tension of drought had been annealed. With the utmost content I awaited FG's return.

During the next few days I felt naive wonder that my own private easement coincided with nature's, but of course it wasn't at all extraordinary. The effects of drought and heat had been universal and the change of atmosphere welcomed by all. Nevertheless for one whose nervous system had for so long been strung up to an almost unbearable degree the effects of external tension had been exaggerated and the release signified much more. Real wonder I might well feel at the adjustment to my world of reality, a balance seemingly attained overnight. But although awareness of such a change had indeed come suddenly, below the conscious level it must have been fermenting for weeks. All that time I had been trying, in often mistaken ways, not to soften or to evade but to come to terms with our capricious and strange misfortune, as well as with the meaning of bereavement. I had sought endurance through occupation, attempted the hardness of an unnatural stoicism, and latterly simply treadmilled my useless empty days. Now, not by conscious thought or action but in some inexplicable way I had come through and a slow spontaneous adjustment of focus had corrected a bent and blinded vision.

The pain of witnessing the undeserved extinction of two good brave spirits long before their time, of realising the loss we ourselves had sustained, of not being in any way able to account for these things, had made acquiescence hard to come by.

Nevertheless this present emancipation meant more than control of feeling, it meant assimilation; it meant that the bitterness of loss and defeat had been freely received and digested by the mind. Our sons' faces at the last had looked neither abject nor defeated but beautiful in their calm acceptance of their lot and such acceptance was now enjoined on me. Better than resignment is reconcilement and to that I had seemingly come though how and where engendered I could not tell; after inquisition, absolution; I had paid my penance and now I was shriven.

Nevertheless more than a decade was to pass before this acceptance was transformed into understanding. There came a day when with good reason and by mutual consent FG and I embarked on a rare evaluation of our past family life. Of course over the years we had often gladly recalled our children, always however remembering activity and involvement, and not disability which had not affected our basic relationship with them both. Now we sought to discover less what their brief presence and their long absence had meant to ourselves but what for them life had been about. For an ultra-microscopic deviation from the norm was only one of the many elements that made them what they were. Had they been different they would have been quite other children from those we had known, loving Philip for himself, all that he was, and Richard for himself, accepting him completely also. The same inheritance that made them courageous and intelligent, balanced and tolerant and gay of heart, also contained the element that would destroy them and deprive us of them forever. "Some parents have such sons," said FG with humble gravity and with truth. Two good brave spirits were lost indeed but two good brave spirits had come into existence and, however briefly, their coming had changed the world they lived in for the most part for the better.

We remembered their own reactions although they had rarely spoken of their handicap and of course these occasions had been widely separated in time since there was a nine year age gap between them, but, despite this, and their differences of character, their attitudes had much in common - objective, realistic, unequivocal. Yes, they had a handicap for which unfortunately science could propound neither cause nor cure and therefore, while saying with honest conviction that it would most certainly have been far better to be "average" they did not waste their brief years and good minds in vain hopes and despairs. For example they knew for themselves that genetic differences may decide pigmentation, temperamental tendencies, special aptitudes, perhaps even genius; also that some are born blind, or stone-deaf, or mentally retarded, all congenital limitations which they regarded as far greater impediments to fullness of life than their own inexplicable weakness of musculature, which at that time we could not ascribe to their heredity. They did not think of themselves as lamed or damaged or crippled or paralysed but simply as suffering from an ultra-microscopical and painless divergence in muscle metabolism. Unlike many physical conditions which affect the entire organism such as toxins and infections and organic defects which undermine vital processes, painful malignancies that slowly erode, or brain damage that may isolate a human being from his fellows, their condition never in the very least impaired their essential selfhood. For all of Richard's life and most of Philip's they had not lost a fundamental sense of well-being and they did not look sad as children on crutches or pushed around in wheelchairs so often do; when they could no longer walk unaided, for years both had been happily mobile on the two tricycles on which they so nimbly propelled themselves. Even when we were disappointed in our once entertained hopes of their ultimate recovery, in some extraordinary way even limitations were incorporated into their wholeness and their youthful buoyant expectancy had remained intact.

FG wondered whether, when they became more dependent on me, they had been unhappy on that account, but I could not think so because once I had accepted my new vocation as a complete commitment I had not found it a burden myself. I found this hard to put clearly. During the Dartmoor years, which had been the most testing, I had not allowed myself to imagine

247

a "normal" existence - home and possessions intact, husband at my side, friends in easy proximity, a future-bound family to rear - by then such vain thinking had become irrelevant. But if clouds obscured the future which had become a lost dimension, yet the prevailing climate was bright enough as I shared their discovery of the world with two avid and growing intelligences, each with wit and will to take it into himself. I never knew them unhappy or repining and the lives they lived, self-respecting and *seemly*, certainly justified their resolution. In the end I realised that two of life's best fulfilments, even for the nimblest, are useful self-deployment, and awareness, to attain which full physical mobility was not an indispensable requirement. So that I had not merely sought that their minds might know "the best that has been known and thought in the world" as Matthew Arnold had described a full life (though I had certainly attempted this, adapted to their age and aptitudes); I had also sought that they might share with me, as partners, the enjoyments I knew while living an unhampered existence, pleasures they could plainly see to be as valuable to me as to themselves. That they might require my help sometimes to attain certain ends we simply took for granted as part of life's normal pattern. If I could get on to the moor to see the swaling fires on the slopes of Nattadon Hill, or watch in the garden for the moon's eclipse, or enjoy the village in new guise glittering in winter snow, then so could they, and the shared objective was everything, the means to attain it almost irrelevant. I felt sure they had never felt themselves at the "receiving end" of a services-rendered situation; I never said, "I will take you," always, "We will go." Thus it was that all of us all the time were absorbed by and into an authentic experience of marvellous variety and interest and scope.

Rather uneasily, seeking absolute honesty, I wondered whether all this might not be an attempt to put a good face on a situation inherently tragic and almost intolerable. No, said FG, in spite of the situation our lives had attained an excellence that it would be a worse dishonesty to deny; even if the outside world could not believe it, we knew it to be true; although we ourselves had each enjoyed more than twice the life years they had known between them we could not say that we had lived *more*, only longer.

Nor should we forget that having embarked on parenthood naturally expecting a normal family and in spite of some initial difficulties not regarded as serious by our advisers we had lived for some years of happiness in that hope and expectation; nor could it be questioned that they had lived gladly and wanted to go on living. Had "genetic counselling" been available could they or we have been better off had neither of them been born? Weighed in the balance what delights we should all have missed! Yet we could imagine that a child *born* handicapped and into an uncaring environment, perhaps treated as a nuisance or a burden, or into the confining miseries of great poverty, or, worst of all, into a world where disability particularly of the hereditary kind is regarded as a kind of disgrace, then such a child, however gifted, might come to wish that he had never been born. Favourable circumstances, their own gifts of mind and character, the knowledge both must have had that their parents recognised and valued their quality, had prevented any such tragic attitude on their part.

It would be cant to denigrate their gift for ardent living by calling it a compensation for disability - as though there were a giver or a withholder, or a balance sheet to be drawn; a ranging mind and honest response are surely absolutes with whatever kind of body they be associated whether one constantly afflicted like Samuel Johnson's or splendidly robust like Titian's. It is never suggested that athletic prowess is "compensation" for a schoolboy's lack of intellect, it is simply deployment in another field of endeavour. Just so our boys had relished their own vitality in the zestful use of all their faculties.

After the premature death of her sister Charlotte Brontë had deplored "a tree in full bearing struck down at the root", but these boys had been at bud not blossom and, unlike Emily, they left no enduring work behind. So in the end our regret is not for the nature of their lives but that an unforeseeable affliction had made those lives brief. Since neither of us believes in personal immortality premature extinction can only be pain of an undiminishing sharpness that two creatures both innocent and good had not achieved their promise. But, as FG said again and again, they had not endured our knowledge to darken our picture of their lives' true reality. Without any pretence that bitterness was sweet we determined not to dwell on images of waste and of loss; and if the natural world and the world of the arts, and especially if other humanity in love or in friendship should become less valuable for us now than with them, we should fail them by being false to all that they stood for. Our living should be enhanced not straitened by our poignant experience of its brevity.

PART THREE

Some Validations

CHAPTER SIXTEEN

Wider Horizons

Thankfully emerged from a tunnel and fully consenting to everything I had set my face forward at last, and although ignorant of the causes I think FG sensed this great change for the very next week he suggested a holiday. We had not been away together since our return from America five years before the war, and his plan was that we should revisit Devon. This seemed an early test of my new-found equilibrium, remembered associations with that county being so many and so strong, and although I raised no objections it was with secret misgiving that I made preparation and eventually departed. But after only a few hours travel I knew that all would be well. The steady forward motion of the car created an unaccustomed and most welcome feeling of purpose, an impulse towards an anticipated goal; the high empty spaces of Salisbury Plain expanded the mind after two years in the flat and over-populated Thames Valley, and by the time we had reached the West Country irrational fear had ebbed away like a tide going out.

Because in the main we revisited places and scenes known to us ever since our marriage, more than thirty years before, this holiday provided recognitions rather than discoveries; nevertheless we saw everything fresh and clear-cut after our long absence just as one rejoices in familiar English landmarks after a trip abroad. And though in the event ours was perhaps a sentimental pilgrimage it wasn't a sad one - at Ashton, Bickington, Kingskerswell, Topsham, Exeter, Gidleigh, Throwleigh and Chagford we looked not with unhappy nostalgic eyes but remembering many heartening fulfilments and delights; outside the old cottage at Ashton FG said quietly: "This is where we began," and did so with a sincere satisfaction that I could wholeheartedly share.

Here it was made manifest that the early life of incipience and hope had flowed through the years of endeavour into our present moment of quiescence, so that this holiday created a link (had he intended it? - for me perhaps, for I cannot think that his lifeline required re-forging) between old and new, which of course had only seemed discontinuous in imagination. For there was no need, no possibility even, of dividing past from present for the two had now achieved coalescence - what bent state of mind could have imagined it would be otherwise? Now I recognised the unreality of the alternatives that I had been posing for myself, the rifting of life into two parts, before and after, without and within, then and now; or imagining the need to devise a "new" life or a fresh identity like the priest in the myth destroying his predecessor. Such "twoness" was altogether mistaken and simply reflected the disintegration of losing a life's central purpose after twenty years of prolonged endeavour. All that was relevant from the past still lived in me so that my life was only different in the sense of growth; I had not changed, I was the same woman. I had never sought to "live in the past" (what a contradiction in terms the phrase is! No wonder that those who attempt it become neurotic), yet it was wholly right and proper that from now on memory, especially "unremembered" remembrance, should exist and continue in my present wholeness. (So it was that a cat crouched on a sagging brown verandah under a moon and mackerel-clouds *meant*, even though I could not have said why.)

But I didn't utter these things because we were absorbed in meeting one another on a new footing, not based on our marriage or our parenthood but simply on companionship. We were grown undemanding and easy; freed from the rigidity of one sole feeling I was accessible to his unspoken encouragement; neither was secretly afraid of the other, nor fearing on my part to enter, nor on his to be invaded; having shed our self-protective armour each met the other halfway and in the open able to give and take; now as we travelled he told me much concerning his outside professional life, his past experiences and present objectives. With shared relief we discovered that I was well again after a convalescence that circumstances had prolonged over sixteen months; the long downdrag of intermittent wretchedness had seemingly evaporated, I could be freely active without punishment, and in this new dimension of well-being could share in everything that FG desired.

Our journeyings did not cease on our return to Surrey because from now on whenever FG had business away from London and it was practicable he would travel by car with me as companion; he was travelling, of course, in order to work, and while he attended meetings and conferences I explored many cities, their purlieus and byways as well as their public buildings and cathedrals, wandered among the colleges in Oxford and Cambridge, sometimes got into the adjacent country. Well I remember sitting on a stile one bright windy morning to watch two horses at play in a field outside Beverley; they rolled exuberantly then pranced and galloped and raced all over their enclosure, manes and tails tossed all ways by the wind; whether or not consciously, they celebrated the magnificent gift merely of being alive just as, after the drought, birds and plants rejoiced in the renewal of their world by rain; the green of grass and blue of sky, the horses' glossy pelts and lustrous eyes composed themselves into a picture of extraordinary brilliance so that I remained on the stile till I was stiff.

Until FG's retirement he and I enjoyed six years of frequent travel in England, Wales and Scotland, building up for ourselves an extensive picture of parts of the British Isles. Contrasts could be startling. A few weeks after leaving the coombes and hills of Devon we drove to Humberside passing in the fenlands through a landscape flat and spreading like the sea where churches in the distance looked like beached ships and a heron hunched over his canal stood out like a landmark. We soon learned that a lifetime might well be required to comprehend thoroughly even one single county - remembering gratefully the work of W G Hoskins in Devon - and for ourselves had to be content with noting the differences between Cumberland and distant Cornwall, between two adjacent counties like Somerset and Gloucestershire, or, in one county, between the three "ridings" of Yorkshire. Place became associated with experience - nightingales in Surrey woods, larksong over the South Downs, moments of silence absolute in Aberfoyle. Surely no other land has such variety of countryside in so narrow a compass, the one thing in common being a simple unpretentious goodness. How many of our writers and their life's works have been shaped by the region that bred them! - writers as diverse as their background, not "descriptive" artists of whom we have many and good ones, but true creators like Wordsworth, Emily Brontë, Clare, Barnes and Hardy and, though Warwickshire was his pastoral background, the universality for England of Shakespeare.

About now we began to take our holidays abroad. In our twenties we had twice visited "the Continent", once through Belgium into the Ardennes, once travelling to Salzburg and Vienna; we had also journeyed extensively by car for a year in the United States with brief cross-frontier excursions into Canada and Mexico, since when, twenty-six years ago, we had not left Great Britain.

Of all their natural features the rivers of the countries I know have been of greatest interest to me, not merely because they composed a bright light-reflecting element with abundance and clarity and often energetic movement, but also because rivers are as diversified as human beings and like them undergo many changes and vicissitudes from their beginning until their end; how natural that the Ancients often gave their river a tutelary deity! For me to name less than a dozen rivers in my own small country demonstrates such differences - think of Tees and Usk and Tyne, or Thames, Dart and Severn, Avon, Wharfe and Wye. In France there is the Loire with its sandy shoals and grassy islets or the lovely little Cher, or the greater Garonne, Rhone and Dordogne, the Sorgues issuing from the rocks in Petrarch's

Vaucluse; in Iberia Tagus and Guadalquiver, in Central Europe Danube and Rhine; in other continents Rio Grande, Colorado, Mississippi and Nile. It is shameless self-indulgence and (for myself) a valued evocation merely to enumerate the names.

I have found that living for long periods of time in one same place may tend to blunt the perceptions and that then to discover a new trackway in the Common or, as once happened, merely to come upon a garden where a veil of rosy tamarisk floats over a bed of grey irises can, by the sheer startle of delight prick the dormant faculties into a new awareness. So the fresh worlds revealed through foreign travel sharpen the senses and I return home much more alive to my familiar environment than before my departure. Of course it would be possible to circumnavigate the world a great many times and return no whit the wiser having merely gone places and seen things; conversely men and women of genius, by exploring in depth a very limited neighbourhood have discovered for themselves whole worlds of meaning without need to travel afield. But, for those less endowed, to experience the strange and new in far places does not merely enlarge the world picture but may also alter the meaning; to cross political and geographical boundaries accepting changes in climate, vegetation and pace and style of living, in lands where sometimes only my companion's speech is intelligible, is for me to extend the mental frontiers also. FG's attitude is less subjective and for him in a new country climate, terrain and natural resources are important as shaping the lives and institutions of its inhabitants.

For him the approach, for me the response made all our journeys significant giving us much more than leisure, change and sunshine. When possible we like to travel independently by car and to avoid motorways and industrial centres, but when to language difficulties is added inability to turn a written script into spoken words as in Libya, Egypt, the Sudan and Greece, we have travelled by air on conducted tours and very good we have found them. Our first visit to Greece was of this kind after which we returned three years later by ourselves; we travelled everywhere by bus and everywhere, Corinth or Crete, Daphne or Delphi, we met helpful kindness; while we ate our lunch of bread, olives and tomatoes with fresh-milled coarse salt we were watched solicitously by the owner of the *taverna*; good host that he was, he offered his finest hard-boiled eggs and brought a selection of his wines for our tasting; frequently we were presented in the villages with gifts of fresh fruits or flowers. Through travel we discovered new sights, new sounds, strange-seeming contrasts. We heard the endless churring of the cicadas in the dried grass on bare hillsides in Spain and Greece, the squealing chatter of monkeys in African trees, the calling of the faithful to prayer from the towers of Islam. We didn't find it strange only soothing and peaceful to see soft-footed camels or oxen gravely transporting their bales or their wagons piled with grapes, but we were mildly shocked when we saw for the first time the burdens carried by Libyan women in the fields while their menfolk drank coffee in the bazaars. Religious observances also impress the traveller from a mainly Protestant country as he moves from the stained glass and decorated statuary of Roman Christianity to the icons and mosaics of Byzantium, or notes how Muslim ritual is regularly observed by the faithful without need of priest or temple very often far from the precincts of mosque or minaret.

During my impressionable adolescence, for a whole year an enthusiastic young teacher had enthralled me and my classmates by the story of Ancient Egypt. How colourful these studies compared with the kings and queens of England, how high-sounding the sonorous names of the pharaohs - Amenhotep, Akhnaten, Rameses - compared with our Williams and Georges or poor Ethelred the Unready! Our headmistress, at a time when such interests were uncommon (ten years before the discovery of the Tutankhamen treasure) worked as an amateur archaeologist during her summer holidays, and we were allowed to pore over her long scrolls of paintings copied from papyri, as she exhibited her photographs, or told some of her adventures. History measured in millennia not in centuries, the colossal size and antiquity of the monuments, the simultaneous reading of Kinglake's classic *Eothen*, captured my youthful imagination, and my interest has been lifelong.

But the mere size and age of pyramids, temples and statuary impressed only my early years, and I have grown to love the Ancient Egyptians for other reasons. It is often said that they were inordinately preoccupied by thought of death and it is true that the desire to circumvent decay and oblivion led to the great monuments and temples, the swathed mummies, the pyramids. But for me not the statues of kings magnified into huge representations of themselves nor the temples erected by a hierarchical priesthood, but the smaller creations of the simpler humble people of more human stature - their delicate wall-painting, their exquisite low relief, their thousands of carvings in miniature, their documentary papyri - more truly reflect the character of their race than the monuments expressing the ambitions of their rulers, priests or politicians. They depict the activities of a people not death-obsessed but life-delighted - in themselves and their daily pursuits so intimately associated with their natural surroundings - birds, beasts and fishes, even insects as well (especially the bee), together with natural and cultivated vegetation. Although I unfailingly visited the Egyptian galleries of local museums wherever we happened to be it was always alone until one morning in Paris as we were leaving the Louvre I persuaded FG to turn back - "for only a few minutes" I promised - to see a new method of lighting Egyptian low relief to simulate the effect of sunlight in emphasising outline. Such a device he thought worth looking at so he came. He was delighted with the fidelity and grace of the modelling on the illuminated pylon, and wandering round the gallery, first in desultory fashion and then with complete absorption he looked at stone friezes, wall paintings, reliefs and statuary. He wasn't impressed greatly by age or size, nor attracted by meticulous craftsmanship in precious metals or jewellery, but he was spontaneously responsive to the depiction of vital human activities in an acutely observed natural world - and he decided that he wanted to know more about it. Thus it was that eighteen months later we visited Egypt.

There we found ourselves again turning from the monumental to the intimate, from the crude animal-headed gods in the tomb of Seti the king to the real creatures depicted in tombs of the less illustrious. There we might see in great detail scenes from a man's world and his life in it: feathery papyri in the swamps, lotus flowers, blossoming trees and date palms; gazelles, hippopotami and cattle, wild duck in flight, geese in procession, cranes (a beautiful pattern this), and once we thought we saw a swallow; men planted, tended, reaped and garnered their crops, built and sailed their ships, went hunting, fowling, fishing, played with their small children; women were weaving, baking, brewing, dancing or playing musical instruments. The vitality, the careful observation and artistry in the tomb of Ti in the year BC 2650, the first we visited, would have repaid hours of scrutiny. I think it was here that we saw the relief of a stubborn donkey, his right foreleg lifted by a straining drover in front while another threatens his rear with a stick; the donkey is resisting with might and main, three legs rooted to the ground and neck extended - yet seems to cast an eye back towards the stick as if gauging just how far he dare go.

Because of its associations and of course its grandeur we were of all the great monuments most impressed by the Sphinx of Gizeh, and perhaps I was a little over-stimulated when I came to set down my reactions:-

"We saw the Sphinx in dazzling sunlight surrounded by hundreds of tourists, deafened by the cries of Arabs, the roaring camels and the babble of many languages, and quite soon took refuge in the monolithic funerary temple close by. What with the stunning heat and all the distractions I had only discovered that the figure was very much larger than I had anticipated - more akin to architecture than sculpture. Seeing the face again close-focused in the 'Son et Lumiere' performance the features seemed altered, perhaps even distorted by the strong and shifting lights and shadows. But at a third inspection in the silent empty desert of two o'clock in the morning it was possible by starlight clearly to see the stone face which, high and remote, gazes away into infinite distance. Originally perhaps, like other smaller sphinxes this figure was designed to protect by intimidation but that is not the

260

effect now. Weathered by the sun and blown sand of thousands of years, the features have grown blurred and the aspect now is calm, dreamy, almost tender. Knowledge of great antiquity and associations with that antiquity thronged my mind; after the Ancient Egyptians themselves, Herodotus and the Greeks, the Holy Family perhaps, the Roman conquerors, Napoleon, then Kinglake, now my contemporaries, had stared up at this bland face and wondered and gone away just as I should do. The duration of this persistence in spite of the changes wrought by thousands of generations of mankind seemed to smooth out human endeavour into a fairly level plane. Since this image was chiselled from the stone we have heard a little more about the complexities of our universe, a little - how little! - about our complex selves, but the mysteries we seek to probe are the same now as then, our world has not changed and is possibly changeless."

Inside the Cairo museum it was good to enjoy the portrait sculpture of individual human beings whose existence had been upon a finite and more sympathetic scale. The group "Seneb the dwarf and family" is almost as old as the Sphinx, yet how almost contemporary the feeling! Seneb is a normal man except for his tiny legs and feet, therefore he sits with them crossed on the plinth that he shares with his seated wife. He looks well pleased with his lot; she smiles and lays an arm across his shoulder. This is not a sentimental grouping but a realistic expression of simple affection, matter of fact and honest and gentle. And a thousand and more years after Ti and Seneb and Sphinx the same loving fidelity to the real may be discovered hundreds of miles away up the Nile valley. On an Eastern wall of the Karnak complex - that vast oppressive concourse of heavy close-set pillars - is an enchanting relief of a gazelle browsing in the herbage; across the river at Deir-el Bahari the Theban reliefs tell how Queen Hatshepsut had sent to the legendary land of Punt for plants for her terraced gardens - we also may see their safe arrival - homely details showing that even a great queen had much in common with her delightful people.

Although unfortunately we cannot read Greek we can scarcely recall a time when the world of myth and legends was unknown to us. Therefore the Lion Gate at Mycenae above the plain of Argos linked ancient Homer's royal house of Atreus with the works of the great classical dramatists; especially for FG Athens meant Plato and Socrates as well as Acropolis and Parthenon; Crete meant the Minotaur and an Ariadne thread through the Labyrinth, Daedalus and Icarus, the treachery of Theseus and the faithful loves of Philemon and Procne; other islands we associated with the Argonauts' Golden Fleece, or with Odysseus and his long years of seeking. Equally with sharing the Egyptians' daily ways of life these myths draw past and present humanity closer together, symbolising as they do man's search in youth for adventure, in old age for safe harbourage, his desire to find a way through the complexities of existence, his carnal and noble attributes embodied in man-monsters, his urge to ascend from the known to the unknown.

And on another simpler level a link in the long chain that spans the centuries and joins us all together is human delight in our fellow creatures, the animals. From the splendid and amazingly photographed television programmes of today whereby millions may observe animal behaviour in places remote and almost inaccessible, see a woodpecker inside her hole and life in the ocean depths, back to the humped bison in the caves of Altamira, the Egyptian proliferation, the bulls of Crete, the horses of Parthenon, the mild faces of sheep and oxen in Christian nativity pictures, in every country that I have visited I have found this affinity with other times, other creatures, other peoples. Such affirmation of continuity in spite of change is for me sustenance and encouragement.

Apart from their associations with what is known of their past, of their affinities with the present, certain intrinsically visual memories of far places may have a very special power; such for

262

me are the symmetry and purity of the Tholos at Delphi among the olive trees; the lofty colonnade at Luxor, the fluted shafts of the columns being bound papyrus stems terminating in capitals of close-clustered buds; very specially at Saint Remy the high stone pillar with two toga-clad youths standing together under the surmounting dome remote against the sky; perhaps also in Seville the Barrio de Santa Cruz, the narrow jasmine-scented white alleys and moon-silvered flowers in patios and on balconies. Seemingly I am drawn to what is simple, direct and clear, indeed I have this moment realised that there is no colour in these pictures. I consciously and very definitely had my preferences demonstrated when one day I had turned away almost overpowered by a richly decorated cathedral doorway, French Romanesque at its most opulent, and entered the little Musée on the other side of the square. There my response to the formal reticence of two pieces of classical statuary, as also to the immense dignity of the lettering on stone of a Roman inscription, was instant and fundamental. Travel did not create my tastes but it has certainly helped me to confirm them, made me more aware of my scale of values; nevertheless artefacts are less important than the affinities found with those who made them.

Always the pleasure of return after travel is intense especially for the restoration to me of our own countryside. At first opportunity I hasten to the Common where all is well, just as I hope to find it and in no way diminished by the wonders I have seen, but even enhanced by them. Truly I have seen sunsets of grandeur in the Arizona desert and over the Sierra Navada in Spain, over Thebes in Egypt as well as Thebes in Greece, but if I recall them now it is the more to wonder at the equally resplendent sky of flame and peacock over this Surrey village here tonight. For us to travel has never been better than to arrive, nevertheless coming back home has always seemed better than either.

CHAPTER SEVENTEEN

Within Four Walls

After our first holiday in Devon both of us had welcomed the return of home life and its regular routine, FG to drive every morning to his day's work in London, I to run the house and care for the flower garden. Less than two years previously the same prospect bereft of Richard's daily presence had seemed so sterile and empty as to throw me into a state of panic fear; now I welcomed it.

I had adequate help in the house in those days and never previously, neither before nor after marriage, had I known such a period of easeful leisure as now ensued; FG told me to take what he called a long "sabbatical" and I learned for the first time the useful art of loafing around, indulging myself and my whims, observing, absorbing, enjoying relaxed uninterrupted hours. After a long night's rest I would lie awhile to watch the first sunlight dapple the tree trunks, hear the first stirring of leaves and song of the birds, feel the first airy freshness blow in at the window. I could go and come at will, a freedom not in the beginning to be taken for granted. One autumn morning I might cut down and divide the monkshood and, remembering that I promised to give a piece to a friend, at the same moment realise that I am free to do so and set forth in the rain with my trug wearing the red waterproof cap that Richard had so detested (recalling his disgusted look). I arrive at a wet wilderness of fallen asters and chrysanthemums wherein friend and I wander propping them up with canes and twine exclaiming at the havoc. On another forgotten commission I find E with her mother and aunt having a tea party under their apple trees and they take it for granted that I shall join them. The narrow stone path curves through grass from gate to doorway, their light summer dresses are flecked with dancing leaf shadows, the garden smells of roses and jasmine and I am reminded of Renoir's evocations of just such luminous afternoons, no feelings stirred, the mood one of freedom and holiday. Afterwards I sit under the walnut tree at home in order to re-read *Lark Rise*. The cat sprawls on the lawn beside me, the garden spray rustles on the azaleas, beyond the shade grass and flowers are almost too bright to look upon. I read, then look up and around and read again; I stop and muse, and again turn back to the book. The evening sun grows very hot and in a curtained room I sit down at the desk then write and post a letter. Presently I welcome FG's return. I haven't been idle but only moderately active, carefree, contented, quiet; and unproductive perhaps a dull day, blissfully uneventful.

From the beginning a proper ordering of home affairs has been the essential scaffolding on which we have sought to build an easeful family life. Apart from the interlude in the Dartmoor cottage this has never been for me a full time occupation because until the loss of Maryfield's resident domestic help, and since, a succession of daily helpers has relieved me of all drudgery and I have calculated that more than five sixths of married life to date I have been blessed by a succession of pleasant and willing helpers and can think of only two exceptions. Their assistance gave me time and energy for my evening work with adult students until the war, and subsequently made it possible for me to devote myself to the family's special needs and interests. I never felt that my reliance on them to free me for congenial activities was exploitation; their lot was not that of my mother's servants with their uniform, their segregation, their complete subservience to her authority. The young women who worked for me became very quickly identified with our family unit so that running the household was really a co-operative enterprise in which their functions and mine had an equal importance; moreover they were devoted to the children and associated themselves closely with all their doings. I never delegated the choice and preparation of food, so basic to the well-being of any household; for some years I obtained wholemeal stone-ground floor in order to bake our own bread, and every autumn saw the store cupboard packed with preserves from the garden.

As well as scaffolding and support home life had also been background, and for me order is a part of civilised living. By this I do not mean tidiness: a desk covered with sheaves of notes and files and miscellaneous sheets of paper may look "untidy" yet may in fact be an ordered and meaningful arrangement of material to its owner. The impulse to tidy away tokens of human habitation that may lie around a room - books, pipes, sewing materials, a spectacle case - can only be a negative perhaps almost an unhealthy instinct. But to see our drive, our lovely grove, transformed from a litter of fallen leaves and twigs and debris into a broad clear expanse over which the trees arch and interlace is for me emancipating, and worth an hour's work every day for a week to obtain. Seemingly a certain comeliness in my surroundings is temperamentally necessary to me and the rigid control of this impulse would defeat its own end - space cluttered by objects is misery; significantly occupied, delight.

At the same time it is crucial that the appearance of things be subordinated to real values. True that on the rare and often tiresome occasions when I have had to choose new furniture, hangings or carpets I have certainly given much time and careful thought to my selection. But once in place fulfilling their purpose without fuss or ostentation, pleasing to the eye because in harmony one with another, then I am always content to leave things alone, satisfied to cherish them unaltered for as long as they will last - for a score and more of years in many instances. And although I respond with intense delight to the beauty of things made with hands I have never desired to become a collector or to make a study of connoisseurship. Certainly we do possess some objects that are by any standard beautiful but, apart from the pictures, these our few treasures consist in old pieces of family silver and furniture, and gifts from generous friends, these last representative of the art of at least a dozen countries. We lost many books when our Exeter house was destroyed and they are probably our most valued possessions. On the whole I hope I have succeeded in getting my priorities right. It may be pleasing when a guest exclaims: "What a beautiful room!" yet I feel more deeply satisfied when a friend says: "I always feel at peace here - I relax the moment I come inside and sit down." And should FG suggest a drive, if I am invited to pay a visit or go for a walk, if unexpected friends drop in, then can there be any question of what is my joyful priority? When all is said and done it is partly to pleasure family and friends that we have a home in the first place.

Nowadays domestic help has become very difficult to obtain and my resident full-timers having been reduced to "dailies" on six mornings a week, these were slowly whittled down to twice-weekly visits until now I have learned how to cope single-handed, my "sabbatical" long over. When I came to full-time domesticity I had some re-thinking to do though at first, because I had come to it so late in married life, the novelty was stimulating, and I even preened myself that I was as successful single-handed as with help. This did not last long. Presently I was shocked and astonished to find the Lee inheritance derived from mother beginning to emerge - urgent haste to complete tasks quickly, unnecessary excitement over the doing of them, brief elation followed by exhaustion on completion - for many I know the driving force of their days, but for me devouring, devastating, distasteful. From the enthusiastic my attitude turned to the critical: domesticity, I discovered, is essentially a lonely way of life; many tasks are drearily repetitive and when finished for one day must be done again on the morrow for all the foreseeable future, while their actual performance rarely requires the active use of intelligence; true you do know whether you have succeeded or not, in which respect manual labour certainly has the edge over creative work; but the continual dealing with details one at a time can make for a fragmentary state of mind. Jane Carlyle once adjured a friend (in a letter, I think) to take courage and determination to lock herself up *in a cupboard* if need be, in order not to be eaten up by little things which, by being infinite and of daily occurrence, may by their very multiplicity tether as strongly as the minute threads of the Lilliputians held Gulliver.

These were perhaps real problems but surely not insoluble for one in my situation? My mother, and for that matter Jane Carlyle too, had lived in large Victorian houses on three floors and in my mother's case with four large cellars as well; for all heating and cooking they depended on coal; they lived close to the pollution of nineteenth century industry; their furniture was heavy and sometimes ornate; their essential tools, dusters, brushes and brooms, often raised as much dust as they removed; my mother's household consisted of my father, grandmother, herself, four children, and a resident servant, while poor Jane Carlyle had to cope with the no less incessant and often grossly unreasonable demands of husband Thomas; every day their servants carried hods of coal up flights of stone stairs to kitchen and living rooms, chapped their hands scouring steps and scrubbing floors, or washed, starched and ironed mounds of linen every week. My mother's temperamental urge to get things done, her almost violent obedience to her favourite precept, "whatever thy hand findeth to do, do it with all thy might", were surely responses to her demanding situation as also was her routine: every single room in the house "turned out" in rotation once a week - my German "au pair" told me this was still quite common in her country forty years later; and in addition there was the dreadful annual ritual of "Spring-cleaning". There was no need whatsoever that I should follow her precept or example; our eight rooms are on two level floors; our environment is clean and our equipment adequate; our furnishings and possessions are fewer and far less elaborate, and finally we are a mere two adults who prefer and enjoy simplicity in our way of life. I discovered that my first over-exertions had been a false start confirming my belief that for me all haste is of the devil. I have to admit that sometimes I succumb to days of effort and of hurry but I never enjoy them as I am sure my mother and all members of her family always did; and generally feel guilty and ashamed when through my own fault I have made them necessary. Quite early on I discovered that choice of priorities - organisation - is the most efficient use of time just as order is the most efficient use of space and, most important of all, that the combination of the two gives freedom.

The excessive curtailment of their freedom by their taskings has long been the grievance of gifted married women; inevitably we know more about the writers' problems than those of frustrated scientists, painters, doctors, musicians and architects (to name only a few) because they have so frequently depicted the situation in their works; few have shown women wholly satisfied with a domestic role. If a delightful woman like Jane Carlyle while recognising her husband's genius yet sometimes felt herself tied down to the very earth so also was George Eliot's admired Dorothea tied to the pretensions of her hollow husband Casaubon; Dorothy Richardson spoke of the "tethered look" of servants, Virginia Woolf of the need for "a room of one's own". Yet to abdicate from their responsibilities may harm both women themselves and their vocation. An unusually happy and well-adjusted writer like Elizabeth Gaskell seems very certain: "Woman cannot drop the domestic charge devolving upon her as an individual for the expression of the finest talents that were ever bestowed", and though she probably never had menial tasks to perform one feels that she would have performed them, and with good grace, at need. Yet Charlotte Brontë, after paying her a visit, wrote asking her the searching question whether she did not sometimes desire to be "her own woman", and Mrs Gaskell, in a rare moment of self-examination, wondered which of "my many '*me*'s" was the real one. On the dust cover of a first novel the publisher speaks of the writer's "illumined moments throughout the busy day" and I imagine that such are the foundations of many works written by women, especially of critical studies in literature or biography which can be taken up or set down as time and opportunity occur; lyrical poetry can also be so conceived and brought to birth. But for long imaginative works a vista of free time indefinitely extended is much to be desired so that the whole self can be brought into play, and it is sad to recall Helen Waddell's long struggle to write the works she had planned to follow her first masterpieces ending in non-achievement once she had left the quiet isolation of her flat for the world of "chores and interruptions".

Such instances scarcely apply to contemporary women; in Western democratic societies there is less cause to complain or to make domesticity an excuse for failure to attempt in other fields of endeavour. We should also perhaps remind ourselves that gifted men have frequently been forced to labour at uncongenial work for years, earning a living until they could give themselves full time to their real vocation. One remembers Berlioz laying aside a theme for a symphony because family responsibilities compelled him to write his regular feuilletons on the works of other inferior composers, or T S Eliot's difficult beginnings. All the same a man has the advantage that he works less frequently in isolation and when his day's work is done he can generally leave it behind, while in addition he is paid for his labour while domesticity is taken for granted, its value seemingly unrecognised. Perhaps here is one reason why many wives and mothers go out to work for money wage. Making the important proviso that I speak as a woman living in easy circumstances in what we call the Western world, I think it may be a mistake to imagine that women without "outside work" are necessarily thwarted and unhappy; surely to devise for oneself and household a way of life that is *agreeable* is not an unworthy objective, and it is no trivial matter to have created the whole texture of daily living for the family group. It is true that now "domestic service" is a thing of the past and in spite of modern improvements, some actual drudgery is unavoidable, but in what is called creative work there is drudgery too: the most glamorous actress must learn her lines, the writer toil tediously over proofs, the eminent scientist spend long patient years accumulating material evidence. Perhaps instead of complaining that the daily round is a waste of the intelligence we might use our brains to improve our lot, for it is a real art to combine efficiency with a proper distancing of the self, to define objectives and choose priorities, to order essential repetitive work so that it demands the minimum of time and attention. It is not a drudgery but an art to make efficiency a means not an end, for while the greatest threat to liberty for the inefficient is an accumulation of tasks undone then for the over-efficient it certainly is engrossment, for absorption is never control and without it, whether over or under organised, a woman will be dominated and never really be free.

As for the demands made by a family much depends on circumstances and for parents isolated high up in a block of flats with restricted space indoors and the nearest outside - if any - a long way off, then the only solution may be to pack the little ones off to nursery school every morning. With them, as for those mothers whom economic necessity sends out to work at often dull and monotonous jobs for the sake of the pay packet I can only commiserate, since the few years of her life that infant care absorbs may be among the most enjoyable and rewarding a woman will ever know, a fulfilment irreplaceable in later years. Happily and increasingly, having devoted themselves full-time to their children's infancy many successful career women today proceed to combine excellence as wives and mothers with productive work in many skills and professions, after their children have achieved independence.

One question remains - if freedom be the goal how will a woman use it when she has attained it? Is economic independence in itself sufficient? I suspect that domesticity is sometimes the scapegoat for other and more basic problems of women and society at large.

To each her own solution. It was largely by trial and error that I discovered mine during the years of single-handedness, giving my problems thought in the beginning in order that subsequently I might not have to think about them at all. But now that FG has retired from work in London I am no longer alone and to our mutual benefit he assists me indoors as well as relieving me of hours of work that devolved on me when he was only a weekend gardener; especially, every morning in his striped butcher's apron, he takes over control of the kitchen sink - breakfast-dishes and often the preparation of vegetables; he doesn't regard this as a tiresome chore but as a daily necessity like cleaning his teeth or brushing his hair every day; with typical efficiency he has devised his own best ways and means so that he appears to enjoy these sessions and certainly would resent any suggestions or offers of help from me; thankfully I leave him alone and work at what I call my "daily monotonies", the result being that by 10.30 every morning - and we still find it extraordinary that almost invariably it is 10.30 almost to the minute - we are free to plan the rest of our day. Even although more tasks will certainly remain they will be immeasurably easier to do because performed against a background of order.

CHAPTER EIGHTEEN

Vignettes, and Sketch for a Portrait

Although life with the boys had never been solitary because we always had a small circle of friends and many acquaintances yet for most of their years I had never sought or indeed felt the need to discover for myself any relationship which they could not also share in and enjoy. Maybe this had been limiting but it had never seemed a deprivation during that time of rich full living. It was not until after Richard's death that I knew real solitude remote from life's general flow, not perversely but unwillingly withdrawn into my private eddy of misery and ineptitude. Once this phase was over I discovered an old source of enlargement as I began to meet my fellows once again on a contemporary footing.

This began as I travelled with FG on his professional assignments; his evenings were usually free and we often spent them quietly with his colleagues - employers, trade union officials, welfare and educational specialists - relaxing together after their long day. For most people this would appear very natural, very ordinary, but for me at that juncture it was a very special thing so to meet and talk with my fellows simply taken for granted as flowing in the current with the stream. With them I was never made to feel outside and ignorant of their concerns though of course I was both, and this profited me as much as did their society, and for many of them over the years I grew to feel respect and admiration.

Some occasions were less decorous - for example the big parties frequently arranged at the end of "weekend schools" which as FG were said were valuable for those whose contact was mainly by letter or long distance telephone, and for the guest lecturers who could now meet their students convivially and forget officialdom. Of individual occasions I can today recall nothing at all, but galleries of human likenesses remain vividly clear: a jolly little person almost bursting out of her skin-tight green satin is happily running amok punching ribs and slapping shoulders; a tall ascetic figure looks on from deep-set dark eyes in a pale face, pince-nez folded glasses hanging from a broad black ribband; a bald pink-pated old gentleman with smooth round cheek like a baby, who, also like a baby, is completely toothless, sits telling outrageous stories to a large circle of listeners; a gaunt energetic woman with enormous hooked nose, nostrils flaring like a horse, waves her monocle in one hand and raises the other clenched as she shouts that she wishes she had been born a man. Of course it was quite impossible - and anyway not the purpose of the gathering - to make intimate contact with individuals; from heat, noise and blue atmosphere, from meeting so many strangers fragmentarily for desultory talk, I would usually emerge more than ever rejoicing in the infinite variety of humankind but glad of the relief of the cool and quiet dark to aching throat and smarting eyes and thankful that we should travel home on the morrow.

Back home in the village I continued to enjoy my freedom to come and go seeing people often as pictures of themselves - it may be remembered that it was of Renoir that I thought when I recorded that summer group having tea under the apple tree - and sharing with them our home and garden. One of my first visitors was a toddler who came with a poodle dog to play outside while FG and his father talked indoors. The little boys fills his toy barrow with windfall apples and small dry pears, and I receive posies of grubby daisies pulled up almost stalkless by this tiny person in flowered dungarees - he tilts his head right back to look at me, one hand in a minute pocket, rounded elbows, downy nape. For an hour there is shouting and the sound of trundling wheels and pattering feet. Meanwhile the dog is less happily employed; after much scuffling he discovers a sleeping cat and the two of them have words after which I give him a bowl of water and he digs a small hole in the lawn by which he sleeps until time to go home. Indoors the little boy and FG play with toy cars, and we give him a miniature wooden pipe to blow bubbles with when he is older; presently the two of them sit side by side, sententious and serious, both "smoking" as they look at a picture book. After two hours of tireless activity he grows quiet and his father decides to go; the child's sigh is eloquent as he puts his arms into the sleeves of his jacket.

Another afternoon I visit old Mr H whose housekeeper takes me first into her kitchen where she is knitting while baking a cake, and here I'm reminded of my Caldecott picture books by the old teapots and jugs and platters ranged along the big dresser, the bright brass on the mantelshelf, the small dog curled up on the rug beside a dozing cat, the old-fashioned grate with its glowing coals, the caged birds twittering and clicking with their beaks at their tiny ladders and wheels. She looks into the oven - delicious the smell that comes forth - closes the door gently and takes the kettle to the tap. "I'll be making some tea. You remember your poor little cat, your first one, the one that died? He was a real friend to our Ginger - now did you ever hear of two animals that'd rub noses when they'd be meeting in the alley?" (Most certainly I have not.) She takes me upstairs to the study where old Mr H tells her to *keep* her tea, and pours sherry for me instead. We sit for an hour beside a small log fire, the cat who has followed me pushing his needle-sharp claws voluptuously in and out of my lap. Big chintz-covered chairs, Persian rugs on the floor, old prints on the walls, fire, wine and talk - this isn't Caldecott, certainly not Renoir, but rather a painting by a Flemish Old Master - soberly rich and mellow, benign.

On impulse one day I boarded a bus at the Green and almost as a painter might I studied fellow passengers. A small light old man with eager face was talking very fast, using his hands enthusiastically, to a man with broad coarse head on a thick neck who, replied with such slow deliberation that he actually held open his mouth - silently displaying a thin tongue lying flat and close inside - before he decided to utter a word. A baby's golden pate and bright eyes lit up the cowl of his hooded anorak and when he laughed he stretched his arms and spread out starfish hands. Reading a book sat a man with youthful face under silver hair, perhaps looking younger than his age with his clear skin and open expression; a line finely etched either side of his mouth suggested discrimination and sensitivity. As in my childhood I observed and speculated about almost everyone that I saw - not always correctly as I sometimes found out. I imagined that an elderly shop assistant with frizzy dyed hair and rouged cheekbones on her powder-pale face must lead a dull and lonely life cooped up with arid millinery perched on wooden stands all day. Not a bit of it. "I'm the next youngest of my father's twenty-two children and all of one mother too!" (So she said, and I supposed that with some twins it might even be possible: Edward Lear was one of twenty-one children.) "And she reared us everyone. We see one another every week though I couldn't tell you how many nieces and nephews I've got now; and of course some of *them* have started families on their own account." She was as proud and happy as if she had herself propagated them all; she packed my cluster of pink silk rosebuds in layers of white tissue talking all the time.

For a period I visited the fortnightly shows of the Royal Horticultural Society, FG having given me a subscription. I was just as much concerned over the people as the plants and often sat on the raised platform at the end of the hall to watch the moving crowds. The majority in the morning were women and most of them "ordinary" like myself - but not at all. Sometimes lady gardeners could be very eccentric indeed. Surely only here could be seen the last ankle-length "dust-coats" as worn by Edwardian motorists. Many wore very strange head-gear: here is a hat like a large inverted basket; here is one "like an explosion" as I once heard Ruth Pitter say; here a small felt basin presses improbable woollen curls over eyes and nose low down as those of a bull calf. Beside me on the platform there comes to sit a weary woman with a pale almost yellow face whose smile as I make room for her makes her momentarily beautiful. She was in London mainly to visit house agents and newly returned from Calcutta where her husband, a surgeon, had died literally on the eve of his retirement. She had two married children in England but India had become home for her - "We used to be called Anglo-Indians, you know." Later I share my lunch table with a voluble small woman wearing almost mauve hair over a raddled rouged face of flaccid jowls and pendulous chins; I am the observed and not the observer as her sharp eyes look me over and she gives me a gap-toothed very knowing grin.

All this was human contact on a superficial and impersonal level and even with our friendly neighbours all remained undemanding, easy-going, at the most a sharing of congenial activity with feelings at a minimum, indeed FG and I sought one another at this time mainly on the basis of familiar comradeship. But it is perhaps a mistake to suppose that the exchange of deep intimacies is a necessary part of friendship, doing things for and with one another may be enough. For example the strong and mutual affection that bound FG and Richard together had been expressed in practicalities undertaken together; theirs was a happy temperamental affinity with nothing deeply emotional about it whereby a most successful relationship had developed between them without either of them seeming aware that it existed and maybe all the better on that account.

Of course I did not at this time neglect the intimate and valued friends that remained from our past and not only those who lived near at hand; although three lived hundreds and one lived thousands of miles away I held on to them all tenaciously.

Every friendship is a unique two-way reciprocity - just as I love one for grace of living, another for his courage and gift of wry humour, one for benevolence not as sentiment but in daily practice, another for singleness of mind and dedicated purpose, with some discovering the pleasure of agreement with others the stimulus of dissent - so each friend calls forth a different response according to the several demands of each relationship. Friendship is therefore a cause of growth and the one I am about to describe brought a robust astringency to bear on some of my most cherished values thus modifying some and paradoxically strengthening others; I like to hope that I benefited her also.

Nevertheless three years after Richard's death I met DC and our relationship lasted over fourteen years, not based on similarity of mind nor yet on unusual affection, but simply on our being helpful and useful one to another as we brought our very different intelligences to bear on the dissimilar experiences and problems of our lives.

We met by fortunate chance neither knowing the other's circumstances or story. She was not a large woman yet seemed so since she was somewhat ponderous and deliberate in manner and movement. Apart from liking her pleasant low voice - she was a Scot from Perth - I thought her at first meeting somewhat hard and severe: her lips were close, her eyes bespectacled, her hair the pepper-and-salt of auburn turning grey, she seemed abrupt and somewhat cold. Yet I warmed towards her and suggested another meeting. Very soon she had revealed her latent geniality, the eyes behind the spectacles were bright with friendliness, her features in profile delicate almost tender, and her seeming hardness the effect of controlled suffering caused by the recent death of her husband a mere three months before. She was less than a year my senior though somehow I always felt her to be much older and she was by no means a forbidding woman but simply very sad and lonely. At this time she found her lot unacceptable; her pleasant anticipations of her husband's retirement had suddenly been disappointed, and she sometimes felt that this should not have happened, that perhaps if the doctors had investigated more thoroughly in the beginning they might have taken earlier steps to deal with her husband's condition; her house and garden were inconveniently large; her new responsibilities were too heavy; and her plans for the future seemed to be, as I felt, made the more hard to devise by the fact that she was left so comfortably off that she could almost do as she liked. She had three grown sons, two already launched in successful careers, the youngest living with her at home while researching for a doctorate in science. Of course to have successfully reared her family was no consolation for her present loss but although I could accept this as so I yet found it hard to believe, since to have brought up even one son, let alone three, would have meant so much to ourselves.

278

So it was harder still to believe that she actually envied me - my early interests and enthusiasms, the people I had met, my travels here and abroad, and, most important of all, that I still had FG. More than once she declared "I have had a *nar-row* life," speaking as though it were all over and done with although she was still in her fifties. The difference between us was that I felt that my life had been challenging, galvanic and rewarding while she thought hers had been drab, monotonous and austere. In spite of its demands I seemed to have valued my living, hers she had merely endured - or so she seemed to think then.

Nevertheless I thought that understanding and acceptance would come to her sooner than had been the case with me and time proved me to be right. She was enduring deep sorrow rather than wild grief and for a long while lived in its shadow - when I called she would often be sitting quietly patient at her fireside, if I glanced her way as we watched a television programme I would see the sadness on her attentive face, heard it when she quietly remarked that "his father would have been very proud of him", when her son achieved his doctorate. But she was immensely reasonable, refusing to be dominated by her feelings in a way I could never have emulated. Once she quoted to me Bernard Shaw's "the ability to live alone is worth attaining at the price of much sorrowful solitude" and from the very beginning she had brought her tough practical intelligence into play, never lying fallow or wholly submissive. Her beautiful house and garden were by no means all-engrossing, and systematically she began to use London; she joined study groups and attended lectures, joined the Fabian and other societies (she was an LSE graduate), visited exhibitions, theatres and opera; encouraged to travel, after two journeys to the Near East she joined the Hellenic Travellers' Association and enjoyed its London meetings.

In course of time she acquired three daughters-in-law, then grandsons and granddaughters; she paid them long visits travelling by sea to the Argentine, by air to the United States; especially enlarging to her was the third son's marriage to a young Hungarian widow with one small daughter, and this not merely through visits to Holland and Hungary.

When her parents were travelling the little "step-granddaughter" sometimes lived with DC for months at a time, attending a local school and taking music lessons. She was then an unobtrusive almost a demure little girl - except at the piano, when she displayed an almost startling boldness and assurance, inheriting her gift from a continental grandmother, a professional violinist. At such times it was hard to remember that she was a ten-year old who still played with her dolls. DC showed me the gay and pretty room she had contrived for her, almost like a folk tale illustration with its brilliant Hungarian rugs and hangings, the peasant shawls, the toys of painted wood, and puppets dangling on their strings. All DC's mellow kindness now came into play; she enjoyed expecting the child home to tea after school, taking her to plays and concerts, planning a day's shopping or a trip to see the sights of London.

Beyond all doubt the company of this gifted schoolgirl and her loving care of her hastened DC's emergence from the rigidity of lonely endurance into a life of flexibility and sharing. For grief can be very self-centred, enclosing its victim within a stony fortress with only a few narrow chinks in the walls thus limiting what might be healing perceptions from outside. It is then that even brief meltings of barriers may ease and however trivial they are not to be despised. I remember Kaye, stricken by loss of her son in the *Hood* disaster, somehow being released from hours of speechlessness after watching an old woman wash an apple at a tap. I remember myself returning from a wintry walk my mind seeming stiffened into a rigidity of dejection, just noticing as I came indoors the new kitten sitting up sleepily in his basket. He stepped out and followed me about until eventually I picked him up on to my lap and we sat together in front of the fire. Presently as I sat stroking and caressing the little creature my hard self-engrossment melted away into a warm protective feeling of tenderness, and I was eased as much by this small waif of a kitten as Kaye had been by the simplicity and beauty of the act that she had regarded so intently. One might almost see the story of Coleridge's Mariner as a myth which symbolises the danger of alienation from the living world outside the self (the killing of the albatross) and the joy of redemption through love of the creatures in that world of whom for so long he had been oblivious. Only when he had stepped outside the circle of his own private despairs had he found release and forgiveness and could return to life among his fellowmen.

For DC things eventually fell into place. When her granddaughter had begun to study at the Royal College of Music she decided to settle at least for awhile in New Zealand whence she has travelled further in Asia and Australia, her life not "narrow" any more. Her re-integration, her so rational adjustments and re-buildings had been wholly admirable and her success beautiful to witness.

One January morning I recorded in my notebook the previous long evening spent in her company:

> "At one o'clock yesterday afternoon the sun shone over the snow-muffled garden, water dripped from the white trees, every twig glittered. Yet the birds remained silent, knowing perhaps that it would freeze again at night. I shuffled out in my snow boots to try for a photograph but after one exposure the shutter stuck.

> "At half past four I set about interlining a silk curtain with flannelette hoping to make the big room cosier - FG being in South Wales for the night I thought to get it finished since I could have an easy meal on a tray.

> "The front door bell - there stood DC looking tired, cold and, as so often, sad. How gladly I brought her in, set her in the big chair, made her take off her boots and borrow my warmed slippers, threw more logs on the fire which blazed up gloriously, carried in fresh tea, and while we drank it saw her face soften, her sorrow relax. Persuaded her to spend the evening here and together we planned the time; presently she settled down with my sewing box and the curtain alone with the cat by the fire and I clattered away cooking in the kitchen. The cold mutton I had thought good enough for myself I now turned into a fine hot curry; I opened one of my jars of home-preserved tomato juice, another of bottled raspberries, and whipped some cream.

"With the sewing finished and folded away we presently sat down to eat together, not silently reading each alone in her own house but with talk adding zest to the food. With curtains drawn close and lights turned down presently we drew up armchairs to drink our coffee by the fire; almost at once DC began to ply me with questions but was interrupted by a vigorous knocking at the back door.

"To my astonishment young John and Gillian had tramped through the snow to return a little oak box I had loaned her. We stood exclaiming in the kitchen while they scraped their shoes and stamped their feet, breath steaming, eyes sparkling in their cold red faces, and then we all trooped back to the fire. Their marriage is twelve days off and they showered their joy all over us, tried to tell us some of their plans, tumbling over one another's words, casting and catching one another's quick glances, the while I gave them hot coffee and we all shared the peppermint creams they had brought.

"When they had gone it seemed very quiet, and DC began again. Apparently she still feels herself to be entirely alone completely thrown on her own resources, and I could only tell her - though she exaggerated their number - that my having friends in my difficult times hadn't helped much, and ultimately I had been thrown on my own resources too. For example, advice to brighten my cheeks with rouge and believe in God had fallen on sterile ground, another's declaration that Richard 'would be very, very angry' if he could know of my grief had seemed merely outrageous; the solace 'you still have one another' (- just as my pointing out to DC that she still had three sons -) had seemed irrelevant, even FG's stoical silence had for awhile seemed almost alien; and my own devisings of activity had merely distracted, perhaps actually hindered understanding. Last evening DC was, as usually, dignified, gentle, deliberate, but comfort and companionship had melted her reserve and she quite forgot to withdraw, to harden herself in order not to be bruised by exposure; as we sat side by side I thought of Charlotte Brontë and her friend Ellen Nussey, their nights of friendly talk, 'with feet on the fender at hair-curling time', a hundred years before.

"Presently she referred to one of my comments: 'Why should you feel dissatisfied with yourself? What do you want, really want to do? What would you have different?'

"'It's not what I want to do, but to be. In the past I seemed to be my best self, now only my inferior faculties seem brought into play. I suppose I'd like to put myself to better use, to have more tingle in my living; I am afraid of drifting, quietly running to seed.'"

"'Do we ask too much? Expect too much? Perhaps we should cease to desire so much more than we actually have. Browning said, that "life the mere living" could be more than enough.'

"'Your mean that dissatisfaction is bad if it cannot in the nature of things be satisfied?'

"'I mean that it is common sense to be prepared for disappointment and of course to be glad when we find something better. You should not repine if your present life is not up to old standards, but be thankful for what you have known.'

"'Certainly,' I said slowly, 'certainly I agree that the past cannot be again, that it is futile to spend oneself searching and feel foiled when one cannot succeed. But should we be satisfied to lose its quality?'

"'If we do not like our present then the only thing to do is to put up with it. It is very important not to be sensitive - I mean perhaps not over-sensitive. Some things are best taken quite superficially, at their face value merely.'

"Silently I remembered those last weeks with Philip, admitted to myself that never since had I lived such excellence, that perhaps I was no longer capable of it. For a forlorn instant it seemed that very quietly an open door had closed.

"Later I took her home. She was, though surely far less nervous in temperament than I am, reluctant to walk back alone to her empty house, and it was pleasant to see her glowing red stove and the cat running with tail aloft to greet her in the hall.

"It was long after midnight with the profound silence of hard frost on snow, white above, below, around, and a cold thin moon. In our drive the cydonia had fallen away from the wall and lay prostrate, birches, ash trees, oaks and cherries all upheld their burden, and with most joyful perception I saw that each yet preserved its individual character, the oaks like coral, the birches silver lace. And suddenly I found myself exultant, burning in the icy world. I might never be able in any medium to express the glory that I had found in living but at least I had once found life to be glorious even if, as I had been admonished, those days were past and 'mere' living, a tepid adjective, must their place. But I did not believe this as I stood there motionless, inarticulate with wonder. Despite DC's quiet scepticism I knew that I should continue as before to await revealments like this one in the snowy drive, that the upsurge of response to the living world remained as intense as when delight was shared with two lost sources of joy, or as when in childhood I had stood transfixed at sight of a glittering Christmas tree."

CHAPTER NINETEEN

Of Records and Of Reckonings

Having completed the long journal entry I read over the scribbled pages and then took the notebook upstairs to its place beside my bed and knew that I had discovered the causes of self-dissatisfaction. I had much enjoyed my sabbatical, it had been a long fallow time when I had easefully sat back on my heels letting the quiet years pass, and if reach often exceeded grasp it had seemed safe then to defer until tomorrow what was uncompleted today so I allowed myself to be beguiled, immersing myself gladly; if it seemed sometimes that I might be taking too much for granted I brushed the feeling aside fearing to disturb the mood of contentment - why stir up the mud at the bottom when the stream shone bright in the sunshine?

A nudge, a jolt to complacency had already been administered - not fully apprehended at the time though now well understood - by a passage in *War and Peace* which I was absorbedly re-reading; I had been disturbed by the description of Pierre's state of mind some years after his return from abroad, when "he no longer meditated on the ideas which the calm sky of Austerlitz had first brought to his soul; dared not glance at the distant horizons of which he had a glimpse and which had looked so bright in their infinitude. The commonplace interests of daily life now absorbed him." He sometimes pondered on his present way of life, vaguely uneasy, saying he would think it out by and by, "which by and by never came," added Tolstoy; nevertheless Pierre like me was afraid of quietly running to seed, and finding "life was mere living" emphatically not enough.

A task long deferred had increasingly weighed on my mind and I knew perfectly well where it lay awaiting my will. So now I crossed the landing and went into the boxroom. On the floor files and cardboard boxes contained lecture notes, prompt copies, cuttings, annotations; the big steamer trunk was stacked - all the drawers on one side, all the hanging space on the other - with more accumulations of papers and documents rescued after the air-raid of 1942; a suitcase was crammed with letters written to FG during the years of our war time separation; my journals dating back to 1930 were tied up together in a tall pile and with curiosity I untied the string and began to look them over. Among the sparse entries made while visiting Yorkshire after Philip's death I found two excerpts copied from my father's Boswell. One was from the letter written by Johnson to his friend Elphinstone to console him for the death of his mother (1750) in which he had spoken of the future "when time shall remove her yet further from you, and your grief shall be matured to veneration". The second was dated 1758:

> "Let us endeavour to see things as they are, and then enquire whether we ought to complain. Whether to see life as it is will give us much consolation I know not; but the consolation which is drawn from truth, if any there be, is solid and durable."

I thought over these words for awhile. Well - I suppose my journals had at least recorded an endeavour to "see things as they are" without evading any of the ways whereby the truth struck home, but doubted that I had thereby received consolation - "if any there be", for Johnson had quite rightly so qualified his statement. Our sons' deprivation, the sense of wastage and parental loss remained the same. At the most maybe my private ponderings, so fumbling and confused, had helped me to see our story with some sense of proportion, to realise that work remained to be done and lives to be usefully lived. Words copied into a notebook many years before now struck

286

me with great force, the "maturing" of grief was a pregnant expression which now I understand but which meant little to me then, and across the centuries Johnson's phrase had meaning; I laid down the book with a sigh and turned to Richard's journals standing in a pile beside my own.

He had been a little boy when they began, a young man when they ended, brief records of his day-to-day life from his tenth up to his twentieth year, every entry dated, with perhaps half a dozen brief gaps in continuity, and I remembered well the October evening of the last entry "...the poplars gold, the prunus bronze and full of leaf, the half moon rising in a clearing sky..." I picked up an earlier volume and read more. Apparently he had enjoyed *Portrait of Greece* by Lord Kinross; had found a Dvorak symphony "glorious"; he described the Sweep with "his ruddy cheeks under the grime, his bristling moustache hung with frosty drops. He put Mummy's half-crown into his pocket and the banknote under his cap on the top of his head". Also an elderly acquaintance: "She looked so *owlish* with her hooky nose and serious face and eyes magnified behind her glasses; I wanted to laugh out loud as I registered her speckled brown and cream tweed coat with her little short legs below."

I closed the books then looked around at the confused accumulation of many years despairfully realising how long a time it would take to sort and reduce all to order - and almost in the same moment I made up my mind to it. I began then and there and for a month worked upstairs every day, at the end of which time the confusion seemed worse than ever: an ancient divan bed, a small bureau, an old card table, the wide flat surface of the steamer trunk and then the floor lay smothered under the contents of files, boxes, suitcases, only very roughly sorted out. Once or twice I panicked and left it for a while always locking the door before I went down. I don't to this day know for certain why I regarded my labours as so intensely private, that not even to FG did I divulge how I spent my spare time over the next months and years - perhaps obscurely I felt everyone's reaction would be "Get rid of it, throw it all out." For myself I never thought of such a solution, knew time and patience would achieve results so worked away, slow, slow, slow, sorting, filing and discarding...

The letters stored so long ago in the suitcase were my first concern. FG had kept my twice-weekly screeds sent to him'during his six year wartime absence in London, each in its original envelope which made dating simple; I also discovered correspondence relating to the children's education and general progress, copies of reports to R E Roper and others, all hand-written, with replies attached; there was, of course, much of no value or interest whatsoever. Eventually I filed away about a thousand letters approximately in chronological order, firmly resisting the temptation to read them all first, many of them smelling still of the rubble and plaster of shattered Maryfield. I did not concern myself at this time with the journals but stacked them up neatly in the corner whence they had come; it was equally easy to cope with the yellowing sheaves of *Time and Tide*, *New Statesman*, and so on, by ruthless despatching them in bundles for paper salvage. Book reviews, newspaper cuttings, reading lists, went into one of the empty cases to be sorted through later. Last of all I examined the many bits and pieces that privately I came to call "Abortions" (appropriately as I think now). Seemingly in the unsettled unleisured years after leaving Exeter I had scribbled down brief notes recording fugitive reactions to experience on whatever writing material was nearest to hand; I was dumbfounded at their number and equally at my having somehow managed to carry them safely through half a dozen places of sojourn before depositing them in their present files and folders where they had lain for at least ten years. I read them all and destroyed most, sending out week by week my little pile of torn notations; this wasn't easy for what was now a suffocating encumbrance had once been part of my life. Much I valued greatly; when I discovered Philip's Gidleigh record of "Richard's Sayings and Doings", even old pocket diaries, they were treasure trove and after copying out brief abstracts it was a real if foolish regret to consign them to the dustbin.

My real difficulties began when I tried to embody the relevant letters, notebooks and journals into one consecutive narrative that should cover the years in Devon 1930-1946. But a private objective wasn't really compatible with my outer life; hence four years elapsed before all was tidied away and I had made my chronological record - that inordinately included everything -

in six large "duplicate" books, each two hundred pages. Not a conscious evasion, this was in fact a substitute for what I might have attempted with more single-mindedness for I had merely tidied into a sequence, I had not organised my material. This must have been why the beautifully clear boxroom and my six notebooks gave me so little pleasure, indeed I felt almost miserable. Maybe I had satisfied an innate love of order and perhaps the discipline of work had been valuable; I had used or destroyed half a lifetime's lumber so that I certainly felt myself less cluttered and encumbered, and at the very least a duty laid upon myself had been wrought to its conclusion.

Before the completion of my boxroom tasking I had embarked on another project which had a more positive result - again after a long endeavour. For some while, since unable in any other way to account for it, I had privately ascribed our sons' inexplicable affliction as perhaps due to a gross overdose of radiation that I had suffered as a small child at a time (1911) when X-rays were still in the experimental stage; the burns had been severe enough to keep me home from school for the best part of a year. After reading a letter in the press I wrote to a scientist in the United Kingdom Atomic Energy Authority, who not only replied at some length but also took the trouble to discuss my letter with two of his medical colleagues. They agreed that it was "possible that exposure of a small girl to a large dose of X-rays could cause a mutation which could result in her sons developing muscular dystrophy." But the main purport of his letter was that the risk of such a mutation was "not likely to be higher than one in 40,000 and ten times more likely to be due to other causes"; "although of course this case could be *the one* in 40,000, we shall never know."

They suggested some factor in the children's maternal heredity and I therefore determined to trace the life history of the six generations already descended from their great-great-grandparents on my side of the family - not in order to solve our individual problem which nothing now could qualify but to allay a private anxiety for the many children of the sixth generation and their possible descendants.

This was possibly an ambitious but not an impossible undertaking; my mother had always been eager to impart all she knew of her forebears and long before realising its possible relevance I had accumulated before her death a sheaf of notes and letters most useful to me now. I began by making contact with all her surviving first cousins, all grandchildren of the progenitors from whom I had decided to start. Having first written I visited the two eldest in Liverpool, complete strangers to me, both octogenarian sons of my great-uncle Dick whom I vaguely remembered; one could remember his grandparents, and since his elder daughter, his grandson and his infant great-granddaughter were all present, on that afternoon I had news of six generations simultaneously. However most of my contacts were by letter, and since in those days I couldn't use a typewriter even with two fingers as now, I had to hand-copy the letters of a considerable correspondence by no means confined to Great Britain. All my informants showed great interest in my project without exception - fortunately, for without their wonderful co-operation I should have worked in vain; I was careful never to divulge the real reason for my interest, and to most of them I was in the beginning a complete stranger who had written to them out of the blue.

By cousinship I presently found myself related among many others to an overseas hydraulic engineer with an annual budget running into millions, to the owner of a tiny hardware shop who himself worked behind the counter, to the Countess of Belmore whose eighteenth century seat is a Palladian masterpiece, to a consultant paediatrician, to an artist potter married to a successful barrister, to the founder of a ballet school, to the director of an art gallery, to teachers, naturalists, musicians; the majority of my correspondents being quite unaware of the others' existence.

It is pleasant to add that regular correspondence with some of my contemporary relatives has grown out of this work and that a warm personal regard has sprung up between FG and myself and four or five who visit Europe fairly regularly from Australia and Japan.

In the end I had completed a long or rather wide scroll (fifteen feet) which was rolled on two wooden cylinders and contained some three hundred names; there were no blank spaces indicating omissions, which was highly important because collaterals have great significance in this form of hereditary transmission. Excepting for premature death in warfare, two in early infancy and an officer cadet who had died after a brief but singularly healthy life (as I knew from close childhood ties with his family) during the 1918 pandemic, all males had grown up into normal manhood most of them marrying and having normal families of their turn. These included my own brother's two sons and two daughters and his nine grandchildren of both sexes. Most important of all, all married women had produced normal children of both sexes who had themselves, in their turn, propagated normally. I found these findings baffling and reported them to three world authorities all known for their researches in this field, and asked for their comments.

All agreed that Duchenne dystrophy is invariably inherited through a mutation in the female ancestry and each separately arrived at the same conclusion. Since I, the mother of two afflicted children, was unlikely to have suffered the mutation myself in my own body but only through the X-chromosomes received from my mother, "on all the evidence supplied an original random mutation must have occurred in your mother who passed the gene to you." One added, "there is a very high mutation rate and the genetic inheritance can appear where never known before" - apparently in even the most healthy family inheritance; another; "if it be of any comfort no individual on earth can be said to be completely immune from the risk of this, or any similarly inherited genetic abnormality"; and, "from all the evidence it seems that you were the sole recipient of the mutant gene", concluding (since my mother's three sisters and my own sisters had not married and therefore had no issue) that "there is therefore no subsequent prospect of the gene reappearing in your family unless of course a further new mutation were to take place; the odds against this are of course astronomical."

I naturally felt the utmost relief at the reassurance contained in this sentence, for the prime concern and purpose of this work had been to know for a certainty that no other members of the family were at risk. To make quite sure I combined the specific purport of the three letters I had received and sent a paraphrase of their verdict to the three scientists for checking. I ended, "Since, always excepting my two sons, all the several hundred descendants of their great-great-grandparents have been unaffected over six generations, the abnormal gene originating in my mother must have been transmitted to me and me alone; therefore the genetic inheritance of the sixth generation is completely unaffected by a mutant gene that can no longer be transmitted." My correspondents accepted my note without reservation: "the reasoning laid out in the statement which you attached to your letter is impeccable," and "Your observations are correct and their application is one that I would agree with."

These two projects had certainly provided an element of ballast that I had obscurely felt to be absent from my life though of course neither had interfered with Johnson's "business of living" - a typically vigorous and invigorating expression. For me this meant husband and friends, travel at home and abroad, the continued exploration of the "world within the world" of English literature, the great outer world of nature, and the delight of little things the importance of which Johnson himself had not despised. "I shall never be *used* to it - life's always astonishment," I recall saying to one of my boys who had grinned sympathetically and wordlessly shared my joy. More fundamentally today my responses are called forth not only sensuously but by the realisation that the whole of nature is affirmative, affirmative of the value of life whether long or short, affirmative of renewal (though never of resurrection), affirmative of one of the strands of delight validating two brief lives.

A great watershed in my living process had meanwhile arrived with the acknowledgement that very much more of life lay behind than could possibly lie in front; and cruelly, it was then that in spite of all attempts to get a grip on the present the days began to crowd inexorably one on another, a spate that I could do nothing to control.

Then I came to realise that in yet another confused boxroom, this time a mental storehouse, files and notebooks long unopened lay dustily at the back of my mind, and that they now must be sorted through and examined or my "by and by" might never come either. I could not halt my present to examine its meaning but the remembered past at least seemed static and I hoped that by scrutinising aspects of a life traversing its brief tract of finite time to discover if not meanings then perhaps values. I knew, of course, that my validations could be only personal ones, that "universal" truth or "absolute" reality were notions too abstract for my comprehension; nor did I seek in the works of modern thinkers for enlightenment for I knew that I lacked the scientific and other disciplines, the training and the aptitude to fit me for such a study; I recognised also that to those with a religious framework or belief my quest would seem grotesquely unnecessary. Philosophies and theologies however, have so far only come up with many conflicting "truths" for which they all make claims, though surely many individual beliefs are not absolute but contingent on circumstance - geography may decide whether one is brought up as Muslim or Maoist, and chronology also has a lot to do with the nature of moral standards. With all such approaches I could have nothing to do.

Almost immediately I discovered that the desire to be honest though certainly paramount was by no means enough because all my views were conditioned by my equipment of intelligence and experience. The Greeks said that each individual's "eye-beam" determines what he sees and complete objectivity is therefore unattainable while time, place and mood may colour and even distort the picture. I discovered that unconscious assumptions might be based on misconceptions tardily discovered or never recognised at all, sometimes I knew insufficiently the facts that had conditioned my behaviour or that of my fellows, my motives were not always those I credited myself with, and frequently I have not known or have misjudged those of other people. The behaviour of humankind continued to present me with an eternal enigma because all lives seem so intensely, I had almost said terribly, private, so separated one from another, that only when sharing certain common experiences perhaps temporarily we may feel at one; much of living and most of the arts are surely endeavours to bridge to gap. How many of us could claim to know and understand even ourselves?

> "For why should we the busy Soul believe.
> When boldly she concludes of that and this;
> When of her self, she can no Judgement give,
> Nor how, nor whence, nor where, nor what she is?"

So wrote Skelton, the Attorney-General of the first Queen Elizabeth and we are asking similar questions today.

With these and probably many more limitations I began to examine in turn the themes of special interest to myself just then - the search for beauty and excellence, the vagaries of chance and mischance, delight in living and the nature of happiness, suffering and endurance, the urge to communicate and its frustration, remembrance and forgetting, old age and transience, the qualities of magnanimity and goodness...I would be hard put to it to decide honestly how much I discovered for myself, how much I owed to others after the years of observing their ways of life or attending to their words spoken or written - literature having played a major role in life, revealing, awakening, confirming and elucidating. It seems to me now that my conclusions were rather obvious ones and that I solved only personal problems. I did learn how, while being outwardly active, to hold a kind of inner silence, a receptivity to revealments or intuitions - for on these perforce I relied, having no gift of reasoning. But often I was denied satisfaction being baffled for instance - to give one of many examples - by the impossibility of defining pain; yet even here it seemed valuable to realise that fear of pain might sometimes be a worse affliction than pain itself. And it was difficult to accept that the search for cause and effect could sometimes be unprofitable, that in certain situations there lay no ultimate reasonableness, many random predicaments being inherently without sense, freakish, arbitrary… In the end my scribbled notes - for always I pondered pen in hand - set out some of my own attitudes, and occasionally how I had come by them; and where I could not find understanding I sometimes found insight and with that I learned to be satisfied.

CHAPTER TWENTY

A Look At Old Age

Although fully aware that ageing is inherent in the life process from its earliest beginning, I lived a long while before considering it as an eventuality for myself. As a child with my brothers I believed that grown people lived on the other side of an invisible barrier where they followed a way of life and cultivated interests that we found incomprehensible. We frequently discussed them among ourselves and always ended by giving them up. It was therefore hard to believe that we might become like them ourselves still less that we might progress from being grown-up (our parents) to becoming old (our grandparents). To be old meant grey hair and wrinkles and walking slowly instead of racing, and spectacles and even false teeth; old people in stories were sometimes unkind; told we might ever become like them we would have reacted with blank incredulity.

It is ironic that my incredulity persisted for so long. Some ten years ago an elderly friend remarked, "When you reach my time of life you will hope for peace and quiet and seek simply to enjoy yourself." The words were spoken with regret mingled with resolution and for a moment I was tremendously startled at the contrast between her objectives and my own - she was indeed considerably my senior - for I was intensely involved in active living, and my own private image of myself was very different from my grandmother's picture of herself as "an old lady" in her sixties. Well, since that day FG and I and our contemporaries have adjusted to many unanticipated events, and thrice endured the impoverishing loss of friends unique and irreplaceable; and now I begin to adjust not to events only but to a piece of knowledge - that a change in the self "too slow to see, too strong to resist" has already begun which, unlike other biological processes already experienced and equally out of my control such as pregnancy, childbirth and the menopause, will not end with a return to normality.

It has been in sudden realisations that the first trivial impairments of faculties, strength or looks have thrust themselves upon my attention - it was for example a mild shock one afternoon to find my exhibition catalogue almost useless because I had forgotten my reading spectacles; on another occasion as I prudently took my stand at the terminus to head a new queue I reflected that not so long ago I certainly would have run to catch the moving bus that now I was content to miss; with contemporaries, half-jocular, half-rueful, I have sometimes lamented a memory less reliable, a slower recall, a dwindling of energy, perhaps the increased time needed to recoup after exertion. (To console has long experience given wisdom, sagacity, enlightenment? In some cases it has. But in present society less honour is given to these qualities in the mature than is their due, a pity, for they might add a useful ballast to the impetuous energy of youth.) Very significant to every individual is the changing locus of the self in time, as day by day the backward perspective lengthens while the forward one diminishes. Surely these first intimations of ageing are not a sorrowful business although often regretted: and the life stream of the elderly man run very smoothly through pleasant country when the demanding struggles of early days and the labours of career-making and parenthood lie behind; when the immutable past and its works have been accepted once and for all; and when also we have come to accept ourselves simply for what we are, at last no longer striving to be more that what we are.

But the process of ageing is not old age itself. It is a commonplace that "age" cannot be measured merely by chronology for in his eighth decade a man may be biologically younger than another much his junior. Still, it is hardly arbitrary to describe as old those who have reached eighty and beyond. And though to my childhood's superficial judgement their lot might have seemed undesirable, today I realise that with one exception the old people I knew from infancy up to my twenties - grandparents, great-uncles and aunts, family friends and neighbours - were both active and happy beings. My mother's dynamic and forceful way of life continued almost to the end; garrulous and nimble old Mrs Storey was bright, light and spry as a bird; musical Aunt Mary, the most ably versatile woman I have ever known, when the time came acceded to limitations gracefully and without repining - her laughter was a peal of bells while Mrs Storey's was a cackle of mirth with a startling crow at the end. Mr Grant the gardener was a cranky bearded patriarch who foraged the countryside for sackfuls of dandelion and nettle leaves which his wife boiled for his dinner. Well I remember how he gravely assured me (a tearful little girl) that the caterpillar that had appeared before my horrified eyes coiled beside the cabbage on my plate would not have hurt me if I *had* eaten it - "What is it made of? Nothing but cabbage itself!" All these attained their ninth decade and remained continually absorbed and entertained by life, themselves entertaining and merry good company.

I imagine that these splendid old people had all their lives been unusually healthy and robust for in their day few weaklings survived into advanced age, hence all were still endowed with great vitality, able to accept inevitable limitations without self-pity nor feeling unduly cast down by their occurrence. Among them were distributed the sticks and spectacles, the grey hair and wrinkles, that my childhood had deplored, and of course some needed to tend individual physical problems which might grow tiresome if neglected (my mother's nightly massage of her neat little feet). But sight, hearing and mobility were not seriously impaired, and most important of all they had retained a basic sense of well-being and enjoyment.

My equally successful old friends of today likewise repudiate any image of themselves as infirm or incapable even when acknowledging their handicaps. Very indignantly the oldest exclaims reaching for his stick in order to walk across his study:

"Fit as a fiddle all my life and now see what I'm reduced to!" For a moment he glares at me then chuckles and stops in his tracks: "What on earth can I expect? I'm getting on for ninety!" He finds the book that he wants and returns to his desk to inscribe my name and a note on the flyleaf - his own brief memoir of his school fellow the poet James Elroy Flecker. Another takes a morning in bed after a strenuous day at the Royal Academy. She exclaims: "I'll never get used to energy not being perpetually available to me like water when I turn on a tap. But am I suggesting that a life of infirmity would have been a useful preparation for later limitations? What a fool if I did!" Two years ago M enjoyed her first flight to Switzerland where she played her cello until her left fingers had blisters ("And I am *very* proud of them!" she wrote - then eighty-four.) Today though musicianship is intact her right hand cannot grasp the bow - to which her gallant adjustment it that she has been immensely fortunate to have played chamber music until her mid-eighties.

These three voice a conviction widely held - that the limitations of age are externally imposed constraints on an inner self that remains in all essential ways unchanged. Tasks may take longer, creativity be diminished, the senses grow less acute, the memory less reliable, competence become clumsiness - the disadvantages of ageing are many and plain to see - yet the individual feels *in himself* unaltered, only the mirror tells the truth. As Wilde said with excellent penetration "the trouble with growing old is that one is still young."

It is a hard dilemma, and how magnificently some men of genius have resisted and overcome the exactions of time, attaining supreme excellence in making music, writing plays, painting pictures until their ninth decade - nor is their creativity to the nth degree the result of quiet easeful living but often associated with passionate involvement and triumph over trials of flesh and of spirit - Renoir painting with the brush tied to a hand too crippled to hold it, the aged Otto Klemperer conducting his noble concerts after years of desperate illness surmounted. It is good to see to what the great may aspire to even if only to marvel and bend the knees.

All the successful old people I have known whether or not gifted had this in common with the great that their aims and outlook were not bound in with self-concerns; it seems that a strong propensity to relish life outside the self may be if not cause yet certainly an attribute of an enjoyable longevity. I recall Mr and Mrs Read of Exeter, grandparents of Philip's school friend, who were in their eighties when they took us in after the air-raid of 1942; subsequently we paid them several visits from our fastness on Dartmoor but as they grew older they did not cease to take a lively interest, not merely in their own pursuits and immediate events but also in our and other people's problems and the distant days of "after the war". When after moving to Surrey we frequently visited FG's parents, she at eighty-four virtually blind, he alert and genial in his nineties, they never elected to concentrate on themselves but delighted to discuss world affairs with their son - of whom all three were remarkably well-informed - both of them deeply concerned for the future though they would not be part of it. But in truth they lived as though they had infinitude.

Yet enough for the most valiant as years increase declension must begin - but how heavily should we let the eventual decline weigh in the balance against long years of unhampered living? My mother lived into her ninetieth year, until, indeed, even her lively mind began to sag, (though well able to note and understand indulgent smiles at some oddity in her speech or behaviour). It was very hard for her indomitable spirit to accept any kind of dependence, and on one of my last visits, speaking with very quiet and matter of fact simplicity, she said to me: "You see, D the whole trouble is that I have lived so long." We were admiring the towering hollyhocks in her large old-fashioned garden - flowers, birdsong, the changing seasons, the whole world of nature - how she had enjoyed them over the years! So now to me her situation seemed sad, and transience a sad word, and it seemed that in the end a price must be paid for long life. But of course there is only one alternative, and who would lose the sum of goodly decades in order not to pay for them? My mother had lived her life with gusto, and for a very long time, so how now should awareness of occasional foolishness or even of her own declension cancel the almost nine good decades that had gone before? It was with robust courage that she paid her debt and there are many like her, old people contented with their lot and making their renunciations bravely.

In addition to their native strength of mind and body the happy old people I have known enjoyed the great advantage of independence, privacy, opportunity to live out their own patterns of life, their root system undisturbed. It is almost a part of human dignity to remain as it were in charge of the self and to resent and resist whatever seems to threaten this right, especially in extreme old age. Many fear lest ultimately bodily weakness should turn them into chattels pushed around at others' whim, regimented into communities where their individuality may be trimmed and adjusted to fit into an organisation; and for anyone - and in this respect financial resources become irrelevant - it is a hard thing to surrender control over his own destiny to nurses, relatives, doctors, institutions and he knows not whom. I remember how FG and I suggested to a friend in his eighties that he accept a vacancy in a community of elderly men and women; he turned it down almost at once. His piano, his choice of TV and radio programmes, his restaurant meals, his private engagements, habits and hobbies, all these he retained firmly in his own hands, which considerations weighed far more than the fact that his house was old and draughty, that he had no telephone and only daily help. With few modifications he continued to live as he had for nearly fifty years and only for a brief while at the end endured some of the hardships we had feared for him. Had he thought about it he would certainly have thought all worth enduring for the sake of the long years of freedom, we were wrong to try to persuade him otherwise and glad that we did not persist.

With such examples to strengthen and reassure I am yet not entirely able to discount the prevalent attitude to old age - that it is "a terrible thing", "awful", "a very sad time", "what I fear to become", a poet entitling his poem on the elderly "The Old Fools" - and dread seems very often entangled with the hope of attaining fullness of years. Yet many elderly people are unhappy not because they are old but because of the often crassly insensitive solutions devised in answer to their problems, and because of prevalent attitudes - many sense a barely veiled resentment at an increasing drain on the nation's resources, for example. Inappropriate living conditions may lead to overcrowding or more frequently to isolation and prolonged loneliness; in cases of poverty "eat or heat" may become very real alternatives; and ignorance, or dislike of being categorised, or a sometimes pathetic clinging to independence may prevent full use being made of such facilities as do exist. And while today more people than ever before may anticipate living beyond the allotted span, at the same time we all know that modern techniques make it possible to keep alive those who have reached an extremity of physical and mental decrepitude, many of them bedridden in hospitals all over the country. The sight of many such elderly men and women thus segregated and grouped together as "geriatrics" (ugly word), or as portrayed in the media or in appeals for charitable aid may explain why I hear more of the miseries of old age than I used to, why the expression too often denotes slow progressive decay of body and brain, de Beauvoir's "life unravelling stitch by stitch like a frayed piece of knitting". Surely this is not necessarily to be undergone, most of us would hope that none would "officiously strive" to keep us alive if ever we should thus come to have outlived ourselves. Therefore by no means all the problems are due to longevity but to unnecessarily unfavourable circumstances which would be found unpleasing to members of any age group, and society could and should seek strenuously to eliminate them.

And yet, and yet - I cannot look squarely at the prospect of old age without seeing that intrinsically sometimes the condition can be cruel. An old Devonian once remarked to FG, "Old Age "er b'aint come alone" (there is a Scots version of this so the saying may be proverbial); thus he referred to the multitude of his physical preoccupations. And surely if the years bring with them a state of continued ill-health his may prove a harder trial of endurance than all the aches and pains. "The days draw nigh when thou shalt say, I have no pleasure in them," warned the prophet; ("Methinks I have outlived myself and grown to be a-weary of the sun. I have shaken hands with delight"). Freud has written of life "with no resonance". "It is to play Beethoven with no sustaining pedal."

Never to "feel well", continually to suffer discomfort, each day a repetition of yesterday's trials with no end to them in prospect, may generate in the sufferer not cheerful endurance or hope of distraction but merely a weary despair. Existence may then become constricted into a dumb or complaining acquiescence in fatigue and bodily preoccupations including the yielding to the organism's demands instead of being adequately in control of them. If the mental as well as the physical powers be affected then the very core of character seems to be slowly eroded and the contrast with what *is* with what *was* is pitiable in the extreme, the price of long life being then inordinately high. Knowledge of this possibility however rarely or remotely envisaged may well qualify our expectation of a hale and hearty old age and daunt even the bravest.

In some societies the old are respected as repositories of wisdom and even if senile are guarded and protected by their families as begetters of their descendants and progenitors of the race. Among ourselves however even where there is some sense of responsibility indebtedness is rarely felt while family responsibility is by no means a simple matter granted our social values and the scale of the problem. In my ignorance I used to wonder why the tender indulgence enjoyed by the infant members of a family was by no means always extended to those in "second childhood" but in truth senile behaviour has little in common with the innocent helplessness of infancy. Few households are able or willing to undertake adults no longer responsible for their own actions, and wilful perversity may be harder to treat with forbearance than the naughtiness of small children. Even patient and good-tempered guardians resort to humouring, condescension, or a sometimes resented familiar jocularity; I know of two cases of a Regan-Goneril resentment and hate. Do these last find it bitter that mere caricatures of former adult creatures survive to cumber this earth? Or are they defensive against the thought that this might conceivably happen to themselves?

Today except for an unfortunate minority old age is by no means synonymous with such sickness of mind and body, yet even when adjusted to their private and personal limitations the elderly have other problems, largely because of their greatly increased numbers in proportion to the rest of the population. After retirement and when the children are reared and away, a family house is no longer necessary, and as yet there is no adequate answer to the question of where to live while competent and able to decide for ourselves, or of what is to be done with us if incapable. Both my grandmothers had remained in their family house, the one with her two unmarried daughters, the other with her son and his wife and family, and such arrangements were not uncommon; today I know only four comparable, yet very dissimilar, arrangements, for these have their own self-contained quarters in the family establishment with privacy and complete independence, assets rather than liabilities to the group. But only a few can count on such good fortune and even these would not expect to stay where they are as of right should they require special care because of mental or physical deterioration. There are of course innumerable "homes", hostels, guest houses, pensions, blocks of flats and converted mansions, but by no means enough of them to satisfy demand. These range from the luxurious, fully staffed and expensive, to single "bed-sitters", some of these last grossly inadequate and exploitative. Often excellent establishments have been set up under local authorities, sometimes with a matron in overall charge, wherein each inmate has private quarters with heating and lighting while able to enjoy general amenities as well. FG and I have visited two of our retired "dailies" who have lived in such institutions for years on their widows' and old age pensions, both maintaining their "standards" - meals on a laid table in their apartment ("*never* on a tray"), and more importantly so far both have filled their new leisure with useful activities enjoyed with other people.

Yet even they may have fresh problems should they attain extreme old age when activity may be replaced by lethargy and boredom.

His last chapter has little to say.
He grows backward with gradual loss of
Muscular tone and mental quickness:
He lies down; he looks through the window.
Ailing at autumn, he asks a sign but
The afternoons are inert, none come to
Quit his quarrel or quicken the long
Years of yawning and he yearns only
For total extinction. He is tired out...

If living alone like Auden's old man, perhaps needing help to dress and undress or to take a bath or simply to get out for change of scene or fresh air, it does seem that some become too tired to bother, listless and inert, ceasing like neglected animals to groom and care for themselves and it is then that they are eventually "taken into care" usually into a National Health hospital, a prospect often and usually quite unnecessarily feared and evaded. Having very briefly given voluntary help in a home for old people, and on two occasions spent some weeks in surgical wards where due to lack of space elsewhere "geriatrics" occupied several beds, and having frequently visited elderly friends and relatives in other institutions, I have seen a little of the conditions.

It is certain that for some hospital may prove a refuge. For little Mrs W a lifetime of companionship had ended with her widowhood, and over the ensuing years I would meet her walking alone in ancient coat and floppy felt hat, her pink cheeks growing faded and sunken, blue eyes bewildered and sad. In her eighties she was moved into a nursing home and with childlike docility she took to her bed. There she soon turned away from nourishment seeking only to be quiet and to sleep; tranquilly she withered and faded until her easy almost imperceptible end, a cause for thankfulness not grief. Nor is hospital always the end: for some it gives renewal. I recall an old woman who had been found lying helpless on the floor of her flat borne in by the stretcher bearers and laid on the bed opposite to mine. She was deeply unconscious, hair a tangled mat and body filthy. Nor did she seem to respond to treatment but lay, seemingly moribund, flat on her back for days on end. To me her plight indeed seemed desperate, yet doctors and nurses cared for her assiduously and within a week, fresh and clean, she was sitting up in bed in a white nightie sprinkled with rosebuds, her hair washed and brushed and combed and tied back with a silky ribbon. Her responses were perhaps limited but she was fully sentient, contented as is any well cared for living creature; she turned herself, intent and bright of eye, when the blackbird sang below her window, smiled like a child at the red jelly on her plate. The long labour for her restoration seemed amply rewarded by her continued existence in a state of happiness. To the lover of life it seemed then, and not for the first time, that dedication to its preservation makes the medical profession at its best one of the noblest in the world.

Generally often grossly overworked nurses treat unresponsive, perverse and even hostile old people with astonishing gentleness and kindness; but I have seen exceptions for different individuals cope differently with the intractable, and two nurses dealing with the same patient's repeated behaviour patterns may show very different degrees of tolerance and understanding. Anyone, young or old, once inside his hospital ward - and the word has unfortunate overtones of custody as well as confinement - is certain to be stripped of some of his cherished privacies in ways that his nurses take for granted. For oneself one accepts the absurdity of being over-squeamish, but it's hard to witness indignities endured by the old and helpless, such as moving them carelessly, unnecessarily exposing their pathetic nakedness and wasted useless limbs - the gentle face of the old lady whose crimson wrinkled buttocks were so unceremoniously hoisted over a commode. And I remember in a different institution the ward festive with paper festoons and balloons where there lay a "terminal" case one Christmas morning; no need to look twice at the grotesque tallow mask agape on the pillow - was under-staffing the reason she had to be there? She was not in any way being neglected for nothing more could be done for her; and her appearance meant nothing whatever to the other old women fumbling over their plates of turkey and Brussels sprouts.

And she herself knew nothing truly enough. Yet - I could not but feel that even an animal might be accorded more privacy in its last hours, and for her I wished more decorum, more respect, whether she knew it or not. (W H Hudson's "In pain and peril let me always be alone, that is an instinct in man as well in the stricken deer".) I was, perhaps naively, surprised above all that riding roughshod over susceptibility, when it occurred, was always taken for granted as normal routine. It would be illuminating but idle, I think to recall a multitude of often contradictory impressions which together simply signify that should we require nursing in our old age, whether by experienced professionals at home, or by our own family, in an expensive private establishment, or an NHS hospital ward, our relative happiness or misery will be largely determined by those who minister to our needs - we can only hope that we fall into good hands.

So it is impossible to know whether old age will be trial or triumph. Browning's "best yet to be" is certainly more bracing than Arnold's suggestion that far from being "a golden day's decline" in the end age is to be "frozen up within". Either is possible and one old person may experience both in the course of one single day. But the slow withdrawal of the valued gift of life is what ageing intrinsically *is*, and this unpalatable fact is true even when decrepitude or regrets for life's griefs and failures are mercifully absent. To be given long life is good fortune after which to age is surely as necessary and natural a thing as it was to be born and to grow; having seen for myself the plight of the unfortunate and the satisfactions of the successful, to accept this reality without self-pity or fear is for me the only way to preserve a proper sense of balance.

And surely old age is a victory, though a brief one, over time and circumstance; small wonder that through the centuries great painters and sculptors have been drawn to portray it so often. Old faces depict the very image of the mind in lines of determination or of disillusion, eyes life-accepting or life-renouncing, aspects sometimes of pathos, sometimes of majestic grandeur. Rembrandt, Titian, Michelangelo? Yes, indeed; but I am thinking now of Toulouse-Lautrec's simple painting, "An Old Woman". She sits alone on a bench with a background of inter-lacing boughs and leaves, her grey dress folds softly about her lax body, and she turns a lined and tranquil face towards the light. She has attained her moment of acceptance, a moment bathed in stillness and luminous warmth, for her "truly the light is sweet and a pleasant thing it is to behold the sun". A very unassuming but a very desirable consummation. *Ut fiat*, one says, *ut fiat*, so may it be.

Chapter Twenty-one

Some Thoughts On Transience

Some knowledge of transience seems to have been implanted in my very first awareness, and attempts to understand and adjust to this knowledge were to become, as probably for most of us, as much a part of life as experience in the external world of people and events. I suppose there was a time when I was completely unaware of mortality but I cannot remember such a time and for all I know this is common experience. Nor was awareness in the beginning a painful thing, it probably dawned gradually - a dead insect on a window-sill, the fallen fledgelings that we children buried under the syringa beside the camomile bed. Eventually I learned that humans, even little children, might die too, but from the beginning I was taught that this was different because all good Christians like ourselves could expect to live "afterwards" forever and ever; I expect I believed this although as I have said biblical stories and teachings seemed remote and isolated from the life of everyday.

In my experience very young children are not moved to fear or sorrow by their first encounters with death unless they suffer personal deprivation; even human demise is accepted without distress though usually with intense interest as their comments and searching questions show. When old Mrs Cartwright died Philip, then six years old, who had known her well, was content to accept that she had lived to so great an age that she had faded and withered away - "died down" as he put it; at the same time he evinced a real sense of the value of fulfilment as he summed it all up for her: "She's all right. She got to *XYZ*."

His younger brother, however, reacted with some feeling when he learned from the robust and hearty farmer's wife which of her flock of fowls was to be killed for our dinner. "I am not," he said firmly, "going to eat that poor little hen."

He had perhaps learned pity - at the age of four; but in both children the reactions were mainly objective: apparently death for others did not suggest as it does for older people speculations about their own. When this happens children make their private adjustments - "private" because children's questions are by no means always satisfied by adult replies however carefully and truthfully they may be answered; alone or with other children they examine or ruminate what they have received. Nor are satisfactory replies always possible. I was certainly unable to cope with Philip's: "If I count long enough shall I come to the last number, and *what will it be?*" As a bewildered nine year old I myself was confounded by notions that no could clarify, lying in bed hot summer nights staring into emptiness while two ideas - infinity, endless space, eternity, endless time - induced, simply *as* ideas, panic and waking nightmare. I could never explain to my mystified parents why I sometimes called them upstairs to me. The hymn, "O God our help," was sung a great deal that June of 1911 when George V was crowned king; the line "Time like an ever-rolling stream" was then an image of frightful import.

However, it was painlessly that - one morning that stays firm in memory - my young brothers and I talked of mortality - three quite ordinary children sitting on a fallen tree trunk beside the ivy todd, eating of out of saucers our eleven o'clock "grapenuts" and milk. We didn't dwell on it long I am sure yet I remember thus distinctly because the boys' attitude was surely more sensible than mine. Since everybody and every living creature must die they could and would accept this for themselves; there was companionship and some comfort in sharing the common lot. But I could derive no consolation from such a thought, feeling that, if every living thing on earth should die on the day I did, it would be no consolation whatever for my own personal extinction. For my young brothers as for Philip and Richard the approach seems to have been unemotional and objective, maybe for them then it was an academic question since perhaps they did not really imagine it possible that their own lives should come to an end while for me the question was more self-involving. For all of us apparently our Christian upbringing, the prayers we had been taught, the many hymns we knew by heart ("There's a home for little children Above the bright blue sky") - were matters belonging to quite another category and were not considered at all.

By this time then death had become for me an unpleasing prospect and eventually there were to be many years when I could think of it only with horror and dread. As I grew older I came to realise that without ultimate death for each individual all species would so proliferate as to smother themselves to extinction, and I learned that a succession of generations means constant modification of the type and in fact that individual existence must continually be superseded for the sake of future development. Easy to accept all this for other people but for myself and those I loved it was another matter.

In nature, plants as well as men and animals, the tremendous urge for self-preservation and propagation for the sake of the species is universal. The animals are quick to sense danger, feint and fight to preserve themselves and their young, their attributes are closely geared to the purposes of survival, and Walt Whitman praised them that "they do not fret and whine about their condition". But unlike humanity they are unaware of their condition and no foreknowledge tinges their undoubted love of life with regret for its brevity or the individual's ultimate mortality. Our continued awareness of transience, our knowledge that once we were not and one day we shall cease to be, our sense of a tragic destiny, is very different from, may even modify the animal's delight in simple existence, so that perhaps human fear of death is not a primal instinct but an acquired emotion which varies according to each man's temperament, situation, experience, or fixation on the supreme value of the individual self.

And then how hard it is that those for whom - at all events in the western world - life is potentially so rich with fulfilments and delights, must one day forego them all - like children enjoying a party who don't want to say goodbye to the fairy lights and coloured balloons, the fun and games, the lovely things to eat and drink, and to leave our friends' good company as perforce we depart into the quiet and lonely dark outside. Yet all the while new guests throng the threshold impatient to enter for their own brief interlude so we must give way and let another generation have a go. La Fontaine speaks of this:

> "...Here Death spoke true. When we are old as he
> We should get up from life as from a feast,
> And take our leave as fits a thankful guest,
> Nor clamour for reprieve that cannot be."

More painful than unwilling departure is the thought that only the great creators will bequeath to posterity any lasting legacy, that not only our physical selves but all the experience of a lifetime amassed and treasured up in the mind will vanish with us into oblivion and "leave not a rack behind". In one week's reading of living authors I came upon in the autobiography of a novelist: "I like the image of a life as a swallow flying in from the darkness into the great hall, and after its moment of light, out into the darkness again. But if it is to be acceptable to me, the swallow, after the second darkness, must come into the light again." In an article by a journalist: "Without hope of immortality - no matter what the humanists may say - the struggle availeth naught and is seen to avail naught and life is therefore a callous mockery." A poet: "If there is no hope of immortality there is no hope and life is impossible without it." For some the thought of oblivion is endurable, perhaps most insistently voiced by Tennyson; for example,

> "My own dim life should teach me this.
> That life shall live for evermore
> Else earth is darkened at the core
> And dust and ashes all that is." (*In Memoriam xxxiv*)

312

The transience of living makes for occasional sadness in all but the crassly insensitive; it is of no use to say; "I never think about it" - a poor expedient since sooner or later that shutter-out of reality is certain to be pulled down. We have most of us seen the *gouffre* of Baudelaire at least once in our lives, experienced Forster's "panic and emptiness". Most men, observed Emerson, behold their condition "with a degree of melancholy". Few are like Socrates who seems literally to have believed that after drinking the hemlock he would presently find himself among the immortals: was it not Bertrand Russell who remarked that this diminishes the courage needed to refuse the ready means he had to evade it? Nor can many emulate the courage of Barbara Wootton's reply to the question, "Of what help are your beliefs to you? How can they comfort you in times of trial?" - "But you see I do not hold my beliefs for the purpose of being comforted by them."

The courage of these fearless ones is to my mind overtopped by Samuel Johnson's courage in facing these fears. His horror of death - whether it meant a new strange state of being or annihilation - was lifelong, and his honesty and strength of mind accepted all its implications. "Annihilation is nothing. But fear of annihilation is terrible," and, "One would rather exist, even in pain, than not exist." As a devout Christian he hoped and prayed for eternal life, but his fears persisted since constitutionally he was surely a melancholic whose temperament was at variance with his convictions. His latter end he found it difficult to contemplate - "the whole of life is but keeping away the thoughts of it," yet, "It must be so; it will do no good to whine." His solution was not to evade but to recognise and resist his fears by living a full and enormously productive life. The monumental *Dictionary* seems alone a sufficient achievement for a lifetime - and it was the first, remember, not a collation of the work of other scholars. Anyone who wishes to see the beauty as well as the immense scope of this production has only to visit the "Cheshire Cheese" pub in London's Fleet Street and go upstairs and examine the copy that stands open there; let him read the definition, the etymology, the examples of usage, with quotations from his wide reading, of one single word, observe the size of the volume, make a rough guess at the number of words it contains and so realise a very little of the years of toil involved. It is not necessary surely to list his formidable literary achievements of the first rank - his biographies, his edition of the Shakespeare *Works*, his journalism, and verses; add to all this activity his foregathering with his friends so inordinately both by day and by night to which proclivity we owe the glorious masterpiece by Boswell, and we may say that English literature would be much the poorer were it not for one man's battle against his morbid preoccupations. But Johnson was unique; Johnson was a hero.

Hopes of immortality are as old as humanity, and men seem to have created their religions at least partly to satisfy them - "the daydreams of mankind" according to T E Huxley but satisfying all the same the basic need of some universal myth to transcend the brevity and capriciousness of most lives. The belief that this life is prelude to an eternity of happier living is intensely meaningful and comforting to those who hold it: happier for some in that the injustices and cruel sufferings of this world will there somehow be compensated; many hope there to attain reunion with their beloved dead; others to find, behind the chaos and chanciness of this life, a pattern and a purpose in existence that they cannot now perceive. But the nature of each individual belief is entirely contingent on the cultural upbringing, the locus in historical time or geographical space, to say nothing of the temperament, intelligence and experience of him who holds it. There is only one absolute certainty - that there is no certainty. W H Hudson's belief that our dead ancestors live in us and in the soil that their descendants till, is all that we can be sure about: we can only speculate about other forms of survival.

For myself I have come to find it strange that some find life unbearable unless it be perpetual ("half dead to know that I shall die") with Wordsworth believing that "in this world we find our happiness or not at all"; a life-enhancing doctrine I have found it, enjoining me to use the utmost of all that I am *now* while alive to know my only certainty. How wasteful of time, the very dimension of life itself, to lose a moment in lamenting that my valued share of it must have to stop.

It is seemingly a human attribute greatly to value the sense of personal identity and to recognise the unique individuality of other people. From the Gospels to Schweitzer, from the Buddha to the Mahatma, in Pasternak and Solsenhytsyn, a "reverence for life" is the mark of a truly civilised mind. To threaten a man's identity, to seek to make it completely subservient to another's will, to violate whatever it is that makes each human being different from all others, are acts universally condemned as crimes against humanity. Nevertheless such crimes are now being perpetrated on a scale unprecedented - whole nations indoctrinated with narrow ideologies with dire penalties for "dissidents", the menace of the Bomb's universal destruction, the impersonal irresponsibility of push-button warfare, genocide - these things horrify because, whether the pretext be ethnic, religious or political, they are absolutely *indiscriminate*, they reduce the individual to a cipher and deprive him of even a limited direction of his lifeline.

The value most men set on their own special selfdom not only makes their own disappearance from the stream of living almost insupportable but also causes death to be associated with that most poignant and universal of all forms of suffering - grief. Those who have died will never return yet in themselves they were so unique, so precious, that they were as we say "irreplaceable". When I attempt to examine the implications of this in the light of my own experience (on which, certainly not on wider pretensions, all my ideas are based) I find myself thinking not of "Death" - capital letter and singular number, the gruesome and surely medieval conception of the arch-enemy of life - but rather of the multitudinous and inevitable termination of all organic identities, each death a separate happening.

When I try to visualise my own individuality I appear to share with my fellows a simple belief that as I am, at any given moment of time, then I exist and all my actions are based on this assumption, reinforced by the fact that other living identities who share the present time with me (*and* the testimonies of identities past and gone) seem to show that consciously or unconsciously most people act positively on some belief. It seems also true that this self-awareness is derived from experience, a complex web of sense impressions in which memory, the imprint on my mind of personal and also of racial history, is also closely involved. Yet I know too that the correlation of past impressions and present awareness results not in a static state of being but in a dynamic organism. At the centre there is energy. Identity for me means not the sum total of all the faculties unique in every individual, nor even the inscrutable awareness of them all as well as of the world outside; the very essence of selfhood is the vitality at the core.

Self-identification is recognisable in the common experience of waking from sleep and especially if from a dream - for a brief while I seem to rediscover and put together the elements of ordinary awareness, perhaps saying with relieved surprise that it was "only a dream", quickly piecing myself together into my familiar pattern. But there are levels of unconsciousness that go deeper than sleep and I have twice known the strange experience of struggle to recover an almost lost selfhood. I remember, in nearly the last stages of food poisoning, the surrender to engulfment in blackness all surroundings having disappeared, pain and discomfort far removed and no awareness of myself as a physical object in space. And yet at the end of a long black vista what I today recall as a spark of light seemed to gleam very far away and my disembodied will fastened itself to that glimmering focus and knew it must not let go. There was no physical effort but a concentration of attention that seemed almost superhuman; with desperate determination I clung to this single perception of reality as if it alone could assure survival thus resisting oblivion until eventually normal consciousness returned. In the second instance I passed into oblivion after anaesthesia, that is to say for a good reason and with my full consent. Mercifully after modern anaesthesia, emergence is usually gentle and gradual but forty years ago the experience for me was so traumatic that three days later I recorded it in writing. Of course this time I has really accepted complete oblivion and there was no spark of any kind towards which I might direct myself when I began to regain consciousness, but though I write as if of a person at first there was nothing whatsoever except a diffused awareness. Somewhere in limbo there was struggle, confusion, frustration, distortion, all in enveloping darkness. There seemed a rootedness in some dreadful element from which no escape seemed possible. Absolute isolation, an appalling sense of being utterly lost, were combined with effort, with emergent will, with a frenzied effort to break out and be clear. Somewhere in a distant other element, which there was endeavour to attain, grotesque groans and cries began to assail the awakening senses. For a long time nothing had meaning.

Eventually the bonds were burst and I knew for an instant that I was I. At the same moment a rush of physical anguish made me cry aloud and sink back into a deep and undisturbed oblivion. Quietly and gradually I emerged once more into consciousness and was aware of self, of my situation, of reality. Strapped in an upright position, cushioned by pillows, my body flaring with vivid pain, weak and profoundly nauseated, yet all was surmounted by my mighty surge of joy at mere existence. This almost unconscious, certainly un-*self*-conscious struggle as in the first experience was not against death but for life, even if only at an animal level. The dominant urge was not fear but will, every ounce of strength directed upon finding and holding together that central core of being that I call myself.

But although I emerged with the spark still alight that cannot always be so - for me as for everyone will come the ultimate quenching. There has been much talk of late as to how death should be defined, and especially concerning the precise moment at which death may be said to have occurred. But nobody disputes the fact that after death the organism has ceased to function as a whole - an "*in*-divid-ual" as we say, meaning a being undivided. What had been an inter-relationship integral and ultimate, of each part with all the others in conditions of continual change, replacement and growth, has become an inert collection of tissues and organs, mere unrelated physical objects that will only briefly hold even the semblance of what they were in life. Each cellular entity, each complicated organ, far from being capable of replacement or growth, function or renewal, can now only disintegrate into its chemical and physical elements. The so valued identity is irreversibly dispersed and the unique correlation begins to fall apart: "chaos is come again."

Throughout life my state of awareness depends profoundly on the efficiency of the central nervous system; if the brain and sensory organs are defined as dead when they have ceased to function, and are certainly "dead" when disintegrated, it follows that then no organism exists to act either as vehicle or recipient of experience. And so, although I may experience the extinction of others, my own I cannot know. A few may remain completely conscious up to their very last moment; nevertheless, after that last moment, for every brain and body experience, in the literal meaning of the word, has finally come to a stop.

Although these are physical and readily verifiable facts they are not always accepted as such, and many fears are caused by imagining the self as dead and at the same time aware of it. Surely this is a contradiction: the dead are incapable of being aware of anything whatsoever; for dying is not an act, something we do, it is a happening, or something that happens to us, and only too often against our will. It is surely false to speak of dying as an action, for it is on the contrary the cessation - whether slow or sudden - of all action. I am bound to fail if I try to conceive merely the negation of all that I know because death is the end of the possibility of knowing anything at all. To project myself imaginatively into "unknown territory", conceive of strange experiences, speak of "passing into a new state of being" or "grim portals" or of "the bourn from which no traveller returns" is simply refusal to accept the end of all states of being, all entrances, all exits. Certainly I shall cease to live, but I shall not "die"; only the living can do that for their dead and should not do so often.

In parenthesis here, language being the image of our thought, it is revealing to see how much nearer the truth of the matter is so exact a tongue as Latin. The verb *morior* ('I die') is deponent, that is conjugated only in the *passive* voice. If it be objected that, like other deponent verbs, it has an active meaning the answer is that this was not so originally; in the beginning the meaning *was* passive, but it has lost that significance - (*deponere*, in Latin meaning to lay aside, from which comes the English derivative to depose) - and thereby surely lost something of its true meaning, not " I die" but rather "I suffer death".

The fear of possible physical ordeals that may precede the end is not fear of mortality but of pain, as when someone says, "It is not death I fear but dying." Yet a terminal illness may cause less suffering than illnesses surmounted in the past, and in any case though bodily distresses be hard to bear ourselves and even harder to behold in other people, good brave spirits will not contemplate them unnecessarily nor meet them before they come. Unhappily for some minds there is fascination in such contemplation, a prurient appetite to feed existing fears by indulging them. How excitedly the village women cluster outside the cottage where an old man died in the night, recounting all they have heard about his rather squalid end, "a judgement on him for beating and bullying his poor little wife." And after the death of the gentleman of leisure, a man fastidious and reserved in life, how distasteful to him would have been the minute by minute recital of his last hours delivered with a strange reluctant horror by his housekeeper, retailed to his old friends over a glass of sherry and a piece of cake. My sense of affront on his behalf is certainly unnecessary, for the magnificent effigy on the bed upstairs is forever now immune, and my sense of outrage is as futile as it is probably foolish. In a very short space of time Lord Moran (of Winston Churchill), Simone de Beauvoir (of her mother), and the Prince of Loewenstein (of his wife), have described with great frankness and most intimate detail the last distresses and frailties of their subjects. Of course such themes are legitimate material for imaginative literature, but it is nonetheless inexcusably bad taste, worse, it is a betrayal of Churchill, of Mme de Beauvoir, of Loewenstein's dear little Princess, to relate details of the end when controls were lost and the body took over. The Prince tells us that he was most concerned that his wife should die in dignity, yet matters that she wished to keep private even from her nurses he shares with all the readers of his book. The writer of *The Pathology of Power* legitimately says that the physical condition of men in charge of affairs, whose decisions may affect thousands of lives, is very apt to affect their acts and their judgement, and should be taken into account by their biographers. This is certainly so. But behaviour *en extremis* is surely a matter for a few intimates who can afterwards keep their own counsel.

It is possible that the writers of these and similar books are finding easement for themselves by recounting the distressing things they have seen and heard. If they are seeking to elicit sympathy these books have failed in their purpose, for I felt less sorrow for Mme. de Beauvoir, about whose death her daughter wrote a whole book, than for Gino, the little son of the Countess of Origo, about whose end his mother wrote a reticent few sentences yet implies so much the more!

The acceptance of death as the inevitable end of each organic life is merely a description of a sterile happening, a kind of negative, yet it is far easier to define death than to define life which remains an inscrutable marvel and mystery. Scientists may produce intricate and beautiful models of the Double Helix, express the DNA formula, indicate programmes of genetic or cellular development but, after all, these are simply formulae, models, descriptions, and do not begin to solve the problem of what life intrinsically *is*.

What is the difference, I ask myself, between the tiny seed of mignonette and a grain of sand, between a pebble and an acorn? Surely it is potency, the power to grow into something quite transcending its inert-seeming physical appearance, which identity will presently reproduce itself in seeds after its kind. Within the egg, human and non-human, the growing embryo; within the bulb, as I showed my wondering children, the perfect miniature daffodil; within the acorn the latent and almost unimaginable tree. The marvel lies not in these small physical objects that I can so easily hold in my hand, but in the urgency, the energy, the mysterious invisible force that, given the right conditions, will propel the organism into attaining its own specific identity - that, and no other, for always " a rose is a rose is a rose" whether it be an oak, massive, enduring for centuries, or the frail blossom of a single season. This is what we cannot explain, still less reproduce or resuscitate - life, so easily recognised yet unfathomably remote from human understanding.

Living in circumscribing mystery as we do, men have always sought to make their own transience acceptable to themselves. Of course for those of certain religious persuasions the end of physical functioning existence is no matter for repining but rather " the climax for which our entire life is but a preparation", "the great consummation", "the threshold to the ultimate", their Celestial City with all the trumpets sounding for them on the other side. Fewer and fewer people today base their lives on such expectation of immortality although millions indeed may desire it; but to validate existence without an outside framework of meaning is often difficult. Without it some turn to lives of thoughtless hedonism, an eddying about from one distraction to another; others, accepting agnosticism like scientist Huxley or stoic Matthew Arnold, discover and promote life-enhancing values for themselves and other people - this has been as I think FG's way and that of some of my admired friends; a few experience the despair of Samuel Beckett's characters acquiescing in an impasse of weariness and loneliness, hardly marking times and seasons, stuck irrevocably in sand or their dustbins, or else moving in some confined limbo "waiting for Godot" although seemingly without belief that he will ever come.

Fortunately few possess the unlimited leisure or the compulsion to endless speculation of Beckett's unhappy creatures. More healthy is the great stress laid, in the western world especially, on the value of objectives, long-term or short-term, the belief that without some over-riding specific purpose life could become a mere drifting. I recollect how often as a child I associated happiness with anticipation - "something to look forward to" as my mother's family used to say. This "something" was generally a definitive object on which to focus; for my mother to plan the annual holiday or perfect some garden project; for my aunts to design and execute one of their church embroideries, or to give a really superlative party. Later on I was to see Philip and Richard engrossed for days in devising and constructing some mechanical model, or how FG really enjoyed the prolonged labour of inter-relating places and people to set up a working organisation, or, as he wrote in Connecticut, how a friend when manipulating rocks, bridging a stream, creating the contours of a desired landscape, would find himself then "possessed, absorbed and most deeply contented". For all such the work is the thing, and they may even feel sorry when it is completed. And to dream, and then seek by labour to turn that dream into reality, action or artefact, is a potent human driving force and when attained an enormous satisfaction.

Although the dull monotony of journeyman labour (absorbing the best hours of so many lives) may block their own attainment, multitudes can and do find vicarious satisfaction in the prowess of their contemporary heroes, and these by no mean only sportsmen and "popstars". Pioneer travellers in outer space or ocean depths, climbers of once inaccessible mountain peaks, lonely navigators of vast unmapped distances, all crossers of frontiers into the unknown, geographic or scientific - these adventurers are watched and reported with a breathless interest that is almost participation. That is not new. The desire to focus on a distant end, the glory not in attainment alone but in a challenge accepted, has long been symbolised in myth and story; quests for the Golden Fleece or the Holy Grail; Ulysses seeking his Ithaca; the long ardours of Tolkein's Hobbit - the more sympathetic perhaps because he is not cast in heroic mould but is at heart a homely hearth-loving creature; Bunyan's Pilgrim; Flecker's Hassan setting forward on his Golden Journey - all tell of seekers of goals beyond immediate horizons, some "beyond the utmost bound of human thought". Therefore the emphasis in these stories is all on the endeavour and the reward, and once it is attained the story ends.

It is important to realise that these myths symbolise only one aspect of man's natural bent, an attribute often heroic and noble, but excluding the ultimate waning of strength and disappearance from the scene of action, so that though at first attractive and plausible the picture of life as progress from one surmounted endeavour to the next and on to the supreme pinnacle of achievement is an image incomplete and unrealistic. I find myself better served when I do not separate human existence from the rest of organic life conceived as potency in action, the long unfolding process. The ties are indisputable and they are many. Like the trees our origin is our parents' seed and our eventual growth is free or stunted according to environment, blighted or unfructified by mishap of disease or injury; some are cut down in their prime, others nipped in the sapling stage; others destroyed by natural disasters, impossible growing conditions, their own inbuilt limitations - the

322

possibilities of failed living are legion. And there are those who grow to full ripeness, deploying their full potential, creating the seed of future generations, and when they perish as all things must, they leave behind an image of strength and tenacity for their posterity to emulate.

The realisation that each individual life consists in the dynamic expression of its own unique potential has greater authenticity than one based on myth or speculation or desire, for it is objectively visible in the whole world of living creatures as well as subjectively true in the private life of each man's self-awareness. "The impulse of all life is to affirm its own essence," wrote Arnold, long before our twentieth century had analysed the drives - sex only one among many - directed to that end. For the picture of life as a horizontal progress towards at best a hypothetical goal we may substitute the reality of the vertical growth, a continual process aimed at self-realisation - a perspective far more encouraging and exhilarating from which to view all life, but for humankind with an important difference. For merely to survive and propagate himself is not necessarily man's sole concern; his dynamism, his own creative energy is in very truth his "eternal delight", its frustration for whatever cause a tragedy.

"Dust in the air suspended
Marks the place where a story ended" -

Eliot's lines are haunted with regret. But the dust by the wayside has always been, remains, and always will be itself and nothing more. Before men are dust they may have made beautiful or useful objects long outlasting the individual that gave birth, or discovered smoother paths for posterity to tread, made it possible for men and women to achieve themselves more fully than those of today, it may even be that they may influence the trend of evolution of this planet. For ill, maybe; yet conceivably for good.

323

Chapter Twenty-two

Last Chapter

When I think of a life I think of a lifetime and find the compound word the more suggestive.

Mathematicians and philosophers today attach great importance to a right definition of time and it is impossible for an untrained mind to understand their arguments. But trained or untrained nearly everyone has a private *picture* of time as the dimension within which our lives are contained, and however unsophisticated or even if positively erroneous, our picture will colour our thoughts and influence our actions. When I was a very small child and had learned to name the days I could picture only one week at a time; this I saw as seven square blocks like my coloured building bricks laid end to end - such a succession of coloured days is apparently a common picture in childhood. After the greens and the blues and the browns the next week lay mistily ahead in the future, while past weeks receded in a long endless scroll - my pictured memories of places, people, events and involvements. Later I saw myself as traveller through a horizontal landscape, a pilgrim through the years. And for me today time future exists only as an abstract idea; the present consists in awareness; and the past is the huge web not of receding but of instant memory over which in moments of reverie I can scan all ways, which memories can sometimes colour my perceptions of the present.

But if the time future does not exist yet the idea of futurity does suggest a vast tract of empty time not yet tied to immediate preoccupations, and the idea of boundlessness invigorates in the same way that spatial distance emancipates - for me the infinite horizons of the open sea, the downs and fells and moorlands of Britain, great deserts in Africa and America, mountains remote from human interference, the coursing of great rivers, even the cosy little gardens of suburbia redeemed from their straitness at night when infinity stretches away overhead - these things "liberate the mind and lift some of the load from it," as V S Pritchett truly remarks. Swiftness of movement is another device for untrammelling the time-tethered self but this cannot be discovered in the enclosed box of a modern car whatever the speedometer reading, still less when confined within a jet airliner even while exceeding the speed of sound. What delight it once was to drive on summer nights in rural Lincolnshire, the old car's hood folded back, hair windblown, the scent of the beanfields almost palpable in the rushing dark; and best of all the one and only flight in a tiny two-seater plane with open cockpit, wind whistling and singing in the fuselage as with engine shut off and wheeling on air we swooped to earth in a long smooth glide that felt like flight itself.

Spatial distance, unimpeded motion, flight - all these connote that elusive invisible, life-giving element of air, uplifting, uncircumscribed and free. Tonight out in the mild wet wind of autumn seeing the lamp-lit trees tossed about, myself air-permeated, I walk on air, feel free as air, could go on forever I feel; all too soon, home and dry, down come the barriers and here is the humdrum world again... I have read that when they came forth from the war's concentration camps men and women at first stood motionless and inhaled long and deeply... Sometimes the mere act suggests a sixth sense. Such intimations are all embodied in my conception of futurity, a time of almost limitless opportunities, of hopes not yet disappointed, of energy and the will to use it; and it can be very terrible when futurity, initiative is withered at the source. Yet even then resolve and resilience may circumvent despair by lowering the sights, each morning like a child only anticipating the day's unfolding while

325

refusing to look further. For me, and I doubt not for thousands like me, futurity spells hope and free expansion, and from earliest childhood an often unconscious search for liberation had been one of the driving forces of my existence.

Such a purpose has naturally been directed according to time and circumstance. The normal urge to grow out of infantile dependence had been intensified for me by fear of domination and I had taken refuge in a world of story book personages where my own enslavement wasn't possible; had gradually freed myself from such self-created hindrances to free intercourse with my fellows on discovering the complete liberty - which later I was to know with my children - of mutual trust between individuals; later struggles had been against the tides of chance and mischance, or there have been brief flare-ups of anger when, rightly or wrongly, I have sensed, and not only when directed against myself, the urge of any one group to dominate another; maybe my attitude to some essential physical taskings is evoked because their performance entails a kind of tethering. As powerful as the desire to love and to be loved has been this search for freedom for myself and for others, that the boys should not feel circumscribed by limitations, nor the lives of us all be controlled by circumstances, nor myself be bound in by dailiness; I would wish for posterity, whatever the omens in the last decades of this sorry century, a future less constricted by poverty, disease, or servitude to others. Often as I have been moved by great human themes depicted in the arts - felt the *frisson* down the spine, the warmth behind the eyes - yet only once have the tears uncontrollably streamed down, and then not for the drama's terror or its pity but at perceivably the light of joy on the faces of the prisoners as they came up from their dungeon with chains struck off to the exultant music of Beethoven's *Fidelio*.

I once believed that the joyous upsurge of expectancy that so permeated my earliest memories and which perhaps has preserved them intact for so long was a childish perception that each moment of time present is poised on the brink of an imminent futurity. And as I look back at a child standing in a sunlight bedroom, or staring up at the pinnacle of a Christmas tree, or recall mornings that anticipated the coming day, and evenings that anticipated the morrow, I realise that must be partly so. But that is not enough to explain the joy, which was, as I feel certain, rooted in the child's own incipience most vividly experienced although not in the least understood; and the pressure which so urgently sought outlet was generated by an immense potential almost like a sentient thing within. In such moments there seemed no let or hindrance to free expansion, and this is part of the essence of a happy childhood.

For most of us this sense of high potential is diminished in the struggle to maintain its integrity in the struggle and flux of other identities seeking their own sometimes opposing fulfilments; we must sooner or later accept inbuilt limitations; eventually we learn that although energy may indeed be eternal delight, yet energy itself is not eternal. Yet although the sense of high potency may be temporal it is eternal too in that it is re-enacted in succeeding generations. With what delight I saw and recognised this during little Richard's growing time at Gidleigh! Even though only a few can hope to preserve this intact to the end many can see it thrice in a lifetime - for themselves, in their children, then their grandchildren. But how narrow, though for me how natural, to conceive as a parental endowment what is maybe the patrimony of all humanity! - evidently my thoughts can still be clouded by remembrance of private deprivations. For the joyful sense of wonder and of potency, combined with freedom to do and to be, is surely, however briefly, all children's birthright.

Yet however fundamental the delights of hopeful incipience and the sense of freedom, I have experienced life most profoundly through a sense of sight, and when I realise myself as a consciousness I seem to exist somewhere behind my eyes. It is a faculty that requires cultivation unless one is to see life only out of the corner of an eye when busied over something else because then perceptions are clouded because unfocused, concentration is also impossible when images of past, present, or future, jostle in the mind for attention, or when bodily sensations obtrude, or emotional states distort the picture. Yet there have been times - of great joy, or great pain, in the almost ecstasy of relief from pain, in the triumph of giving birth, after perfect sexual union, in aesthetic response to life or art - when perception has filled consciousness to the brim all else excluded. I imagine that apart from the mystery of their unique creativity such an un-self-preoccupied clarity is a constant in the vision of great artists. Rembrandt's self-portraits look at us from the canvas with a disinterested observant gaze that seems to comprehend our wholeness without bias or judgement; we are told that Tolstoy could look at an event and see all its significance as well as its immediacy; the imagined characters of the greatest literature are often presented to us quite without slant to be judged only in terms of themselves (hence the arguments about how we should interpret them); a simple drawing of an ash tree by Constable seems to suggest what is to *be* an ash tree - it seems possible that while he sketched, forgetting himself, unconsciously the artist knew.

Perhaps it is presumptuous in one lacking their creative skills to claim to have seen, however rarely, with the artist's clear purity of vision, yet I am glad to believe that this has sometimes been so for me, which moments are the more precious because of their rarity. Primarily my mental life is visual - I have sought less to understand than to see the actual reality of the situations into which I have been thrust by life; and I would probably speak of "seeing" what were the impulses and motivations of other people rather than of comprehending them. This has been as much a part of living as the sequence of events.

Entirely apart from visual or other sense perceptions I treasure moments when the thing seen and the seeing self have been so wedded and welded together that neither can be separated from the other. There is seemingly no emotional involvement whatsoever, although a period of intense feeling may have preceded the experiences. For example when I had news of the arbutus tree planting to commemorate the boys of

328

happy memory it was with a pain so intense that I could neither plumb nor believe its hugeness; I walked upstairs with the letter in my hand, lay down on my bed and seemed at once to sleep. After about forty minutes I awoke; outside the sun glittered on the pine needles, birds flew and sang, and trees, birds, myself, our lost sons, the turning world, seemed suspended in space all at one with some long enduring timelessness. After this I knew a spate of such experiences always without premonition, often triggered off by preternaturally clear perceptions and yet which always seemed mindless when I thought about them afterwards - for I could only recognise that such moments had occurred at the moment of losing them. Very significant was the winter evening when I walked to a favourite larch plantation overtopped by a single cedar. The sun was setting red behind distant ilexes and where I stood it was already dusk when suddenly, very high, a long skein of homing gulls flew over, pink as flamingos in the reflected light. As I watched them sweep silently across for what was perhaps only a brief instant there occurred a moment of cessation when the personal self of memory, feeling and perception and also all that lay outside and beyond that self merged together into a universality of which all things were a part. That these experiences are of the briefest possible duration was confirmed for me at least once. As I stood at the open door of an aircraft just arrived at Tunis very late at night a long scroll of lightning silently unfurled across a sky of deepest violet and the dark faces of long-robed men standing together at the foot of the steps were suddenly illuminated. In memory I stood transfixed for an endless moment - which nevertheless must have been as brief as the lightning, a bare instant of time.

Such moments, not of heightened perception but rather or unconscious identification have become increasingly rare for me and I fear that I no longer hold myself constantly open to such experience; in my case I have found that such insights arrive not as a result of will but of waiting. Timelessness is of the essence, the moment is a still thing, utterly still. But maybe this is an illusion like the seemingly motionless apex of a spinning top when it is turning so quickly that as the boys used to say it "has gone to sleep"; like the undeviating wide bell of the Dervish's robe held taut by the speed of his dancing feet. However this may be I emerge after my moments of equipoise with some sense of Eliot's "point of intersection of the timeless with time".

It seems an odd paradox that one whose main delight has been to appreciate and sometimes to promote individual differences, and to respond to the sharpness of immediate reality, should have grown with the years more and more concerned with the abstract future wherein neither she nor they will play an active part. It is perhaps somewhat ludicrous to realise that for most of life I have lived in the hope that human antagonisms and entanglements might at least begin to straighten themselves out before my departure. Today I sometimes feel doubt and misgiving. But I pin my hopes first on the present breaking down - however painful this process now seems to be - of the many barriers that have so long hindered communication between peoples, and secondly to the urgent conviction, everywhere spreading and growing among all peoples, that their only salvation is to work with and for one another, that all are in the same boat to float or to founder together.